POSITIVE PSYCI

POSITIVE PSYCHOTHERAPY OF EVERYDAY LIFE

A Self-Help Guide for Individuals, Couples and Families with 250 Case Stories

NOSSRAT PESESCHKIAN, M.D.

Positive Psychotherapy
since 1977

authorHOUSE®

AuthorHouse™ UK
1663 Liberty Drive
Bloomington, IN 47403 USA
www.authorhouse.co.uk
Phone: 0800.197.4150

Original Title: «Schatten auf der Sonnenuhr»
Medical Tribune GmbH, Wiesbaden 1974

Translation from the Revised Edition
«Psychotherapie des Alltagslebens»
Fischer Taschenbuch Verlag GmbH, Frankfurt am Main 1981

«Psychotherapy of Everyday Life»
Springer-Verlag Heidelberg Berlin New York Tokyo 1986

Positive Psychotherapy (PPT after Peseschkian, since 1977) has applied in 2015 for a Community trade mark (Word mark) at the Office for Harmonization in the Internal Market of the European Union (OHIM). The application number is 014512578. The same application has been made for Canada and the United States of America.

Published by AuthorHouse   06/22/2016

ISBN: 978-1-5246-3143-7 (sc)
ISBN: 978-1-5246-3142-0 (hc)
ISBN: 978-1-5246-3141-3 (e)

Library of Congress Control Number: 2016908601

Print information available on the last page.

Any people depicted in stock imagery provided by Thinkstock are models, and such images are being used for illustrative purposes only. Certain stock imagery © Thinkstock.

This book is printed on acid-free paper.

"Enquires should be addressed to
International Academy for Positive and Transcultural Psychotherapy
– Professor Peseschkian Foundation –
Langgasse 38-40, D-65183 Wiesbaden, Germany
foundation@peseschkian.com
www.peseschkian-foundation.org

For further information on Positive Psychotherapy,
please visit the international website of the world of Positive Psychotherapy at
http://www.positum.org"

Nossrat Peseschkian, M.D. was a specialist in psychiatrics and neurology and a psychotherapist, as well as specializing in psychotherapeutic medicine. He was born in Iran in 1933 and had lived in Germany since 1954. He did his medical studies in Freiburg, Mainz and Frankfurt and received his psychotherapeutic training in the Federal Republic of Germany, Switzerland and the United States. From 1969 to 2010, Professor Peseschkian had a psychotherapeutic practice and day clinic in Wiesbaden. He was the founder of Positive Psychotherapy and a professor at the Academy for Continuing and Further Education in Medicine of the Hessen State Medical Association. In 1997, Nossrat Peseschkian received the Richard Merten Prize for his work, "Computer Aided Quality Assurance in Positive Psychotherapy". In 2006, Nossrat Peseschkian received the Order of Merit, Distinguished Service Cross of the Federal Republic of Germany. (Bundesverdienstkreuz). The International Academy of Positive and Cross-Cultural Psychotherapy – Professor Peseschkian Foundation – was established in 2005. Nossrat Peseschkian passed away in April 2010 in Wiesbaden, Germany.

A list of the books by the author Nossrat Peseschkian is included at the end of this book.

CONTENTS

CHAPTER I:
DIFFERENTIATION ANALYTICAL THEORY
(POSITIVE PSYCHOTHERAPY)

CHAPTER II:
ACTUAL CAPABILITIES
(PRIMARY AND SECONDARY CAPABILITIES)

Chapter III:
Misunderstandings in Parenting, Partnership and Psychotherapy

Chapter IV:
Education - Self-Help - Psychotherapy

Editor's Preface

*"If you want something you never had,
do something you never did."*
Oriental Wisdom

As the author himself intended with the above quote, coinciding with the fundamental vision in mind that arises in many of the theories within his books, there can be no development without an aspect of change.

From the time the book was first published in 1974 under the original title, "Shadow on the Sundial," until the present republishing of the author's great work, the world has changed many times over. Over the last 40 years unimaginable technical advances have occurred, so much so that the children of today can hardly grasp that humanity once danced to radios, connected with friends via telephone boxes, or let alone waited on delayed dial up Internet. The social world of the 1970's was thought to be smaller and more readily available with the introduction and increase of air travel, the broadcasting of live television, and the delivery of daily mail. Nowadays we are constantly connected with every corner of the world through Internet platforms containing live personal information updates and detailed self-imaging.

Although rich in change, our society still has similar problems in the areas of health and mental health that, with the pressures and shifts of time seem to develop in their own unique ways. While this book was written with the problems of 1974 and earlier in mind, the theory and practices are still relevant to those problems we see some 40 years later, arguably, even more so. To say that Dr. Nossrat Peseschkian was way ahead of his time would be an understatement. Not only was he able to see the direct correlation between "illness" and mental health, he was advanced enough to write his theory that expanded across all cultures, religions, medical perspectives, and most importantly across all time dimensions. He created a cross-cultural theory that is unscathed by the advances of time. Alike the immortal power of his theories, his use of stories, parables and myths effectively work like medicine for the soul in order to open doors that we didn't realize were closed.

With the modern day influence of those who further the teaching and practice of Positive Psychotherapy, the basis of the author's theories have transformed into an even more direct approach to the individual, while creating the vision of a healthy world beginning with the transformation of the self. This idea of transformation postulates, in accordance with the author's original vision, that every person, family, society, culture, the entire human race, has the potential to develop healthfully and justly, in order to live together peacefully in the present world.

In the following pages of this book and the revelation of the theories of Positive Psychotherapy, Dr. Peseschkian waters us gently as he would his very own peaceful garden. The reader is treated like an essential seed set in rich, fertile soil, full of capabilities, needing only to be developed and maintained. The author gracefully nourishes us with his wisdom, giving us the proper support we need in furtherance of our expansion and growth. Ultimately, as the author intends, it is up to us readers to take the insightful chapters of self-help and education as to blossom into our own responsible beings, fully developing our capabilities, thus creating sunshine in those we meet along our individual paths, creating a better world for everyone around us.

We hope you enjoy the contents of the book and we wish you success on your journey,

The International Academy for Positive and Transcultural Psychotherapy – Professor Peseschkian Foundation, Wiesbaden, 2014

In addition to the original foreword intended for the 1974 version of Psychotherapy for »Everyday Life« ("Schatten auf der Sonnenuhr"), Professor Dr. Battegay has written a supplementary foreword after the many years of work with Professor Nossrat Peseschkian and his theories in Positive Psychotherapy.

FOREWORD (1974)

In this book East and West are united in a total vision which gives the reader an expansive view of inner lives and behaviors, some of which are healthy and some not. The author presents an analysis of contemporary social relationships and the attitudes associated with them. But he does far more than this. He also vividly describes the «primary» and «secondary» capabilities of the psyche, capabilities that are valid for all times and all situations. Peseschkian draws on his experiences in the Middle Eastern homeland of his youth and also on the insights he has gained through his psychotherapeutic practice. He does not stop with special examples, but draws conclusions that are valid for people everywhere. He then molds these conclusions into an illustrative system. Uniquely interesting are the passages where the author describes errors in the development of a child and erroneous punitive behaviour of parents: «Right from the start a child must learn to obey;» «There must be punishment;» and «You have to break the child's will.» Or when he shows how tensions between the parents are transferred to their children: «You're just like your father. He doesn't know what punctuality is either.» The author attempts to integrate his faith in psychotherapy with his vision of the world and also tries to understand the world's religions as an expression of their times. Accordingly, the Bahá'i religion, of which the author is a follower, is a stage of further development on the way to ward a higher perfection. The author emphasizes that faith is a part of man's path. He distinguishes between two aspects of religion: a spiritual and transcendent aspect, and an aspect consisting of temporal values and norms. If a religion does not take into consideration the principle of time, it can easily confuse the primary and secondary aspects. It is therefore important to see the core of the religion and not to push it aside because of temporal views. Peseschkian strives to open up this religious core in psychotherapy as well. He places great importance on the misunderstanding that can develop in the parent-child relationship. Frequently the parents try to make their child into something he simply isn't. The author emphasizes the uniqueness of each individual and the resulting necessity to let each person develop the uniqueness that is in him. Drawing on Middle Eastern folk tales, he describes education and psychotherapy as a process whose goal is the development of self-help and an expansion of goals in the sense of the fullest possible unfolding of all one's mental, somatic, and social capabilities.

This book will be of relevance not only to those with a professional interest in psychotherapy. It is also a rich treasure full with psychological and pedagogic insights for parents, educators, and others who are concerned with pedagogic tasks.

Professor Raymond Battegay, 1974
Psychiatric University Polyclinic, Basel

Foreword (2013)

The author (1933-2010), a gifted psychotherapist had the ability to help his patients improve their lives by using simple words and wisdom taken from the orient, where he had passed his youth, as well as of the occident, where he lived as an adult. It was important to him to help his patients live a better life, not only by treating their symptoms of disease, but also by caring for them as active partners.

With his Positive Psychotherapy and Differentiation Analysis Nossrat Peseschkian focused mainly on the capabilities and virtues of his patients which helped promote their potential of reintegration. It was of major importance to help his patients develop their own creative capacities through psychological treatment, with the practice of «Positive Psychotherapy.» In this way he put emphasis on the significance of the patients' inherent primary capacities in which were developed during socialization, in addition to the secondary capacities of the psyche, which have an impact on how people react in many situations. Nossrat Peseschkian also demonstrates how parental misbehaviour (e.g.: insistence on obedience; constant conflict between parents) hinders the development of their children's capacities.

A central issue of Positive Psychotherapy is to reinforce the qualities of an individual in a positive manner. In this context, the author illustrates the impact of misunderstandings not only in education, but also in partnership and possibly in psychotherapy, too. He emphasizes that a considerable number of the human conflicts are caused by these misunderstandings. One of the most important goals of Nossrat Peseschkian was to create a psychotherapy that positively reinforces the central capacities of the individual. For this reason he made the effort to help each patient develop their own uniqueness during their psychotherapeutic treatment. This book proves his intent to help individuals using psychotherapy in order to unfold their own psychic, somatic and social capabilities.

Nossrat Peseschkian, M.D.

Nossrat Peseschkian was not only an extremely gifted psychotherapist and author, but also a man with an extraordinary understanding for people in need. With the foundation of Positive Psychotherapy he has brought great progress to psychotherapy - both in theory and practice.

Professor Raymond Battegay, 2013

Author's Preface

Every book has a date of origin and a date of formulation. The development of a book is like the growth of a tree. Its fruits do not ripen overnight. They are the result of the growth and maturation of a seed that unfolds and is helped along by favorable conditions until it becomes the fruit that is harvested and taken home.

Positive Psychotherapy (differentiation analysis) has had a short history and a long past. Since 1958 I have been working on a new method of psychohygiene and psychotherapy. I have based my work on extensive experience in therapeutic practice with a psychosomatic orientation.

Although the fruits came to maturity in Europe, the tree from which they grew is rooted in the Persian Middle East, the place of my birth and youth. This book, and, I hope, my work as a psychotherapist, represents my attempt to combine the insights of the Middle East with the progress of the West. I am aware that there are a lot of problems inherent in such an approach. But in our times, when geographic distances are no longer a problem, a sense of unity in the world is very useful, if not necessary. The times we live in, despite the many misunderstandings, reveal a hopeful longing for unity in multiplicity. Goethe summed it up in the following lines of his book *Westöstlicher Diwan,* and their meaning will come up again and again in the pages of this volume:

Whoever knows himself and others
will recognize the truth here as well:
East and West can no longer be separated.

The development of psychotherapy has shown that it is not practical to proceed exclusively from the nonic principle and to center psychodynamics only on the recognition of disorders. It seems important also to be concerned with man's inherent capabilities and virtues.

According to Freud, the goal of psychoanalysis is to make the unconscious conscious. According to Alfred Adler, the goal of individual psychology is to intensify the sense of responsibility. According to Victor Frankl, the goal of existential analysis is to increase both consciousness and responsibility. Positive Psychotherapy has as its goal a refinement and expansion of one's ability to make distinctions in the realm of actual capabilities.

Special thanks go to my colleagues Dieter Schoen, MD, and Hans Deidenbach, psychologist in Wiesbaden, for their helpful suggestions.

I would like to express particular gratitude to the translator, Mrs. Martha Rohlfing of Chicago, and also to my secretaries. Loving appreciation goes to the friends whose wisdom and encouragement have on many occasions been like the bread of life. Finally, I am thankful to my wife, Manije, and sons, Hamid and Nawid, who inspired and stimulated many of these thoughts.

This book could not have been written if it had not been for the cooperation and openness of my patients who have so willingly allowed me to include their case histories in this publication. Naturally I have changed names and dates to preserve their anonymity. But to maintain their documentary value, I have included the oral and written reports word for word insofar as this was possible.

This paperback edition differs from the first edition in several ways. In addition to changing the title, I have expanded the contents and added an extensive section called «Tips for the Reader,» which presents an overview of the book, gives information concerning its development, and offers the reader some help in dealing which the themes of education, self-help, and psychotherapy.

Nossrat Peseschkian
Wiesbaden, October 1985

THE PROPHET AND THE LONG SPOONS

An orthodox believer came to the prophet Elijah. He was motivated by the question of hell and heaven, for naturally he wanted to live his life accordingly. «Where is hell - where is heaven?» As he said these words, he approached the prophet, but Elijah did not answer him. Elijah took the man by the hand and led him through the dark alleys into a palace.

They passed through an iron portal and entered a large room crowded with many people, rich and poor, some huddled in rags, some adorned with jewels. In the middle of the room, a big pot of soup, called «asch», stood over an open fire. The simmering casserole spread a wonderful aroma throughout the room. Around the pot, crowds of hollow-cheeked and empty eyed people jockeyed to get their share of the soup. The man who came along with Elijah was amazed when he saw the spoons the people carried, for the spoons were as big as the people themselves. Each spoon consisted of an iron bowl, white, but from the heat of the soup, and way at the end, a small wooden handle. The hungry people greedily poked around in the pot. Although each wanted his share, no one got it. It was hard to lift the heavy spoon out of the pot, and, since the spoon was very long, even the strongest men could not get it in their mouths. The more impertinent people even burned their arms and faces or spilled the soup on their neighbors. Scolding one another, they fought and hit each other with the spoons they should have been using to quiet their hunger. The prophet Elijah took his escort by the arm and said, «That is hell.»

They left the room and soon were no longer able to hear the infernal cries behind them. After a long journey through dark passages, they entered a different room. Here, too, there were many people sitting around. In the middle of the room there was again a pot of hot soup. Each of the persons there had a gigantic spoon in his hand, just like the ones Elijah and the man had seen in hell. But here the people were well nourished. Only a quiet, satisfied humming could be heard along with the sounds of the spoons being dipped into the soup. There were always two people working together. One dipped the spoon in the pot and fed his partner. If the spoon became too heavy for one person, two others helped with their implements, so that everyone was able to eat in peace. As soon as one person had had enough to eat, it was another one's turn. The prophet Elijah said to his escort, «That is heaven!»

This story, which has been a part of oral tradition for thousands of years, is an accurate picture of life. It represents the things we see when we look at the problems within individual families - quarrels between parents, fighting among children, and the battles between parents and their offspring. We see it again in the way the individual confronts his surroundings and even in the disagreements between groups and peoples. The «hell» in the story exists when people work against each other or simply next to each other. «Heaven», on the other hand, comes about through the willingness to establish positive relationships. Both sets of people, those in heaven as well as those in hell, have the same kinds of problems. How they solve those problems determines whether their life is heaven or hell.

This book leads the reader to the fountain,
but he must drink from it himself.

TIPS FOR THE READER

Upbringing and education are generally accepted as concepts that are obvious to everyone. Self-help, however, is like a foreign word to many people.

Some expect that when they have problems or succumb to illness, a doctor will immediately recognize the problem and prescribe exactly the right cure, almost as if doing it in his sleep. Given this expectation, psychotherapy is still faced with the problem of concocting an effective potion for internal and external conflicts. We see the problem when we hear statements like that uttered by the mother of a 5-year-old child: «We don't have time now to deal with him. Later we'll take him to a therapist.» Although the child was suffering from bed-wetting, stuttering, and behavioral disorders, the mother adopted a casual attitude, thus forcing the therapist into the role of miracle healer, a role to which doctors cannot always do justice in good conscience.

On the other hand there are people who have no faith in medicine, doctors, or therapists. These people tend to say, «My mother was under a doctor's care, but she died anyway. I want to stay around a while longer. Let the optimists go to the doctor if they want.» Such people are often do-it-yourself healers who, in their inimitable way, pass on their advice to others: «It worked for me. I will help you, too.» If they could, they would go so far as to perform their own appendectomies.

Between these two extremes of passive expectation and stubborn mistrust of specialists, there should be an area where the desire to be cured and the willingness to accept professional help can meet on common ground.

Self-help should serve as a guideline. In order to be effective, it must be based on a small number of basic processes. This gives it the advantage of being relevant to a relatively large group of people and a wide array of problems. Self-help does not provide directions that can automatically be applied to the individual case. After all, every relationship is unique; self-help must acknowledge this uniqueness. As a practical approach, it must not dispense prescriptions; its job is to reveal guidelines for preventing problems and for dealing with them when they do occur.

WHO IS HEALTHY?

Many people need psychological help. When they realize it, they perhaps go to a psychotherapist. But in the process something unforeseen can happen: The patient doesn't understand the therapist and consequently feels that he isn't understood either. If he tries to read a book on psychology, he often gives up after a few pages and lays the book aside. The book remains a mystery.

As a general rule, psychotherapy doesn't necessarily mean curing an outright psychic illness. Rather, it must be practical self-help. Without this orientation, actual illnesses could develop, or there could arise what are commonly known as «quirks.»

So very often one is tempted to ask «How should I raise my children?» «Why do I hate this or that?» «How should I behave toward my wife in this or some other situation?» These questions are the domain of psychohygiene. From everyone you ask, you get a different answer; you end up as ignorant or confused as ever.

We are all faced with conflicts, problems, and difficulties in our relationships with ourselves, our partners, our fellow men, and ultimately our life goals. This is why we need new points of view and new methods of psychotherapy and self-help. We need new methods that are both practical and effective.

A healthy person is not one who is free of problems, but one who is in a position to deal with them when they occur.

LEARN TO MAKE DISTINCTIONS

In my therapeutic practice I am frequently confronted with a misunderstanding. If a child has fever, a headache, stomach pains, or a heart ailment, we treat that child with special care: But if, in our eyes, the child acts «funny,» i.e., in a way different from that to which we are used to, or is even impolite and unruly, our tolerance reaches its limits quite fast. In other words, we react in a negative or aggressive way. We too often overlook the fact that the behavior could have the characteristics of an illness. There are definite consequences of our tendency to place more value on physical illnesses: if one feels ill, one is inclined to go to a doctor. But one seldom thinks about consulting a therapist, even when it is a clear case of psychic disorder.

PSYCHOTHERAPY INSTEAD OF PSYCHOPATHOLOGY

People rarely say how a person can do something better. More often, one hears what a person shouldn't do. There is an anecdote about the British Queen Victoria. She once complained in a letter how her mentors constantly reminded her of what she couldn't do as a future queen. «But what I was supposed to do, and how I could do it, that no one told me.»

We find the same principle in psychotherapy and medicine. One speaks of illnesses and silently assumes that if a person does not have an illness, he is healthy. The philosopher Lichtenberg put it this way: *One first gets a sense of health when he is sick.* Freud formulated it with these words: *Only when one has studied sickliness can one understand what normal means.*

As a result of this idea, one is more concerned with what one can do with regard to illness than with what one can do for health. From all appearances, our interpersonal relationships, partnerships, and child rearing follow this idea to a great degree. Even our language, the means by which we make ourselves comprehensible to our partners, proceeds from this negative principle: «Don't do this, and don't do that.» «Why are you home so late?» «I can't stand the mess around here any more.» «I just can't deal with that cutthroat.» «You're lying to me again.» «Why are you so unfaithful?» «Your laziness is driving me crazy.» «He doesn't know how to behave.» etc.

These attitudes inevitably give rise to aggravation. But one is usually not certain as to how far-reaching the consequences will be:

Does one have to be divorced in order to realize for the first time how good a marriage is? Does one have to suffer a heart attack to be convinced of how important physical health can be? Does one have to have committed suicide to understand the importance of mental health? Does one have to have sat in jail to know how wonderful freedom is? Does one have to turn a car into a pile of junk to know that driving recklessly in heavy traffic carries a big risk?

Conflicts and disorders, as a rule, originate in everyday life, not in psychotherapeutic practice. Marital problems, for example, develop initially out of the partners' relationship and in connection with their other social contacts. In the case of infidelity on the part of a spouse or lover, for instance, there are other ways to react besides seeking «justice,» and the restoration of «honor» with a gun or knife. One can drown sorrows in alcohol; one can try to find a better world by taking drugs; one can get back at the partner by also being unfaithful. But one can also seize the opportunity and tackle the problem in an active way. All of this is self-help. But some forms of self-help have the disadvantage of provoking even more trouble and anger. It is ultimately a matter of finding measures that are acceptable and feasible for both partners. This book points to such methods. *For this reason I adopted the goal of writing a book that one could give to patients and clients within the framework of a medical and psychological practice, as well as in connection with consultation for specific problems. I felt that the book I envisioned should prove useful as an aid in the therapeutic situation or the consultation process. The book was thus not conceived for specialists, but for a wide range of readers: students, young people, parents, business people, teachers, and educators, as well as physicians and therapists.*

That means that I could not remain fixed on the description of pathological, i.e., disturbed or diseased conditions: Instead of a *Psychopathology of Everyday Life,* as Freud wrote, I saw it as my task to present a *Psychotherapy of Everyday Life* in response to existing needs and to the development of psychotherapy as it is today. I could not limit myself to manifestations of the unconscious. I had to proceed from interpersonal relationships and from the capabilities inherent in man. Suppressed and overly expressed capabilities were shown to be possible sources of conflicts and disorders in personal and interpersonal areas. They can be expressed in depression, anxiety, aggression, conspicuous behavior, and psychosomatic disorders:

From childhood on I was trained to succeed... My job is a pleasure for me, but I don't have close ties to other people. I can't even do much with my kids. Leisure time is a torture for me... (42-year-old attorney suffering from depression)

Conflicts grow in the course of a person's development in confrontation with his environment; they are not unavoidable acts of fate. They are tasks and problems in which we must try to solve.

The term «positive» is usually used as a moral category. Regardless of the value judgment designated as «positive,» it depends on the value system, which sets the standards for good and bad. This relational system is what positive family therapy investigates. Here «positive» takes on an additional meaning: As in its original usage (Latin positum), it refers to what is factual and given. Factual and given things are not necessarily conflicts and disorders, but also the capabilities inherent in every human being. I don't mean that everything should be looked at in a positive light; rather, Positive Psychotherapy tries to differentiate between the critical behavior and the capabilities. Only through this process can we separate stable, less conflictual behavioral components from the symptoms. This process prepares the patient and his environment to deal with existing problems in more effective ways.

The ability to make differentiations is basic to all our physical, mental, and social functions. Therapeutic intervention, regardless of the particular method used, is ultimately an attempt to make it possible for the patient to make more precise and appropriate distinctions. This ability enables him to respond to the demands of a situation in ways appropriate to his own particular goals (differentiation analysis).

According to traditional views, the illness stands-between the therapist and the patient:

Therapist	Illness	Patient

Traditional Process

As soon as we concentrate on the regenerative power of the patient instead of exclusively on his illness, the relationship between the therapist and the patient takes on a new quality:

Therapist	Capabilities Illnesses	Patient

Positive Process

SELF-HELP?

An important feature of the model for differentiation analytical therapy is that education and self-help are integral parts of the psychotherapy itself. Psychotherapy as re-education refers directly to what was formed and learned in the upbringing. Through self-help the patient is encouraged as an active partner; he isn't merely the one who has to endure something. Self-help is a method of prevention and psychohygiene. It is an essential element in the psychotherapeutic process.

As forms of self-help, internal medicine offers such aids as fitness training & diet guidelines, and charts for keeping track of progress. Under the direction of a physician, the patient learns to actively do something to improve his health. In a similar way, educational problems, career conflicts, and marital difficulties can be approached by way of self-help.

Self-help already starts in child rearing, when we parents and educators think about the consequences of our educational methods. Often it is not the big events that lead to disorders in the child, but the little recurring emotional injuries that eventually form the character trait that is particularly conspicuous for individual conflicts. If a mother constantly complains about how messy her child is, for instance, neither she nor the child benefits. In this case it would be better if the mother were to become aware of how the child has developed his own sense of order. She should come to realize that people have different concepts of what orderliness really is. For the child, it would be better not to be criticized, but rather to be told and shown how he can behave better.

Another example: A person, who has learned that he is valuable only if he accomplishes something and has career success, will suddenly face a severe defeat if he is given a task he is no longer capable of accomplishing. Here we touch on a problem that strikes the very form of our upbringing. Let's compare driving a car with raising children. You will all agree that raising a child is just as hard, if not harder, than driving. To drive a car one often enrolls with a driving school, learns the rules, and, of course, has to pass an exam. But to raise children it is enough simply to have children in the first place. The rest, it seems, happens automatically. At times it seems to me that some parents are like a driver who drives blindfolded and without a license through rush hour traffic in a big city.

A chief task of this book is to encourage people to adopt self-help as I have described it.

WHY STORIES, PARABLES, AND MYTHS?

In my practice and in seminars and lectures I have found again and again that parables and Middle Eastern tales have captured the interest of audiences and patients. For me, parables are like pictures that come in the form of language. As such they lend support to understanding and have a central didactic value. Many people feel overwhelmed when confronted with the abstract aspects of psychotherapeutic topics. Psychotherapy does not take place just among experts, but must be a bridge to the layman, the patient. This is why it is important that psychotherapy be comprehensible. One way to make it easier to understand is to use an example, a mythological story, or an image. In their own way, all of these deal with personal, interpersonal, and social conflicts, and present possible solutions. Stories help the patient free himself from the direct world of his own experiences and from his resistance to revealing his own conflicts and weaknesses. These stories, if used in a conscious way, help him gain a more distanced relationship to his conflicts. One does not think only in abstract and theoretical concepts. Rather, an understanding of his problems is determined by vivid and imaginary modes of thought and by fantasy that is charged with emotion. This realization led me to include imagination and hence mythological stories and fables as aids to comprehension in the therapeutic process. Another concern in my book was to unite the wisdom and intuitive thought of the Middle East with the new psychotherapeutic discoveries of the West. The wisdom of Middle Eastern and Western philosophers and scientists, and also the foundations of the great religions, are viewed in the light of modern psychotherapy.

HOW DID POSITIVE PSYCHOTHERAPY
(DIFFERENTIATION ANALYSIS) ARISE?

Since 1968 I have been working on a new concept of psychohygiene and psychotherapy, *differentiation analysis*. I may have been motivated in part by the fact that to a certain degree I live in a transcultural situation. As a Persian (Iranian) I have lived in Europe since 1954. This perspective made me aware of the importance of psychosocial norms in socialization and the development of spiritual and interpersonal conflicts. With American and European patients, as well as ones from the Middle East, I found that behind the symptoms there were usually conflicts that went back to a series of recurring behavioral norms. I tried to collect these norms, to assemble them into concepts that relate to each other, and to set up an inventory for describing the central areas of conflict. I called these behavioral norms *actual capabilities.* I used this term because it includes norms that operate in our everyday interpersonal relationships and thus have a continuing significance. Differentiation analysis starts with the actual capabilities as potentials for both development and conflict. We do not deal with some mysterious concepts known only to the specialist, but with norms and concepts that everyone encounters every day. What is really behind it all when we get angry, feel furious with someone, retreat with great indignation, feel wronged, or want to jump out of our skins? I have delved into this question and have tried to grasp the conditions behind the problems and conflicts of my patients and clients. Step by step, over a period of eight years, I set up the actual capabilities in their present form. At first I was struck by the psychotherapeutic significance of politeness and honesty. These two categories offered a guideline for completing the inventory of actual capabilities. This inventory was repeatedly checked and enlarged through what I discovered in the course of my practice. These investigations, carried out not just by me but also by my associates and colleagues, were based on some 50000 psychotherapeutic sessions. Let's look at some examples. When a mother says, *my son is a devil;* behind this utterance is the assertion that the boy is disobedient and messy.

A married woman said, *my husband and I aren't compatible. We are two different types of people.* Behind this statement several things were hidden: The husband had little time, the wife had to wait for him for hours on end, and the husband was not as well-groomed as the wife wanted him to be. A young man was suffering from depression. Although he was very competent, he had been sacked from his job because he had rarely arrived there on time.

If we direct our attention to these connections, we can see what contents play a role in the examples: fidelity, honesty, politeness, justice, achievement, ambition, and many more.

We can say that practically all conflicts stem in some way from a particular content area. Although we deal with them every day, and our behavior and experience are influenced by our expectations and experiences in these behavioral areas, we are seldom aware that there really is a connection. If a person fails in a particular situation, we say he is a failure. If we aren't able to achieve a certain goal, we think we are worthless. If a child is lazy, we label him a lazy person and consider him as someone who has no concept of cleanliness or politeness as we do. We view him as bad and asocial.

So that we have a picture of these social norms and can view them with a critical eye, I have tried to compile a list of the central norms that operate almost everywhere and form the base from which most of our conflicts develop. We call this inventory the differentiation analysis inventory (DAI). When problems and conflicts occur, one can work through them by using the DAI. We no longer say things like, «My partner is a monster. I can't stand to be with him any more. He makes me angry all the time. He's driving me crazy.» Instead of making such statements, we try to grasp the contents of the particular problem. From the statement, my partner is a monster, we perhaps derive the assertion, «Today I felt I was treated rudely and unjustly by my partner. He kept me waiting too long and then didn't even apologize. I place a lot of importance on courtesy, but my partner doesn't always give it the same priority as I do. Why do I put so much emphasis on politeness? And why was it precisely today that my partner treated me this way?» In this process we can recognize the difference between the two utterances: on the one hand the emotional generalization which often makes it impossible to handle a conflict objectively; on the other hand the attempt to make differentiations, to look into the sense of the anger, to give the problem the weight it deserves, and to find new possibilities. This distinction or differentiation is one of the basic functions of self-help.

Differentiation analysis, a new form of conflict-centered psychotherapy, includes a series of methods that are also important for self-help.

The described procedure suggests that one investigate the patient's susceptibility to conflict in terms of the actual capabilities. Let's assume a patient always becomes anxious when she has to wait for her husband at night. In such a case the anxiety is focused in terms of content on the psychosocial norm «punctuality». Isn't it therefore appropriate to work on precisely this area? Such a procedure would be radical in the best sense of the word. It starts with the root and not with some symptom, i.e., the leaf.

Treatment Shortened?

After its inception in 1968, my psychotherapeutic procedure was developed further and has established itself as a method of psychotherapy. It has been discussed at a number of national and international conferences.

Differentiation analytical therapy has a focal orientation. That is, we direct our attention mainly to the capabilities surrounding the conflict-laden areas and try to mobilize the existing re-integrative tendencies of the physical–spiritual–mental entity we call man. This takes place in a plan of treatment comprising several stages. I'd like to give an everyday example to illustrate the plan:

When we are mad at someone who has been rude to us, we're inclined to feel upset, to complain openly about him, or to gossip about him and his shortcomings. Suddenly we no longer view him as a person with many capabilities, but only as the rude person, the boor who insulted us. Because these negative experiences overshadow our relationship with this man, we are unable to deal with his other, more positive traits. As a result, we are unable to deal with him; the conflicts remain destructive; communication is limited. This chain of events can lead to psychic and psychosomatic disorders, but, if we use it as a point of departure, we can follow the following phases of a treatment plan:

1. *Observation and Description:* An account is given, preferably in writing, as to the reason for being upset, who caused it, and when.
2. *Inventory:* By using the DAI, we determine the areas of conduct where the patient himself and his partner have positive qualities

as well as the ones under criticism. In this way, we can counter the tendency toward generalizations.

3. *Situational Encouragement:* To build up a trusting relationship, we strengthen individual traits that we find acceptable and that correspond to the negatively labeled traits.

4. *Verbalization:* To overcome speechlessness or the distortion of speech in the conflict, communication with the partner is developed step by step. There are discussions about positive as well as negative traits and experiences.

5. *Broadening of the Goal:* The neurotic narrowness of perspective is consciously broken down. One learns not to carry the conflict over into other areas. At the same time, one learns to open up new goals that have perhaps never been experienced before. The treatment is thus based on two procedures that run parallel and are intertwined: *psychotherapy,* whereby the relationship between therapist and patient is in the foreground; and *self-help,* whereby the patient takes over therapeutic talks within the circle of people he is closely involved with.

These are, in brief, some of the essential steps in differentiation analytical psychotherapy. We gathered the results of using this methodology with marital problems, educational problems, depression, phobias, sexual disorders, and psychosomatic ailments such as stomach and intestinal problems, heart and circulatory problems, and difficulties with rheumatism and asthma. Several psychopaths and schizophrenics were also treated.

The success rate showed that as a rule there was either a cure or considerable improvement after just a short time (six to ten sessions). Check-ups after a year generally showed that the success had continued. There were particularly favorable results with neurotic and psychosomatic disorders. Differentiation analytical psychotherapy thus proved to be a favorable alternative to the customary forms of therapy.

THREE FOCAL POINTS OF DIFFERENTIATION ANALYSIS

Differentiation analysis has three focal points that can be summarized as follows:

1. The conflicts, problems, confrontations, and disorders like inner unrest, anxiety, sleep disorders, and aggression, as well as the so-called psychosomatic disorders, have their sources in conflict potentials that occur again and again. We describe them by means of an inventory of actual capabilities. This enables us to work on conflicts and disorders in terms of their essential contents. The actual capabilities are compiled in the DAI. The following psychosocial norms are included among the actual capabilities: punctuality, orderliness, cleanliness, obedience, politeness, honesty, loyalty, justice, thrift, diligence/achievement, dependability, and exactness, as well as model, patience, time, contact, sexuality, trust, confidence, hope, faith/religion, doubt, certainty, and unity.

2. The actual capabilities are central factors for the development of the individual. Grounded in the capabilities inherent in every person, they are stamped by the person's upbringing, and are then differentiated or hampered in their development. In this sense one can be very orderly, but not prompt, or orderly and not patient. In addition, the actual capabilities become the contents of disorders if certain expectations about the capabilities are not fulfilled. «For me cleanliness is very important,» a woman complains. «If my husband doesn't take a bath I don't have the slightest desire to have sexual contact with him. I find him repulsive at times like that, and wish I'd never met him.» While cleanliness is important for one person, politeness is important for another, and for the third person it's honesty or orderliness.

3. The actual capabilities acquire their stamp in the course of development of the individual as he is influenced by his environment. Since the actual capabilities are learned, there are three ways to react to them as potentials for conflict:
   a. In the sense of prevention through education
   b. In the sense of self-help
   c. In the sense of psychotherapy, that is, relearning

A GUIDE TO THE BOOK

Chapter I:
Beginning with the example of the sundial, the theory of differentiation analysis is developed. Special attention is paid to the situation of education today, which can be described with the terms helplessness and hope. Through examples of social conflict situations in education and psychotherapy, the actual capabilities as a central aspect of differentiation analytical theory are developed and related to concrete questions. As a basis for the theory, the basic capabilities, the abilities to know and to love, are introduced. The actual capabilities are compiled into a typology that can be used in practice.

Chapter II:
Now that the actual capabilities have been depicted conceptually, I attempt to describe them in terms of their content, development, and significance. At this point particular weight is given to examples from therapeutic practice. The primary capabilities are presented in a type of developmental chain. For practical application, the secondary capabilities are depicted as conflicts between the values of what is and what should be. The examples of the is- and should-be-values are likewise taken from psychotherapeutic practice. The should-be-value is not a precept or prescription, nor is it a general statement; it is the alternative that a patient has found to be the most appropriate for his particular situation. In the «situational check» the reader can work through the is- and should-be-values on his own, relating them to his own problems.

Chapter III:
We present 22 misconceptions, with many examples. We do this under the assumption that personal and interpersonal conflicts stem in large part from misunderstandings like these. The reader is made aware of the significance of the actual capabilities in these misconceptions, even if they are not stated explicitly. The misconceptions can be categorized as follows: general misconceptions, misconceptions in upbringing, misconceptions in interpersonal relationships, misconceptions regarding sexuality, and misconceptions about religion and death.

Chapter IV:

This Chapter deals with the possibilities for applying differentiation analysis in upbringing and self-help. Please note that self-help should not replace therapy carried out by a specialist. Rather, it represents better ways of dealing with the problems and conflicts that confront us every day. The differentiation analytical self-help is divided into five stages: the stage of observation/distancing, inventory, situational encouragement, verbalization, and broadening of the goal. These five stages are explained in great detail by means of an example. Special attention is paid to the possibilities within the family group, the parental group, and the partner group. Finally, we look at differentiation analytical psychotherapy, illustrating its main features by way of case examples dealing with the themes «conspicuous behavior in children» and «sexual disorders.»

Children can read individual passages of the book. In particular we recommend the Middle Eastern stories and the is- and should-be-values.

This book cannot solve all problems or give patent prescriptions for them; nor does it try to do so. It was designed to direct the reader to individual circumstances and problems, to make him more sensitive to them, and to present the possibilities that exist in making distinctions. In this sense one should not view this book as a closed entity, but as something within a continual development. But this can have practical consequences only if the reader is willing to continually ask questions. The Fischer Publishing Company has come out with a new work of mine, *Positive Psychotherapie - Theorie und Praxis einer neuen Methode*. This book presents a more extensive portrayal of differentiation analytical psychotherapy. It includes new aspects, methods, and therapy models as well as the basic starting points for the book you are now reading. All of this can fundamentally expand, complete, and revolutionize psychotherapy and psychohygiene.

PSYCHOTHERAPY TODAY

Some 60% - 80% of all illnesses are at least partially determined by psychic causes.

In West Germany today there are about 300 divorces per day. The number of alcoholics is growing steadily. Approximately 40% of men and 70% of women in West Germany have to quit their jobs prematurely because of illness. There are around 1,500 practicing medical psychotherapists for some 9 million potential patients. We need about 20,000 psychotherapists.

A patient must wait from 1 to 2 years before he receives psychotherapeutic treatment. For psychosomatic disorders, the waiting period is about 6 years - if the patient can get the treatment at all.

Why is this so?
- Because one treats the symptom and not the person.
- Because one deals with the form of the conflicts, but not with their contents.
- Because the therapist and the patient speak different languages.
- Because psychotherapists are hardly able to communicate among themselves any more.

What can be done?
- Free psychotherapy from its ivory tower and from the customary impression that it is a secret science.
- Use the potentials that are found in self-help.
- Don't view conflicts abstractly, but also concretely, in terms of their contents.

What this book wants to do
- Not to speak solely to people with psychotherapeutic training. The book is designed for a broad audience.
- To provide physicians and psychologists with useful Information.
- To confront psychiatrists and psychotherapists with a new theory and new therapeutic methods.
- Through its concepts, particularly those of the actual capabilities, differentiation analysis attempts to overcome the language barriers. It will thus be possible for the therapist to communicate with a member of the working class, and to give the patient the feeling that we can understand him and his problems. Differentiation analysis can thus contribute to giving all people an equal opportunity, at least in psychotherapy.

- The more it is realized that psychic and psychosomatic disorders are related in content to the actual capabilities, that is, to psychosocially relevant norms, the more the methods of differentiation analysis will be recognized by science and by the public.

Chapter I:
Differentiation Analytical Theory
(Positive Psychotherapy)

THOUGHTS ON (POSITIVE PSYCHOTHERAPY) EDUCATION

SHADOWS ON THE SUNDIAL

In the East, a king once wanted to please his subjects. Since they did not know what a clock was, he brought back a sundial from one of his trips. His gift changed the lives of the people in the kingdom. They began to differentiate parts of the day and to divide up their time. Becoming more prompt, orderly, reliable, and industrious, they produced great wealth and a high standard of living. When the king died, his subjects wondered how they could pay tribute to his achievements. Because the sundial symbolized the king's generosity and was the cause for their success, they decided to build around it a splendid temple with a golden cupola. But, when the temple was finished and the cupola soared above the sundial, the rays of the sun no longer reached the dial. The shadow, which had told the time for the citizens, had disappeared; the common point of orientation, the sundial, was covered. The one citizen was no longer punctual, the other no longer reliable, the third no longer industrious. Each of them went their own way. The kingdom collapsed.

The fable about the sun, the sundial, and the splendid palace that became darkened can easily be carried over to the situation of education. Each individual has at his disposal a number of capabilities that he develops in the course of his growing up and in confrontation with his environment. At first the parents are the most important people in that environment, but other people involved in the upbringing can also support or block the capabilities that are sensitive, undeveloped, and malleable when the child is still very young. Quite often there is an obstructive process similar to what we find in the fable. So that the child will mature into the kind of person he envisions, the educator places certain socially desirable qualities in the foreground. In many cases they appear as highly stylized and cultivated into a perfect one-sidedness. In this connection some qualities in the child are developed and differentiated, often even stretched too far; and other qualities are

2

suppressed and forced into the shadows, as was the wondrous invention, the sundial, in the splendid temple.

EDUCATION AND RE-EDUCATION

It may seem strange to some readers when we mention problems of upbringing in the same breath with problems in partnerships, marriage, and interpersonal relationships. Whenever we wondered whether this kind of juxtaposition and intermingling was even admissible, our thoughts forced us to abandon the narrow concept of upbringing as merely parental influence on children. In all forms of interpersonal influence, even the way attitudes and expectations are formed and conflicts are settled, we repeatedly found the basic principles of education: Parents are not the only factor in their children's upbringing; the way the children behave can also have an educational effect. The parents' behavior, on the other hand, is marked by the upbringing they themselves received. The same holds true for the relationships within the partnership. When we use this term, we are referring to a close relationship such as a friendship, a marriage or a work relationship where interpersonal contact plays a central role. Long-range interests perhaps common goals, and, at any rate, strong emotional ties characterize partnership, in general - in this case also the relationship between parents and child. Harmony or strife, both created by the partnership, are not just the result of rational decisions and well-founded attitudes: The whole realm of experience which a person has from the start of his existence, and which he partly derives from tradition, gives its own stamp to his feelings, reactions, attitudes, expectations, and mode of thought.

Since each person brings his own «educational sphere» with him, it happens all too often that other people's expectations are unfulfilled, people simply talk right past each other, and finally hate each other. And what happens if we transfer these considerations to other social relationships, including groups, peoples, nations, and cultures? One could go so far as to develop a social theory that emphasizes interactional difficulties as well as economic factors.

Conflicts do not strike like lightning out of the sky, leaving one as defenseless as if only a lightning rod were at one's disposal. Rather, our conflicts have their own developmental history. This is the basis for what we optimistically call reeducation: the attempt to reduce conflict potential by means of education after the fact. The social institutions responsible for reeducation are psychotherapy and psychological consultation. But they are meaningful and successful only when they go beyond the therapist-patient relationship. Unfortunately there are too few practicing therapists for that. It seems more practical, meaningful, and effective if the conflict partners themselves are incorporated into the re-educational process.

Education and reeducation are thus not limited just to children; they touch on general questions of human coexistence:

How did I learn to hate?
Why is it that I can't stand this particular person?
Why does this particular trait of my husband drive me up the wall?
Why does my wife's conduct make me so angry when I can accept that same conduct in another person?
Why did I lose my temper with my child?
How is it that I could hate someone yesterday and accept him today?

We want to try to study these questions in which concern every individual. We want to look into causes, test assumptions, and find suitable solutions.

If you give someone a fish,
you feed him only once.
But if you teach him how to fish,
he can feed himself forever.
(Oriental saying)

DESPERATION AND HOPE

Education is a process of confrontation; it comprises various levels and a number of parties. Without a doubt, the focal point is the mutual relationship between parents and child. But this relationship is further dependent on the relationship between the parents, their own ideas on education, their relationship with society, and the influence of its moral institutions. Education is not just a matter for the parents; it involves everyone who in some way communicates with other people and, whether by intent or not, exerts a lasting influence.

Hand in hand with social changes there is a change in the customary educational styles and their contents. In our time we have witnessed an expansion of the possibilities and directions that the individual can take as he unfolds. In many cases the possibilities also create a lot of uncertainty for parents, teachers, and educators. Parents react in different ways: they can be prudent, be shaken in their confidence, or defiantly express themselves in a provocative show of self-confidence.

«*When I come home at night,*» so a father reports, «*the children are in bed. If they don't want to go to sleep right away and disturb me, I give them a little slap on their backsides, and then there's peace and quiet. My wife has finally come to realize that this is an old and reliable way to do things.*» «*I don't spank my children,*» another person says. «*You shouldn't do that anymore. After all, we live in the twentieth century. I bought my kids a dog that they play with in the evening. They have a lot of fun with him. They take him into their room and play with him so much that we can enjoy a peaceful evening. It is important, you know, to have some peace and quiet after a hard day's work.*»

The terms «authoritarian,» «laissez-faire,» and «anti-authoritarian,» as they refer to educational styles, do not hide the fact that almost everyone has developed his own particular educational practices, which nonetheless, are marked by the situation in which they are applied. We are dealing with a pluralism of educational styles for which there seem to be no common standards of measurement and no common basis for communications. There really isn't a lack of educational practices. But we do need criteria for judging which practice is timely and appropriate for the situation at hand.

The insecurity, desperation, and hope that confront people all have a general significance. This forces us to see educational problems in the general framework of the individual's situation, and of the situation of the particular society and of mankind.

FUNCTIONAL CHANGE IN EDUCATION AND PSYCHOTHERAPY

The principles of education and psychotherapy have always been dependent on the conceptions about mankind that prevailed in a particular era. Included in this vision of man are the experiences one has with one's own parents and fellow men, as well as the experiences derived from tradition or from other people. Education teaches one to behave in a manner that is desired by the particular social environment. It is tied to particular groups and is also dependent in a greater sense on the value systems of the prevailing philosophy of life and religion. This holds true for every type of education, regardless of how different it may otherwise be. In other words, education transmits norms that offer the child a point of departure for a life that is relatively free of conflict. The process of adapting to such norms we term «socialization».

How do these norms work when faced by the changes that a society undergoes in its development; how do these norms work when faced by what Toynbee sought to circumscribe as the destruction of values? In fact, no firm, static relational systems today can be asserted as the «right education». In earlier times religion provided the point of departure, the criteria, the standards of measurement, and the goals for education. It showed what was right and wrong, good and bad. But since religion and churches, as moral institutions, did not pay timely attention to the demands and needs of the people in their social environment, these institutions were replaced by an emancipated society as the transmitter of social norms. Viewed in this way, there is not a destruction of values, but a shift in values in terms of a functional change.

There emerged a number of views about what factors determine a person's behavior and about the factors responsible for development and its disorders. In earlier times the body was considered the cause of physical and mental illnesses, but today segments of the environment (home, school, social and moral institutions) are viewed as the responsible factors. An important change has taken place. *You inherited this from your father. He lies all the time too.* Today such a statement has become, *I'm like this because my parents raised me this way. I can't go back and change the way I was brought up.* The physical and environmental factors are themselves dependent on another dimension: *the dimension of time.*

In reference to incongruities in educational practices, the dimension of time means the following: One treats the child the same way he was raised himself (identification), without considering the demands which the current times place on the child. *My child should have it just as nice as I had it.* Another untimely attitude can be seen when parents criticize the upbringing they had to endure, and now practice just the opposite. *My child should have it better than I had.*

This attitude likewise disregards the child's capabilities and the demands of the times. Unconsciously this attitude usually contains mostly parental wishes and conflicts (projection).

Probably the most common reaction is indifference. The parents are unsure of themselves. They know, of course, that the learned style of education is problematical, and they try to modify it, but they can't free themselves from identification and projection. They cloak their inconsistency with tolerance: One raises the child according to momentary (variable) ideas, information, and whims (generalization).

The dimension of time is not only important for the educational style. It is also crucial as a human capability. While an animal lives primarily in the present, man is able to look at the past, present, and future. Because of his experiences, discouragements, disappointments, and impressions, he is fixated on one of these three areas. Escape into the past (in loneliness and illness), escape into the present (work), and escape into the future (daydreaming) are the result. In this way most human conflicts can be interpreted as a disorder of the time dimension, that is, the lack of an integration of past, present, and future. If the time dimension is not given consideration, the result is fixation, resistance, and indifference. The consequences can be found in politics, religion, and science. Giordano Bruno was burned at the stake as a heretic, because he taught, among other things, that the earth revolved around the sun. A few years later Galileo was forced to retract his views, even though he knew they were true. When Sigmund Freud used a case of male hysteria to present his new theory to the Viennese society of physicians, he was repudiated in such a way that he never again visited the group. Examples such as these could be cited ad infinitum.

Education depends on the vision of man that prevails at a particular time in a particular society. In the development of the personality there is more at play than just the body and the environment. Indeed, these can only be understood when one considers also their variability under the dimension of time.

Social Conflicts - Norms

The importance of physical factors, just like the importance of the environment, is generally recognized. But what are the behavioral areas to which psychic disorders and interpersonal conflicts are related? A systematic look at these behavioral areas can pave the way for new and effective methods of psychotherapy and psychohygiene.

Examples of Social Conflict Situation in Education

When company comes, don't forget to watch your manners.

Let's inquire into social norms, those norms that determine human interaction. They are transmitted by education. Corrections, as related to the individual's processing of his experiences, are brought about through psychotherapy. Observation of everyday confrontations between parents and child, between child and school, and between the parents themselves and in their dealings with other people all show an abundance of contents which are carried out as in the following way:

Get up, or you'll be late. The only time you were on time was when you were born. (Punctuality)

You don't even need to say hello. But when company comes, don't forget to watch your manners. (Politeness)

Don't contradict me all the time. If I tell you to come, you have to do what I say. (Obedience)

Your clothes are flying all around the room again. Will you finally put your things where they belong? (Order)

If you keep being so lazy, I'll be ashamed of you. You can't leave the house until you've done your homework. (Ambition).

When you bring company home, the house ends up a total wreck. The next time you invite someone over, you can clean and straighten up the place afterwards alone. (Order - Cleanliness - Contact)

Interpersonal communication and social relationships seem related to these kinds of themes in similar ways. A mother's conversation with her two-year-old, for instance, consists almost exclusively of demands, wishes, praise, and reprimands.

EXAMPLES OF SOCIAL CONFLICT SITUATIONS IN PSYCHOTHERAPY

For my husband punctuality and order are like a sealed book

In psychotherapy one finds that behind the complaints, fears, depression, aggression, and psychosomatic disorders, there are motives that are related to definite social norms. Headaches, sleeping disorders, tension, or aggressiveness after confrontations at work can appear as the result of educational problems with one's children and in connection with unyielding mental problems.

But when we say that there are stresses behind these disorders, we have not yet said anything about the nature of these stresses. Generally people tend to see only job stress. But in fact there exists a whole spectrum of behaviors and attitudes that become potentials for conflict and erupt into conflict when the situation is ripe. The following patient reports can provide examples:

When I find out that there's a special math exercise being done at school I'm very nervous until my daughter Renate (9 years old) comes home with her grade. If her work is good, I feel better. But if she did poorly, I get a bad headache. (32-year-old mother of three. Heart trouble and circulatory problems)

I had to give up my last job, even though I enjoyed working there... because I didn't do a few important assignments right... I wasn't orderly enough for my boss. He always got upset over the way my desk looked... Frequently I was five or ten minutes late... (27-year-old secretary, depression, circulatory problems)

For my husband punctuality and order are like a sealed book. I always have to wait for him, because he never tells me when he'll come home. And he just leaves all his things lying around. I really get upset about that. (28-year-old patient among other things, severe headaches, depression, sexual disorders, but with no internal or neurological cause)

I get in to bad moods and feel terribly depressed. At night I can't fall asleep, and if I do, I wake up screaming a couple of hours later. Then I feel very afraid and don't know where I am. Once I've found the light switch, I can slowly start to calm down. I feel everything is beyond my control. I'm very irritable. These problems started two years ago when my husband died of a heart attack. He was much too overworked and worried too much about the company's finances. A colleague of my husband's, in whom my husband confided a lot, didn't do the bookkeeping properly. So we got into trouble with the auditors and taxman. And on top of all that, there was the problem of some of our supplies disappearing. When he died, I was left with the business and all its problems. I don't know whom I should entrust the business to. I don't trust anybody anymore, not even myself, because I never learned the business and still feel overwhelmed by it. I panic at the idea that because of my ignorance the business is slowly heading for bankruptcy. (48-year-old businesswoman with depression and anxiety after the death of her husband. There are underlying conflicts associated with the areas of exactness, order, honesty, trust, and confidence.)

I'm developing a heart problem because obedience and order are like a foreign language to my son Mark (5 years old). The 27-year-old mother suffers from heart trouble and depression; for an entire week she keeps a record of her son's behavior:

Sunday: Today Mark is supposed to go to a church procession, either with his father or with his classmates. He decided to go with his father. But he didn't stay there very long. Came back home right away. But I sent him right back. The procession was in the park. Mark went back there, but didn't take part in the program. He just wandered around by himself. Only did what he wanted to. Today he was neat. At dinnertime he changed clothes without being told. Even put his clothes away.

Monday: Once again, he didn't listen to his grandparents. They ended up aggravating themselves with him. But he couldn't care less. They can threaten to tell me everything when I get home. He just laughs. They ought to give him a good spanking one of these times. I think that's what he needs. As far as neatness is concerned, things were okay today.

Tuesday: Right after his bath he went out in the rain. I called to him several times and said he should come in. He already had a little cough. My words didn't even register with him. He had to go to bed early because he had gotten up so early. After a while I wanted to look in on him to see if he was sleeping. He had moved his whole Lego box to the bed and had started building things. He was asleep on my bed. He had just taken over. I really didn't know how there'd be room in bed for me. A big mess everywhere. His neatness left a lot to be desired today. His room and my kitchen were a no man's land. Everything all over the floor, regardless of what it was - toys, building blocks, model cars, and all the stuff in his little tool box. He brought home some old boards and tubes again. He likes it when things are a mess.

Wednesday: Today he made a mess of his room again. Cleaned out his closet. Threw shoes and trousers on the floor. Right along with his cars and building blocks. All his stuffed animals were on the fur rug by his bed. I was barely back home and called him in to start cleaning up. At first I was going to do it myself, but that was too much for me. He's got to do it now. After all, he made the mess all by himself. He doesn't need any help for that.

Thursday: Mark hasn't tidied up his room for days, but that doesn't bother him one bit. Before I left for work I said, « Mark, when I get home tonight, I want to see this cleaned up. Or I'm going to be mad.» So he cleaned it all up. I said, «See how nice you can do that? You did a beautiful job. You should start taking better care of your things, then they'll be even more fun for you,» He agreed.

Friday: He was disobedient after he got up, and he really should have been well rested. He threw his pajama pants in the hallway, and the shirt on the floor of his room. I hollered, «Mark, please pick those things up after you. People don't go throwing their clothes around like that. You're old enough to know that.» Mark again acted deaf and dumb. And I had to do the work myself.

Saturday: He was a little devil again today. Nothing suited him. When he got up he was determined not to join his regular playgroup. The whole day he dawdled around on the street. Again, he didn't listen to his grandparents. His room and the kitchen looked like a battlefield. In the evening it was my pleasure to clean up the place. He watched like a good little boy and didn't make a move.

In looking carefully at these statements we see that certain behavioral areas appear again and again: order, cleanliness, obedience, politeness, honesty, punctuality, ambition, thrift, etc. We use these and similar concepts to express our likes and dislikes, our satisfactions and our displeasures. We need them when we are upset or happy. They are the subject of many of the wishes that we have about our partners, but often unspoken. The importance that is given to them depends on our individual and collective systems of relationships.

While ambition is important to one person in a relationship, the other might emphasize order, punctuality, politeness, honesty and thrift. Each of the concepts can be used in a broad emotional scale: challenging in a well meaning way; urgently pleading; angered or desperate. It can even go so far that a mother takes order so seriously that she says in desperation, «*My seventeen-year-old daughter now shares an apartment with a girlfriend. The place looks like a pigpen. I'd rather see my daughter get pregnant than have to look at that mess.*»

Problems of parenting - as a special group of problems in a partnership - rarely become critical exclusively from the side of the children or the parents. More often it is a question of the relationship between the children and their parents. Because of this, we will not look at children as an object of education. Instead, we will focus on their confrontation with the parents. At the same time, we will try to include the parental problems and marital confrontations as aspects of the educational process.

Social conflicts, hence also educational conflicts and problems in the marital relationship, can be traced back in large part to differing attitudes about the social behavioral norms.

DIFFERENTIATION ANALYTICAL THEORY (POSITIVE PSYCHOTHERAPY)

We have seen that the principles of education and psychotherapy depend on the image of man. Let's try to present an image of man that comes closest to contemporary man according to the most recent psychological and religious views.

When man is born, he is not an unwritten page, but, if we can retain this metaphor, an unread page, or a page that cannot be read. Capabilities and possibilities - the foundation for the person's development - need to mature, and they need the help of the environment. But it is hard to talk about capabilities. After all, one doesn't notice them until they express themselves as accomplishments. It's much like black ants sitting at night on a black stone. You just don't see them. But they're there. And when the situation is right, they can make their presence known. Every person has capabilities like that. But whether they are expressed in the course of his development depends on the condition of his body, his environment, and the times he lives in. These conditions can either support or obstruct the development of those capabilities.

We can start with an investigation of interpersonal conflicts. We look at the standards used to judge others and ourselves; we investigate the criteria of education and psychotherapy; and we question the conditions in which lead to the known psychic and psychosomatic disorders. If we do all that, we find that behind the disorders, to a certain extent as deep structure, there is a lack of distinction concerning one's own behavioral pattern and the pattern of others. These behavioral patterns can be described by means of an inventory of social norms. They are characterized by the fact that they operate as conflict potentials in human interaction. The list includes: punctuality, cleanliness, orderliness, obedience, politeness, honesty, loyalty, thrift, justice, ambition, achievement, reliability, diligence and love, model patience, time, contact, sexuality, trust, confidence, hope, faith, doubt, certainty, and unity. We call these behaviors actual capabilities.

ACTUAL CAPABILITIES

These psychologically valid norms can be grouped according to their contents into two categories, which we will label the secondary and primary capabilities.

Secondary capabilities are an expression of the transmission of knowledge and, hence, the ability to know. In them are reflected the norms of the individual's social group. The secondary capabilities include: punctuality cleanliness, orderliness, obedience, politeness, honesty, thrift, justice, ambition, achievement, reliability, exactness, diligence, etc.

The secondary capabilities play an important role in everyday descriptions and evaluations and in the way that partners judge each other. If someone finds another person nice and likeable, he bases his opinion on these terms:

He's decent and orderly. You can count on him. But if he has the opposite opinion, it goes like this: *He's not likeable because he's sloppy, late, unfair, rode, and stingy and doesn't show much ambition.*

Equally common are the effects that corresponding experiences have on one's mood and on how one feels physically. For example, pedantry, messiness, ritualized cleanliness, lack of cleanliness, excessive demands for punctuality, tardiness, compulsive conscientiousness or unreliability can lead to psychic and psychosomatic reactions, in addition to social conflicts. These reactions - like anxiety, aggression, and imitations - can take place in the psychic area, in one's breathing, in the circulatory system, in the gastrointestinal area, in one's apparatus for movement, in the nervous system, in the urogenital area, and in the skin.

When I think of how unfair my boss is, I start to tremble and get sick to my stomach. Afterwards I have headaches and pain in my stomach. (28-year old employee with psychosomatic disorders)

Only on the basis of emotional relationships can one understand the great affective resonance that occurs in disorders of the secondary capabilities. The primary capabilities are their means of expression.

Primary capabilities deal with the ability to love. From the day of birth they are formed through contact with other people. The primary capabilities include: love, patience, model, time, contact, sexuality, trust, confidence, hope, faith, doubt, certainty, and unity.

In normal language use, some of the concepts are rarely included as «capabilities» in the narrow sense of the term: model, doubt, certainty, and unity. In part they are psychic processes in which specific capabilities are manifested; in part they appear as the results of these processes. As typical forms of appearance they can be included in the group of capabilities. With these capabilities it is not a question of «pure isolated factors.» Rather, they stand in close connection with each other.

When we speak of primary capabilities we don't mean that they are more important than the secondary ones. The term «primary» refers to the face that these capabilities deal with the emotional area, the area close to the ego. The primary capabilities represent the foundational phenomena on which the secondary capabilities are built. As far as content is concerned, the primary capabilities refer to experiences in view of the secondary capabilities. An example of this is a statement from a 22-year-old female patient: *I don't trust my husband any more because he's unreliable and always late.*

On the other hand, the primary capabilities have an intensifying effect on the secondary capabilities. In this regard a 29-year-old female patient said: *The area I react to almost allergically is the concept of orderliness. I get sullen when my 8-year-old daughter doesn't do her homework neatly enough. Then I become impatient and react aggressively.*

Secondary and primary capabilities function like a weapon, a shield, or a pretense: *I don't like my husband. I don't like to have sex with him because he doesn't keep himself clean, and leaves everything lying around. When I think of his body odor, I lose all desire to be near him.* (24-year-old secretary, sexual disorders and circulatory problems)

The Differentiation Analysis Inventory (DAI) of the Secondary and Primary Capabilities:

Secondary Capabilities	Primary Capabilities
Punctuality	Love/emotions
Cleanliness	Model
Orderliness	Patience
Obedience	Time
Politeness	Sexuality
Honesty/openness	Contact
Loyalty	Trust
Justice	Confidence
Ambition/Achievement	Hope
Thrift	Faith/religion
Reliability	Doubt
Exactitude	Certainty
Conscientiousness	Unity

The list of actual capabilities can be taken further, but the thirteen secondary and thirteen primary capabilities (actual capabilities) constitute the behavioral areas that occur most commonly in interpersonal relationships. In addition, other behavioral areas can be taken as gradations and combinations of the capabilities listed above. Veracity and candor, for instance, are included in honesty, prestige and success belong with ambition; and honesty in the marital relationship can be viewed as loyalty while in social communication it could be termed openness and forthrightness. Social norms can be understood systematically as actual capabilities. Man's development is based on them. They are the content of socialization. The actual capabilities operate in all cultures. Only their forms show cultural divergences.

Actual Capabilities and Unity

In the entity which we understand man to be, the factors of body, environment (to which the soul and experience correspond), and time (epitome of consciousness and the human spirit) play a central role. The actual capabilities shape themselves in close relationship to these three dimensions. At the same time they influence one's attitudes to these three areas.

Actual Capabilities and Body
Under the body dimension, we understand the biological factors that form the basis for life. Here we find metabolic processes, reflexes, genetics, physical maturation, the functions of body organs, the functional capabilities of the senses, and the vital needs. Through the means of satisfying the vital needs, individual capabilities are developed or are blocked in their development. In this sense the development of punctuality, for instance, can be viewed in connection with vital rhythms of awakeness, sleep, and hunger, Cleanliness is associated with early toilet training. Depending on the way a person reacts to the child's individual needs and physical peculiarities, the seed is sown for his later self-image and personality.

The actual capabilities thus exert an influence on the person's development. They can also influence how the person is situated: Experiences and conflicts based on actual capabilities affect the psychosomatic realm. They can produce mood changes, anxiety, aggression, and depression. In many cases there are further effects in psychosomatically conditioned organic ailments. Messiness and tardiness in a person can «strike the gallbladder and the stomach» (Peseschkian 1973).

It isn't simply biological factors that influence a person's behavior. He is also influenced by his physical features as they are recognized by himself and others. One's attitudes about them are deeply rooted in one's emotional life: a child is rejected by others because of his red hair; a mother particularly loves her child because of its baby fat; an adolescent thinks his long arms and legs are too gangly; but a lover will gaze in wonder at the long legs of his beloved.

Actual Capabilities and Environment
Like a seed that has an abundance of capabilities that will unfold under the influence of the environment, man also develops his capabilities in close relationship to his surroundings. The environmental dimension is oriented according to the individual's relationship to his social

surroundings. The actual capabilities influence our expectations about the behavior of others as well as the behavior itself - directly or indirectly - by means of rules: *We seek a conscientious, neat, and dependable employee for an interesting position.*

Every inner and external conflict can be described with the concepts of the actual capabilities. Every day we are confronted by their effects in personal and collective areas: when a marriage takes place or is dissolved, when a friendship breaks up, when someone is fired, when the relationships between groups and peoples acquire the potential for conflict. Through the influence of tradition, individual patterns of actual capabilities become the specific characteristics of a group, exerting a strong influence on the group's cohesiveness and on its relationship to other groups (Peseschkian 1970, 1971).

Actual Capabilities and Time

Disruptions in the development of the individual, which are related to the areas concerning the body and the environment, are disruptions in the dimension of time: *I don't trust people because someone abandoned me once. How can I ever again trust my child once he's lied to me?* The contents of the actual capabilities become fixations and thus develop into conflict potentials. The actual capabilities cannot be differentiated according to time because past, present, and future either are not distinguished, are viewed as isolated parts, or are not integrated. Because of misunderstandings, one's own behavior and that of others appears distorted. Fixations mean that the measuring stick for acquired behavior has been made absolute. Fixations are the opposite of understanding and the effort to achieve understanding. An example can be used to show the relationship between fixations and their opposite, flexibility and the ability to change:

I've become a completely new person. I don't quarrel with my husband so much any more. I used to always get upset over his messiness and sloppy habits. Today I am in a position to discuss it with him. I try to understand my husband. If he doesn't take a shower, for instance, I tell him that he should. But I don't make a big issue out of it anymore. (26-year-old patient who previously suffered from headaches and sexual disorders)

The actual capabilities are not abstractions. They frequently appear in behavior via the developmental dimensions of *body, environment,* and *time.*

Significance of the Actual Capabilities

The secondary and primary capabilities (actual capabilities) are not just terms or random phenomena. As specifically human capabilities they are shaped in the course of socialization, then acquired and affectively taken into possession. They are a component of the personality:

When I find out that my daughter has gotten bad marks in school, I develop pains in my heart, and break out in a cold sweat. (34-year-old father of two children)

The actual capabilities have two functions: they offer categories for making descriptions and provide an encompassing inventory of human behaviors.

They are not primarily the language of the specialist, but can be understood immediately. In addition, they are important to us as factors in the development of the personality, the psychodynamics, and the social relationship: They are the contents of socialization, are incorporated into the personality during various periods of life, and lead to the development of individual and social patterns for attitudes, value judgments, and evaluations.

In this regard differentiation analysis does not confine itself to general assertions like the parental home, strong ties to the parents, tyranny, idolization, and hand or soft double-bind upbringing. It doesn't just talk about conflicts of self-esteem, inferiority complexes, or a far-reaching indefinite super-ego. Rather, it presents the concrete contents (actual capabilities) of inner and interpersonal processes.

In psychotherapeutic and medical literature, particularly in the case of behavioral disorders, psychosomatic disorders, neuroses, and psychoses, there are sufficient allusions to individual actual capabilities. According to Sigmund Freud, orderliness, thrift, and willfulness are the products of training from the phase of toilet training. Carl Jung, F. Künkel, and Victor Frankl emphasized the importance of faith. Erich Fromm talked about hope. Mitscherlich expounded on the importance of the demand for achievement and the motivation for achievement. R. Dreikurs discussed

21

success, prestige, and exactitude in connection with educational problems. G. Bach and H. Deutsch pointed to the importance of an open relationship (honesty) in a partnership. E. H. Erikson formulated a sequence of virtues that are built up according to the development stages of the individual and according to the maturity of the psychic functions. He listed trust, hope, will, determination, and loyalty as virtues in adolescence; concern and wisdom as features of adults.

But despite all this literature, the systematic connection to the content components hardly receives any attention at all.

In medical, psychological, pedagogic, and psychotherapeutic literature one returns again and again to the actual capabilities as a unit of behavior, but these actual capabilities remain isolated. Only in differentiation analysis is systematic attention paid to the actual capabilities as a set of all-encompassing categories.

Actual Capabilities and Conflicts

The secondary and primary capabilities can only unfold their full power when they are in harmony with each other. Shifts in this area narrow one's field of vision for making evaluations: Man emphasizes one capability in which he represents at that particular moment. He is so blinded by its value that he becomes blind to other values and capabilities:

A person counts with me only if he conducts himself well. I don't care how successful he is. If he's not courteous, he just doesn't get anywhere with me. (53-year-old patient, headaches and circulatory problems)

The disorders depicted by the actual capabilities can develop out of a dissonance within the secondary capabilities (one can be ambitious, but not orderly), out of a dissonance within the primary capabilities (one can trust others, but not oneself), or out of a dissonance in the relationship between the two (one can be orderly, but not patient). Looking at them from this perspective, we can interpret many things as reactions to conflicts between primary and secondary capabilities; we can thus treat them as the result of a lack of differentiation. Examples of behavioral disorders are educational problems, generation conflicts, child– parent difficulties, marital problems, and conspicuous behavior.

Along with being categories of description, the actual capabilities are also factors of personality development, psychodynamics, and social interaction. We basically understand psychic and psychosomatic problems as the result of a lack of differentiation of the actual capabilities.

BASIC CAPABILITIES

The foundation of differentiation analysis is the view that every person regardless of his stage of development (age, sex, rate, social class, typology, illnesses, or social «abnormalities») - possesses the two basic capabilities, the *ability to know* and the *ability to love* (emotionality).

Ability to know

Each Person tries to discover the connections in reality. He asks why an apple falls to the ground; why a tree grows; why the sun shines; why a car goes; why there are illnesses and suffering. He is interested in what he really is, where he came from, where he is going. Man's ability to ask such questions and to look for their answers is the ability to know. Educationally, this ability is built on the transmission of knowledge. The ability to know is divided into the complementary abilities to learn and to teach, i.e., the ability to make discoveries and to pass them on. Out of the ability to learn there develop such secondary capabilities as punctuality, orderliness, cleanliness, politeness, honesty, and thrift.

Ability to Love

The ability to know is correlated with success and failure, satisfaction and denial - all experiences that are common to everyone. When a child shows poor achievement in school, he soon loses all enjoyment of school. He'll try to avoid doing homework, since for him it is associated with failure. The parents, of course, do not remain indifferent to the child's failure either. But the reverse is also true: Positive achievement can change the entire atmosphere. This refers not only to achievement in the narrow sense of the word, but also to the secondary capabilities. Attitudes and reactions to the various areas of the ability to learn belong in man's emotional realm, the sphere of his feelings. One can designate this sphere as emotional relationships, as the expression of his ability to love. Two components are particularly important here: the ability to actively take up emotional ties (to love) and the ability to accept emotional attention (to be loved). In its further development, the ability to love leads to such primary capabilities as love, patience, time, contact, trust, confidence, hope, faith, doubt, certainty, and unity.

The transmitters of secondary and primary capabilities are religions, cultures, forefathers, parents, and cultural institutions (school, society, and moral institutions). The actual capabilities thus depend on the social and historical conditions. The abilities to know and to love, on the other hand, belong to the essence of every person. This means nothing else than: *Man is essentially good.*

Disorders have nothing to do with the basic capabilities. There is no such thing as bad people. If we can't put up with someone, it may be due to the fact that he looks different than we want him to, maybe because he has a different skin tone, a different facial expression, or certain physical qualities that we don't want to accept. If we detest someone, distance ourselves from him, and become upset because of him, it may be because he doesn't hold the same views we do, that he isn't courteous enough, that he keeps us waiting, is unreliable, and makes demands of us that we find unpleasant and unusual. If we dislike someone, it may be because he disappointed us once, or that others had bad experiences with him and we have thus lost our confidence in him. But we can't hate the ugly person because he is ugly, the rude person because he is rude, and the unreliable person because he is unreliable. Some whom we find ugly are beautiful in the eyes of others. Some who seem rude to us have not yet learned courtesy, as we understand it to be. Some whom we no longer trust deserve our confidence in other areas and at other times. The ideal of beauty has changed over the course of time; the ceremonies of courtesy, highly stylized in earlier times, seem artificial to us today.

Decisions in education and partnerships often require the courage to abandon an objective pose and to admit, *I can't yet help this child, this adolescent, this partner,* instead of saying, *there's nothing anyone can do for him.*

All people possess the two basic capabilities, the ability to know and the ability to love. The three developmental dimensions of body, environment and time are responsible for disorders of the personality.

ACTUAL AND BASIC CONFLICT

If one analyzes psychic and social conflicts, two conflict areas can be identified, both of which affect the type of conflict and its unique features. These two conflict areas are actual conflict and basic conflict.

Actual Conflict

This is the term given to conflict situations directly brought on by pressing problems such as excessive demands at work, marital strife, problems with children or parents, and problems of interpersonal relationships. In terms of content, the conflict situation is played out in the behavioral categories of the actual capabilities, and can be described by them: A child comes home from school and tosses his school bag into the corner of the hallway. His mother sees it from the kitchen and becomes very upset. Does she really have to get so upset? Aren't there perhaps other ways for her to react? Her anger stems from the belief that orderliness is of extreme importance. The conditions for this belief are found in what we refer to as basic conflict.

Basic Conflict

This deals with experiences that a person has in the course of his development, particularly in childhood. These experiences, which usually receive their particular stamp from education, appear in long-held attitudes, expectations, susceptibility to conflict, and conflict thresholds. Why does the mother in the above example believe that throwing the school bag into the corner is important enough to cause her to become upset? This question leads us to find an answer by looking at the mother's own past, particularly in terms of things she has learned. The following situations are plausible: The mother was scolded or punished as a child because she was not tidy. Or: When she was a child, others were responsible for keeping things in order. Now she still expects others to do it. This example could also be extended to such areas as punctuality, cleanliness, politeness, and ambition.

We will now briefly present the conditions for the development of basic conflict, viewing them from a typological aspect. It is thoroughly possible to transfer the typology to chances and risks in education.

The Secondary Type – Overemphasis of the Secondary Capabilities with Insufficient Emphasis on the Primary Capabilities

Development:
The secondary capabilities stand in the foreground of education. People close to the child try to familiarize him as soon as possible with social expectations like achievement, orderliness, punctuality, cleanliness, frugality, etc.

I could rarely invite friends over to play. My mother said they messed up the house too much... (26-year-old engineer, contact disorder, inhibitions, heart trouble)

The educational style is strictly organized in terms of time, and is aimed at developing the child's obedience: *If you adopt do what I say, you'll never amount to anything. Look at how I've turned out, and use it as an example...*

People who are motivated mostly by the secondary capabilities react in typical ways:

As long as I'm successful, I'm worth something.
You can't depend on anything, but your own achievements.
I can do everything by myself.
I don't need help from anybody.
Let the other people work for you.

In such an educational situation, justice is given predominance over love. The main educational means are warnings, threats, the withdrawal of love and physical punishment.

Forms:
There develops the «success and prestige» type; the «object» type, who sees his partner only as an object for satisfying his own needs; the «perfectionist,» who frequently leans toward compulsive behaviors; the «compulsive» person; and in the religious realm the attitudes of intellectual opposition and bigoted superstition.

The Naïve-primary-Type – Overemphasis of the Primary Capabilities with Insufficient Emphasis on the Secondary Capabilities

Development:
The primary capabilities play a dominant role in the education. Here the people close to the child try to clean away all difficulties. The child is thus freed of all burdens and responsibilities.

My mother took care of everything for me... (28-year-old patient, anxiety, difficulty falling asleep, marital problems)

It is characteristic that the child should not be placed under too many demands in his upbringing; he shouldn't exert himself.

You can't do that, sweetheart. I'll do it for you.
And the child responds: *I can't do it alone.*
Others have to help me.
If I don't get help, it's all over.

In the educational situation characterized by this type of reaction, love is more dominant than justice. Typical educational methods include the threat of withdrawal of love, rewards, and gratitude.

Forms:
Several types develop: the sufferer; the modest type; the killjoy; the « naïve-religious» type; the fanatic; and the passive expectation type (in areas of sexuality and achievement). In all of these an attitude of passive expectation predominates. The person expects that other people will smooth out all the problems for him, just as his parents did.

The Double-Bind Type – Primary and Secondary Capabilities Are Emphasized Randomly by One or More Person Close to the Child

Development:
In the educational situation, the people close to the child are unsure, or are not in agreement. They act ambivalently and allow for tendencies of the naïve-primary and the secondary reaction types. Their behavior toward the child is not consistent.

Mom, you want me to play outside. But if I get my shoes and my clothes a little dirty, you scold me. And you barely get done scolding me, and you give me candy. I don't know what's wrong with me... (9-year-old girl, difficulties in concentrating, and compulsion for washing herself)

Characteristic expressions of this type are:

I can do everything by myself... but can't you help me?
I don't know what I want. I want something, but at the same time I don't want it.
I don't like it when you help me. But I'm not happy if you leave me alone either.

Education goes back and forth between justice and love. The means of education change, often irrespective of the fact that, in the child's experience, they are contradictory.

Forms:
Many types result from the double-bind orientation: the insecure one who has trouble making decisions (Hamlet type); the type that wants sexual satisfaction, who loves his partner only until he can feel that he possesses her; the person who is neurotic about being exonerated (occasional heavy involvement in a project, followed by sudden withdrawal from it); and the eternal seeker (ambivalent attitude toward religion).

The various accentuations with the actual capabilities result in typical educational forms and consequences for the educational process. Particularly noticeable are the secondary type, the naïve-primary-type, and the double-bind type. Certain susceptibilities to conflict correspond to these three types. But they do not necessarily lead to open conflicts.

PARENTAL TYPES

The particular educational forms responsible for the reaction types we have depicted are determined by the behavioral patterns of the parents.

Within the framework of various ways for taking over a role within the family, there are different parental types, which, in their extreme cases, look like caricatures. In practice they frequently overlap.

Various types of mother
The professional mother: This mother is basically there for the children. She cooks, cleans, and keeps everything in order for the children.

The doll mother: This mother's love goes only to young children. She loves and takes care of her children only as long as they are small and helpless. As they get bigger, she withdraws her love and attention. She becomes remote.

The sacrificial mother: This mother takes great pains in raising her children. For her it's important to be a good housewife. She sacrifices her freedom and her time and forgets herself. Neglecting her own interests, she is happy to offer herself in this way. Later she develops a need for the children's gratitude.

The anxious mother: She tries to shield her children from everything dangerous and difficult. Everywhere she sees danger, negative elements; she is overly concerned.

The alien mother: This mother does not show her children that she loves them. She saves her love. She often kisses her children secretly while they are asleep. Her style of raising them is exact and perfected.

The movable bookcase: This mother regards the education of her children as her duty. She raises them by the book, according to plan. She is overly exact, but is lacking in natural attention and love.

The jealous mother: This type of mother becomes upset when her children begin to become independent and loosen themselves from the home. The mother then feels superfluous and accuses the children of being ungrateful. She tries to hold on to her dominating position by criticizing them even when they are already grown up. She disapproves of the way they dress, the way they look, their friends, and the way they keep house.

The buddy mother: She is her children's pal, the exact opposite of the alien mother. She empathizes with them, feels their hurt, and can't say no. She postpones their education until later on.

The part-time mother: Because of her career and other activities, the upbringing of her children is neglected. The part-time mother tries to make up for this when she gets home in the evening. She then smothers her children with attention and toys.

In our experience we have found that all these types are the result of various educational situations with their different educational style. The various types of mother can be categorized with the three educational forms as follows:

- Emphasis on secondary upbringing: the movable bookcase, the alien mother
- Naïve-primary upbringing: the professional mother, the doll mother, the sacrificial mother, the overly careful mother
- Double-bind upbringing: the part-time mother, the jealous mother, the buddy mother

Various types of father
The patient angel: The naïve father who removes himself from his children's problems, but is concerned and shows emotional attention.

The theoretician: Words are his force; deeds are not his thing. He raises his children according to theory. He pays less attention to the uniqueness of the child.

The stubborn father: His children should work, not play. He wants his children to amount to something. His child rearing is stubbornly aimed at achieving this. He determines what the child can and can't do. He allows for no freedom or latitude for the child's own activities.

The dictator: He raises his children like soldiers. His strict discipline requires absolute orderliness, obedience, ambition, and punctuality. He insists on all of these. Deep down he's often very good-hearted, but he doesn't know how to combine strictness with tenderness in the educational process. The dictatorial father makes sure his orders are obeyed, but he does allow a certain latitude.

The magician: He gives his children total freedom, allowing them to do what they want if it suits his fancy. The children regard him as a companion, but the mother often suffers quite a bit from the father's attitude.

The sovereign: He treats his children like adults. He doesn't praise or reprimand them. He thinks that through his mere presence he can raise his children; and that as a «silent servant» he can do his duty in raising them.

The various father types can also be placed into three categories of educational form:

- Emphasis on secondary upbringing: the theoretician, the dictator, the stubborn father
- Naïve-primary upbringing: the patient angel
- Double-bind upbringing: the magician, the sovereign

Most parents are probably oriented toward the double-bind upbringing, but the father role seems to lean toward an emphasis on the secondary capabilities. An overemphasis on the primary capabilities could be typical for the maternal role.

Types are by their very nature abstract summaries of common characteristics. Reality is much more colorful. Here there are fewer pure forms, but more mixed forms in their various shades and degrees.

A major difference between these typical attitudes and behaviors on the one hand, and the customary typologies on the other, is that with the former we grasp the reaction type dynamically because of the conditions for its development. Basic temperament and talent play a secondary role here. This means further: The educational form, even the parental role, is not a necessary fate, but can change over the course of time.

Like the parental types, such reaction types are characteristic attitudes that we have often found in psychotherapeutic practice in connection with corresponding disorders. But to prove these connections statistically under the aspect of the actual capabilities is a task for the future.

The educational forms and their results can be distinguished according to the concepts of the actual capabilities as follows:

The naïve-primary type: Overemphasis of the primary capabilities with insufficient emphasis on the secondary capabilities.

The secondary type: Overemphasis of the secondary capabilities with insufficient emphasis on the primary capabilities.

The double bind type: Primary and secondary capabilities are emphasized randomly by one or more persons.

CHAPTER II:
ACTUAL CAPABILITIES
(PRIMARY AND SECONDARY
CAPABILITIES)

Actual Capabilities

The Sightseers and the Elephant

The elephant was supposed to be the main attraction at the show; the people came in throngs to see it. But since the elephant was kept in a dark room at night, the sightseers couldn't see him. Each could only touch one part of the great animal, and describe him accordingly.

One of the visitors, who had grabbed the elephant by the leg, explained that the elephant looked like a strong pillar; a second one, who touched its tusks, described him as a pointed object; a third, who got hold of the elephant's ear, described him as a fan; and a fourth, stroking his hand over the elephant's back, said that the elephant was as straight and flat as a couch. (After J. Rumi, Persian poet)

Everyone sees correctly, but not everyone sees everything. One person wants to have a good child; another wants a child that is alert and achievement oriented; and yet another wants one that is dependent. The one woman chooses her mate on the basis of how successful he is; another wants a man who is gentle and considerate. One man dreams of a tidy woman who is the housewife type; another wants one who is ambitious and independent. They all try to envision and comprehend their spouse, but they do this from only one perspective. They view a person only as the bearer of a few particular characteristics, not as a whole personality.

The diversity of the actual capabilities is found in varying degrees in every individual. It could be a new experience for a partner if he went beyond the previously observed capabilities and inquired into his partner's other qualities and investigated to what extent they were present.

The actual capabilities play a significant role in our professional and private lives. Contemporary civilization is grounded in them. Education continually draws on them. Marital and interpersonal relationships are played out against them. What's remarkable is that nearly everyone deals with them in some way, but only a few really know what they mean. They are given short shrift in even the most well known dictionaries and encyclopedias. They are either barely mentioned, or receive only a brief explanation. As a result, they are underestimated or overestimated, generalized into whole areas of life, or projected onto other people. This can lead to conflicts in one's experience and behavior; it can also produce psychosomatic disorders.

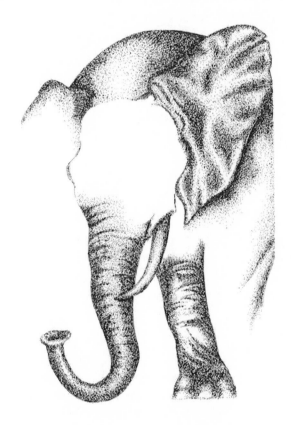

Nossrat Peseschkian, M.D.

WHAT ARE THE FUNCTIONS OF THE ACTUAL CAPABILITIES?

They are descriptive categories
Behaviour can be described from the perspective of interpersonal and personal conflicts and also from the perspective of an extensive conflict potential going back into the concepts of the actual capabilities.

They are socialization variables
The actual capabilities are the contents of education. In accordance with the needs of a society, they are transmitted to its members. Industrial society is based on characteristic expressions of punctuality, exactness, orderliness, ambition, and dependability. The desired behavioral patterns in an industrial society are marked by a certain neglect of the areas encompassed by the *primary capabilities*. Other conceptual systems express this state of affairs with the term «renunciation of drive.»

They can become a substitute religion
As absolutes, they are taken out of their context of functional balance and are placed in the center of a person's view of the world and mankind: *Orderliness is what life's all about. I'm somebody only if I'm successful. Organization and success are what separate man from animals. I can't stand my job anymore. The guy I work with is so arrogant. I dropped out of school because I couldn't put up with my teacher's lack of fairness.* Means and ends become confused with each other.

In various situations they function as masks
In some cases it seems useful to fake individual actual capabilities in order to attain a particular goal. This deception does not always take place unconsciously. An example of this could be the politeness and attentiveness of a fiancée who, after the marriage, becomes a complacent and demanding pasha.

They can serve as a weapon or a shield
The affective resonance of the actual capabilities turns them into unique weapons: *Since you aggravate me with your messiness, I'm not obliged to be nice to you. Since you upset me with your impatience, I'll just keep you waiting. If you are going to be lazy and disobedient, we're going to have you clean up*

the hallway. Because you have so little time for me, I'm not attracted to you anymore. In such situations one is not aware of treating the other person in a sadistic way. I use the term sadistic in its classic meaning here: One derives pleasure from the punishment and suffering of the other person. The «weaponry» of the actual capabilities can also be pointed at one's self, leading to both pleasurable and unpleasant experiences: *I'm too polite to tell an unwanted guest that I have an important meeting; because of my lack of honesty I cancel an important appointment and then feel angry with my visitor and with myself.* Other people might develop a remarkable talent for arriving late or for missing appointments. This is how they bring punishment upon themselves.

The primary and secondary capabilities relate to each other in the personality of the individual. The secondary capabilities are behavioral categories; the primary capabilities are emotional categories. This differentiation receives its particular weight from the organization of behavior and experience. Behavioral forms acquire their emotional resonance on the basis of the primary capabilities. Only through a lack of patience, for example, can we get upset about someone being late. Our aggravation itself is an expression of emotionality. The primary capabilities represent the basic phenomenon to which the secondary capabilities are related.

Secondary Capabilities
Primary Capabilities

The emotional area thus offers intensification, rewards, or punishment for a behavioral area of the secondary capabilities. And on the other hand, there is an affective resonance, in the sense of the primary capabilities, on particular secondary behavioral forms. One is more likely to develop trust or confidence in someone who is obedient and reliable, than in someone who does not show these qualities. Disobedience or unreliability, viewed in this context, is frequently experienced as a breach of trust. Conflicts between people such as parents, children, and educators are often based on such a relationship between obedience and trust. Still accustomed to childlike obedience, parents and others are often helpless when confronted by a youth's striving for self-realization. At such times, people may feel doubt or outright mistrust. The outward signs of personal independence - one's own handling of time, and personal taste in clothes, career, and social interaction - become the symbol of a crisis in trust. Parents and teachers mistrust their children (and the consequences of their education). Adolescents feel their parents don't understand them, and for this reason consider them unsuitable for maintaining or developing a relationship of trust. And just as trust can be connected with obedience and reliability, it can also appear in connection with other secondary behavioral areas, for example politeness, punctuality, ambition, and the general ability to accomplish things. These processes are not limited to the narrower field of upbringing and education, but also occur in marital and interpersonal relationships.

The secondary and primary capabilities, as we have pointed out, relate to each other in the development of the individual and also in partner relationships and in the interaction between parents and the child. We express this fact by referring to them as corresponding capabilities. Experience has shown that a shift to one side or the other within the actual capabilities, particularly within the corresponding capabilities, can lead to a restriction of the entire field of values.

IS ONE ACTUAL CAPABILITY MORE IMPORTANT THAN ANOTHER?

Alternatives are the result of various educational circles: for one person, reliability might be the ideal behavior, while contact ranks at the second level. Someone else may value contact very highly, but pay no attention to reliability. The difference between educational circles can be even more pronounced if one looks at the level of development. Parents, children, and spouses can be more different than people of different cultural groups. But at the same time, people can often use their biographical similarities to establish an understanding in various areas of the actual capabilities.

Not everyone must have the orderliness of a bookkeeper, the punctuality of a stonemason, the exactness of a tailor, and the cleanliness of a surgeon. Separated from the situation and the point in time, which gives them their full justification, these capabilities become caricatures; indeed, they even become the potential for conflict. Before and after an operation, a surgeon washes his hands several times, each time from three to five minutes. If he does the same thing at home and if he requires it of his family as well, they will see it as a farce, even though it is justified and essential in the other situation. But at home it has no purpose. The child resists, the mother gets upset, and family life is disturbed.

In the following sections we will present the basic features of the actual capabilities. But only a few important correlations can be treated here. It remains for the reader to think about the aspects in which there is no space for here.

We have tried to do justice to the dynamic cohesiveness of the primary capabilities by presenting them as a developmental or communication chain. The actual capabilities are expanded on in the chapter entitled «Misunderstandings.» This is particularly the case with sex/sexuality and love, which, in our world, seem particularly susceptible to misunderstandings. The most commonly occurring conflicts and disorders will be presented in connection with each actual capability.

From the patients' stories we gathered frequently recurring disorders and conflicts that often appear in connection with individual actual capabilities. When the image of a disease is associated with a particular actual capability, one must keep in mind that other actual capabilities can also be at work, but the one being described occupies the foreground.

Primary Capabilities

When a child uses every aggressive means at his disposal to get what he wants, the parents often feel they don't understand the world any more. Aggression is thus viewed as something threatening, alien, and even sick. People with this opinion fail to realize that aggression, just like anxiety and imitation, is a central component in the child's development.

Capabilities: The Influence of Anxiety, Aggression and Imitation

EVERY ACT OF BRUTALITY HAS ITS ORIGINS IN A WEAKNESS.
(Seneca)

A child's capabilities thrust their way outward. In principle they develop much like the child's ability to walk: they unfold into complete functional capabilities. In learning to walk the child displays expansive tendencies; his urge to move forward and outward is controlled by his fear. The child wants to walk, but also wants to avoid unpleasant experiences such as being injured by falling down. The child reveals certain insecurities and the need to have more security. In this sense man's progressive development is based on the interaction between anxiety and aggression.

Learning with models, the process of imitation further these learning experiences. It all depends on how the mother reacts to the child's developing capabilities:

Anna Freud found that during bombing raids in England in World War II the children became frightened only when their mothers were anxious. When the mothers remained calm, so did the children.

Anxiety and aggression have their own position in parenting. In West Germany the number of children murdered by their parents each year is ten times greater than the number of children who are sexually murdered. And this doesn't take into consideration the number of children who are abused by their parents day after day. But aggression as an innate drive in man is not the factor. Aggression is related to anxiety and imitation, and is a learned behavior. In terms of content these experiences are associated with the actual capabilities.

The model for these behaviors is a person closely associated with the child. Their relationship is characterized by very definite attitudes.

Disorder and Conflicts
See «Anxiety, Aggression and Imitation as Conflict Potentials»

MODEL

EDUCATE YOURSELF AND INFLUENCE OTHERS THROUGH WHAT YOU ARE. (Wilhelm von Humboldt)

A model is a person or his actions insofar as someone imitates them or selects them as a measure of his own behavior. In adopting new behaviors into his repertoire, a person undergoes three processes:

- The child imitates his parents because he feels the imitation is rewarding in itself. He smokes those awful cigarettes because they make him feel like his father.
- Imitation takes place because it is rewarded. *«You tidied your cupboard just the way I've done it for twenty years. You're a smart child.»*
- Imitation does or does not take place because the model was rewarded or punished. «I'd have said something too, but after I saw my brother get *spanked, I decided to keep quiet.»*

For the child's self-image, the model behavior of the main people surrounding the child and his siblings is of great importance. The parents' behavior toward each other serves as a model for partner relationships. And the parents' attitudes and behavior toward neighbors and others outside the family help to form the child's relationships to these groups. Whether the child asks religious questions, or questions the meaning of things (and how he answers them), depends in large part on the model in his earliest environment. The model is always the concrete observable behavior (secondary and primary capabilities) of the persons close to the child. When parents punish certain behaviors in their child, they are really punishing the model that they themselves presented: A father spanked his child for piling books, folders, notes, and other items on his desk. And at the same time the father's car was littered with all sorts of things.

Disorders and Conflicts
Tendencies toward imitation; restriction of one's ability to make a judgment; affective rejection of the model; excessive self-reliance; ambivalent attitude toward the model; wavering between love and hate; inhibitions when with a stifling model; unrealistic expectations of oneself and the model; impatience.

FAITH

BELIEVE IN GOD AND TIE YOUR CAMEL SECURELY. (Mohammed)

The person close to the child (for instance the mother) automatically establishes a relationship with the undeveloped and hence unknown capabilities in the child. Although she doesn't know what capabilities the child possesses, she believes in them.

By associating with the child's capabilities, she supports their development - assuming that she herself has access to corresponding capabilities within her. If her own capabilities are not sufficiently differentiated, it is hard, or impossible, for her to relate to them within the child.

The example of learning to walk can be applied to the development of other physical capabilities as well as to the actual capabilities. The capabilities are at first unknown areas in which unfold continually or only in spurts. Usually we perceive unknown things outside and within us as possible threats to our security. We are faced with the task of coming to terms with the unknown. Only when these as yet undifferentiated capabilities are confronted by our physical requirements and the needs of our outer and inwardly accepted environment is it finally possible for us to integrate these capabilities into the structure of our personality.

And here the question arises as to whether a person has sufficient tool functions to come to terms with the unknown. In this respect faith is a fundamental capability of man. In his attitude and expectations about the unknown he draws not only on the unknown in him, but also on the unknown in his environment and on the incomprehensible in the universe. This is also referred to as the concept of *God*. Even science, which thinks of itself as being objective, is based on faith. Through faith, the small individual steps of the hypothesis, one moves step by step toward the unknown.

The potential capabilities of a person are a part of his reality. They are the basis for his future development and must be recognized by others and by himself if they are not to be stifled because of lack of attention to them. *I don't think there are still capabilities in me that someone could develop. I've built up a firm theory that goes like this: «I can retain nothing.» That gives me poor prospects for my career. Why should I accept myself? After all, everybody rejects me anyway.* (33-year-old schizophrenic)

Man doesn't develop his capabilities in a linear fashion; nor does the process correspond in its details to the expectations one holds about them.

Disorders and Conflicts

Fixation; superstition; bigotry; anxiety; aggression; imitation; resignation; mood fluctuations; existential fear.

TIME

PEOPLE WHO NEVER HAVE TIME DO THE LEAST. (Lichtenberg)

Neither a child nor an adult partner can be molded like putty. In relating to those close to him, a child doesn't just adapt to that person's expectations; the child also follows his own inner laws. The person close to him must face this fact. He must be ready to allow the child or partner some time.

My daughter always had to be ahead of the other children, in toilet training, in learning to walk, in talking, and in school. (32-year-old mother of a 12-year-old child with learning disabilities)

Time means giving the other person time for his development. But it also means giving him time in appropriate measure and in sufficient quality - in other words, attention. When a mother says, «I'm with my children all day long,» she is not telling us anything about what she does during this time with her children. If a mother uses this time to criticize impatiently, to scold, nag, and impose her idea of «parenting,» she has used her time differently than a mother who allows her children some latitude and occupies herself with them accordingly. Along with its significance for development and for parental or partner attention, time also touches the characteristic human capability to consciously manage the past, present, and future, and to integrate these time dimensions.

Disorders and Conflicts
Excessive demands; insufficient demands; neglect, anxiety; fear of being alone; escape into company; impatience; isolation; excessive preoccupation with the body as a substitute for attention; escape from home; dependence on friends; egotism.

DOUBT

HE WHO SEEKS TO KNOW RIGHT MUST FIRST HAVE DOUBTED IN THE RIGHT WAY. (Aristotle)

The discontinuity in a person's development, its often unpredictable course makes the people close to him feel insecure. This lack of sureness, this fluctuation in one's belief about the person's capabilities, is called *doubt*. Doubt results from a certain disappointment in the expectations one has for the child. One finds oneself in a state of indecisiveness. Doubt is characterized by a distorted time dimension, which is represented as an imbalance between the child's developmental time and the other person's expectation time. To the extent that the person is able to view the childish behavior within its developmental time, the person's doubts and the associated anxieties and aggressions will be channelled.

... But then I began to have my doubts. Before I was very authoritarian. I believed you had to break the children's will. The children had to be home when I wanted them to. I didn't allow stylish clothes or haircuts. They all had

44

short hair like in the army. But then I started wondering if I was right, and my doubts grew stronger. Our oldest son rebelled. He wore ragged jeans and the typical olive jacket. A girl's hair could hardly be longer than his was. I was furious. Oliver, 14 years old, didn't even react. My wife urged me to give in. She said it wasn't that important. Finally it happened: Oliver disappeared. We had the police look for him. My wife blamed me. Believe me, I never want to go through those three weeks again. After three weeks the police caught Oliver and brought him back. I don't know how it came about that I got up the nerve to talk to him and reveal my doubts. I was so unsure of myself that all I could do was retreat. To better understand what was going on, I even went to a counselor. (41-year-old attorney)

Some people are so frightened by even a temporary loss of orientation, that they quickly choose the other extreme. To protect themselves from their doubts, or, better said, their state of desperation, they escape into a rigidity that they then interpret as loyalty and strength of character. In order not to have to change their behavior, they disregard information that could intensify their doubts. Along with this clinging to a set idea, there is a second erroneous attitude that can develop out of their fear of insecurity: Without acknowledging the possibility of doubt, they accept the opinions of others - a group, a person in authority, a famous person - and adopt these ideas because this gives them a feeling of security, of belonging to a group.

Disorders and Conflicts
Insecurity; anxiety; ambivalence; envy; excessive sensitivity; changes in mood; moodiness; impatience; uncertainty; indecisiveness; helplessness.

HOPE

EVERY DARK NIGHT HAS A BRIGHT END. (Nisami)

Everyone sees in a partner his future developmental possibilities as well as his current behavior. One's expectations go beyond the current moment. We hope that something will happen tomorrow, next year, or at an indefinite time. Our attitude toward the future, an attitude that makes relative the events of the present, is *hope*.

The development of hope depends on what experiences a person has had and how he perceived them. If he were never shown that every difficulty has a solution, he would tend to feel hopeless. Hopelessness can also result from an undifferentiated attitude toward the future. This is the case when hope is limited to a few areas and when other areas are not recognized. People with this attitude tend to be disappointed and to want to escape. They are simply strengthened in their hopelessness: *As far as my career goals are concerned, I am fairly confident. By contrast, I think it's almost impossible that I will ever find a woman I can trust.* (38-year-old businessman, disorders in establishing contact with people)

There are many degrees of hopelessness, ranging from almost complete, and resignation to pessimism about one's purpose in life. The manifestations are equally varied. They extend from «psychological death» to disorders in one's sleep patterns. The hopeless situations can be sharply delimited, or blurred. Sometimes difficulties in a particular area are generalized. The way and degree to which a hopeless situation is experienced depends en the person's upbringing (basic conflict). Correspondingly, timely situations can function as releases from the situation.

Every activity has died in me. I'd like to learn to have hope, but I spend my time daydreaming. I get hungry, but I can't eat alone. I want to do something, but I feel paralyzed. This makes me conscious of how meaningless my life is. It all came to a head when my boyfriend left me. We'd been quarrelling for months over little things. We'd fight because he wanted sex with me, even though he had bad breath. Or we'd fight because I was never on time, etcetera. I was completely thrown off the track I'd followed since I was a child. (26-year-old female employee after suicide attempt)

Disorders and Conflicts
Hopelessness; dissatisfaction; pessimism; resignation; escape into fantasy; attitude of passive expectation; naïve optimism; fear of living; fear of death; inability to take action.

TRUST AND CONFIDENCE

TRUST IS A DELICATE PLANT. IF IT IS DESTROYED IT DOESN'T REAPPEAR QUICKLY. (Bismarck)

Hope looks at a person's future. It fosters trust in the particular capabilities that the person has, or that one expects of him. Based on the confirmed trust, that is, based on how those expectations do indeed develop one develops trust in that person as a total being. One accepts him as he is. Trust therefore depends not only on one's isolated experiences with the individual, but on the totality of one's experiences in life. These very pre-experiences make it all the more imperative that the child be accepted as a unique being and that this uniqueness be considered within the structure of one's expectations. Along with the confidence that grows step by step with the confirmed trust, there is another kind of trust that still has its original character. It is frequently found in a particularly developed form in the mother –child relationship. «I have faith in you, because you are here.» The subsequent self-confidence reflects the trust that that person has shown to the child.

I never trusted myself to do anything. I started a lot of things, but never finished them, because I believed in other people, but not in myself. I always saw myself as just a failure. People had been telling me long enough that I wouldn't amount to anything. Again and again I got the message, «You may as well forget about that. You can't do it.» (28-year-old student with depression)

Disorders and Conflicts
Breach of faith; mistrust; blind faith; fear of defeat and of disappointment; jealousy; hate; envy; rejection; exaggerated expectations; disappointment; expectation of failure; inferiority complex; resignation; overestimation of one's self; excessive demands; insufficient demands.

PATIENCE

PATIENCE IS A TREE WITH BITTER ROOTS BUT VERY SWEET FRUIT. (Persian proverb)

One needs patience in order to accept a person as he is, according to his capabilities. Patience means supporting the development of the capabilities appropriately, and putting up with the person's own way of developing despite one's doubts and expectations. Patience is thus equivalent to the ability to wait, to postpone partial satisfaction, and to give the other person time. One is most aware of patience when either oneself or other people are lacking it.

I get terribly upset when Jürgen doesn't do his homework.

When Manuela comes home late, I don't immediately greet her with an angry voice, like my husband does.

I hit the ceiling when I look in the office and see that the dust has just been swept into the corners.

When my husband thinks of me in unflattering terms, I just let it go right by me and give him the cold shoulder.

The educator's patience can stem from two sources. Someone can be patient out of fear. Through patience he would like to avoid confrontation. The father whom everyone admires for his tolerant patience, and who let's his children do everything, conceals a great deal of insecurity behind the mask of patience. The childrearing is generally left to the mother, as are unpleasant decisions. The relationship between the partners makes it essential that both be willing to bear the «lows» as well as the «highs».

Lack of patience could cause every friendship to shatter. Here we mean by patience, that one leaves time for the other. Impatience can be viewed as just the opposite, that is, the urgent desire to have here and now those things that actually require time. Impatience can also be traced back to a misunderstanding, as when a person does not know, or perhaps misunderstands, the reasons behind a particular action: A husband might show up at home at 2 o'clock in the morning, even though he had said he'd be there at 6 p.m. The wife doesn't say a word, nor does she let her husband give a word of explanation: *Don't say a word, because it will only be a lie anyway; I just hope you had a good time. The* wife doesn't hear - and wouldn't believe it anyway - that her husband had taken a colleague to the hospital and then had a flat tire and no chance to phone home. *I've run out of patience with you. If you like the other woman better than me, then go ahead and take her. As for me, I've got a good lawyer.* And no less dramatic is the misunderstanding that often leads fathers and mothers to become impatient: just when the living room has been cleaned, the child sits in the middle of the room with his crayons and practices his drawing skills on the hardwood floor. The parents had their idea of neatness and cleanliness, and their little boy a different one.

Disorders and Conflicts

Impatience; patience out of fear; unpredictability; excessive sensitivity; expectations that are too high; ambition; mood fluctuations; moodiness, egocentricity, inability to «belong,» silence, lack of consideration for others.

CERTAINTY

CERTAINTY IS MOSTLY THE RESULT OF OBSERVATION. (Shogi Effendi)

Insofar as patience bridges the distance of doubt and the development of a person is recognized in its possibilities, there is certainty in the relational figure. Certainty does not refer to the fact that the child or partner would become a model of one's expectations a «certainty,» of this kind would lead to disappointment. Rather, certainty refers to the unfolding of the particular person's own unique qualities. This certainty is not an abstract certainty of belief. In fact, it has practical consequences in one's dealings with the other person. Doubt represents a lack of decisiveness and expresses ambivalence toward one's partner. Certainty, on the other hand, indicates that one is sure of the partner's potential. Certainty enables one to accept one's partner in all his uniqueness and to allow him to make his own decisions on the basis of his capabilities:

I finally realized I wasn't married to my mother... I'm finally at the point where I am breaking away from my mother's and my sister's domination. Both are real fanatics when it comes to cleanliness. So was I. Then I got married. My husband wanted a comfortable home he said, but I was making it sterile with all my cleaning and fussing. Since I didn't want to ruin my relationship with him, I gave in, and look what happened: I actually liked what I used to despise. Things really improved between us; I now had time for my husband and for my hobbies. Until one day my mother and my sister arrived from Bavaria for a visit. «Good grief, child, how awful it looks here» etc., etc. I began to waver; I was caught between two fronts. I had the choice of going to pot with my husband or with my mother. I was constantly torn back and forth. I felt guilty toward my mother. She said she was ashamed of herself because of me, and that it was all her fault. And while all this was going on, the apartment wasn't really all that dirty. Sure, sometimes the beds didn't get made all day, if we didn't have time. And the dishes didn't get done until my husband helped me with them in the evening. And I didn't dust every day. Finally I realized I wasn't married to my mother. Wasn't the main thing that my husband and I felt good; When my mother visited us the next time and started criticizing again, I calmly told her I respected her opinion, but that she couldn't expect me to think exactly the way she did. The result: she left in a huff. I can't change that. Maybe she needs time to realize I'm not so wrong, and will come back. At any rate I'm sure I did the right thing. (38-year-old mother of three children)

Even a child cannot avoid doubt. When he begins to walk, he doesn't know whether he'll fall right away again. When he cries for food, he doesn't know if someone will feed him. As the mother turns her attention to him again and again, his doubts make it necessary for him to find ways to communicate. Certainty then appears when he solves his problems of doubt as they relate to the demands of the particular instant.

Disorders and Conflicts
Exaggerated certainty; fixation; lose of unity; defensiveness; unrealistic expectations; uncertainty; doubt; mistrust; anxiety; compulsive thoughts; compulsive behavior.

LOVE - CONTACT - SEXUALITY

LOVE BEARS THE SOUL LIKE THE FEET BEAR THE BODY.
(Cathenne of Siena)

The feeling of certainty is the most stable basis for the phenomenon we call love. Love is an emotional relationship that can be directed to a series of objects in various degrees of intensity. Love is thus an encompassing capability comprising a number of different aspects. Parents are often baffled that their child has this or that disorder, despite the fact that they have given him so much love. But a closer look shows that their love was not differentiated enough. The general advice of «give the child more love» doesn't do much good if there is no instruction as to exactly where the love is lacking and what kind of emotional relationship is to be emphasized. A person's love can be directed toward himself. To a certain extent it *must be* directed toward oneself in order to create an unbroken relationship. The earliest form of love occurs in the relationship between mother and child. The child needs the emotional attention of the mother or another person. At this basic stage the child develops a fundamental trust. But if the child's vital anxieties are not addressed, he can develop a basic feeling of mistrust.

Emotional attention - love - does not exist in a vacuum. It is always associated with various behavioral areas and qualities. A distinction must be made between the ability to love and the ability to be loved. One person acts in such a way that positive feelings flow toward him; another person may put forth a lot of emotional effort, but receive no positive response because he doesn't act in a way that corresponds to expectations. Love and attention can often be used as a weapon:

Love as a «hot weapon»
Through word, gesture, mimicry, and deeds a person praises or shows gratitude at every opportunity, or does all sorts of tasks for the partner. The person thereby develops a gratitude complex, difficulty in breaking away, too strong identification, problems with new surroundings. The secondary capabilities are not sufficiently developed.

Love as a cold «weapon»

This operates through withdrawal of love, threats, warning, and punishment. People treated in this way appear well trained, inhibited in their aggressions, or overly oriented toward achievement and success. The emotional spheres are not sufficiently developed.

Hot and Cold

Various, unpredictable practices are used in upbringing. People treated in this way become incapable of entering relationships or making decisions. They are easily influenced and adapt to the norms that are the most advantageous for them.

Love to a «thou» is the conventional form. The «thou» can be one's own mother or father, siblings, playmates, friends, live-in partners, and spouses. Love is not the same in all these cases. But certain relationships, e.g., with a puppy or other beloved pet, or a comrade of one's dreams, can become a substitute for another relationship that is missing. An essential source of the relationship to the «thou» is *sexuality*. We generally speak of sexuality when we are referring to sexually mature individuals. Indeed, sexuality directed toward the «thou» first occurs at this age. But already in young children there is an egocentric sexuality directed to one's' self. In the sexually mature individual this form of love appears as passive expectation: *I am here. Love me.* The naïve-primary form of upbringing is at the root of it. People with this kind of expectation, as a rule, are disappointed. When we love, we must enter into a relationship with the object of our love. To do that, we must first know how to do that. And it is precisely this skill that is missing in an attitude of passive expectation. A 23-year-old student complained: *I'd really like to have a girlfriend, but simply don't know how to approach women. I don't know how you do that. When I see a nice girl on campus I suddenly feel paralyzed and can't utter a word. So there's nothing for me to do, but keep on masturbating.*

The disorder here was not in the ability to love. Instead, there was a deficiency in knowing the behaviors and conventions for showing love. The crass opposite of this is the *object type*. This person is not short on technical knowledge. He knows how to turn on a woman; a woman in this category knows how to catch a man. The problem lies in the willingness and ability to develop emotional ties with the partner.

In other words, the ability to love the other person and to be loved in return.

With many people it's a problem of developing emotional ties to others. They love and act in such a way that they will be loved. But they lose interest in their partner at the very moment when their goal is reached: when the boyfriend or girlfriend has been won; when the man or woman has gotten married. Other situations are significant in this respect: One's professional studies are completed, there are no financial worries any more, and the children no longer live at home. After achieving these goals, after being released from the tensions that accompany them, the couple is beset by a feeling of emptiness and weariness. We designate this form of reaction as the unburdening type. It's development links it to the double-bind form of upbringing.

Although many people would want nothing more than to live on a Robinson Crusoe Island with their partner (for some, of course, this idea makes them feel very anxious), our social relationships go far beyond the one-to-one relationship with just one other person. We live with other people and are dependent on them.

When we speak of the ability to make contact, we mean the ability and willingness to turn to other people, parents, partners, colleagues, and social groups, and also to animals, plants, and objects. In some people this is closely linked to anxiety and aggression. Social contact, after all, is not just a confirmation. It also represents a certain threat. Through confrontation with another person one's own sense of worth is put on the line. For some people this is sufficient reason to seek contact only where they can count on positive reaction, where the same models of the actual capabilities predominate. We all know that we make friends with people who think like we do, who hold the same views, and whose tastes and enjoyments don't differ too much from ours. If a group is formed whose members have such similarities, a solid repertoire of responses is developed, and thus a common base is built for understanding each other. After a while the people have nothing new to say and are content to hear and repeat the same things because it is comfortable for them. But in a group made up of different cultures and backgrounds it is easy for tensions to develop. As a rule these tensions stem from the fact, that there are different behavioral patterns and different expectations.

Imagine, for instance, that a group member has learned to place a lot of importance on politeness. In his dealings with the other members he will avoid aggression, while at the same time he will try to develop a low tolerance level toward their rudeness. In contrast, another member may find this attitude hypocritical and dishonest, since he may have been raised to speak his mind. The interplay of these two members alone will provide enough fuel to perhaps drive the group apart.

But people don't just have contact with people they know well, with entities like «I,» and a group. A person also has ties to things he doesn't yet know, or that he in principle cannot know. By this I mean man's questions about the meaning of his life and about God. On the one hand man is finite. There are limits to his earthly existence. But his consciousness reaches beyond these limits and tries to find, in some way, a relationship with a past that has no origin and a future that has no end. The answers to these questions are various. But the question is always the same. It is the question that everyone probably asks at some point during his life.

Disorders and Conflicts
Anxiety; uncertainty; fear of love; mistrust; jealousy; excessive sensitivity; exaggerated expectations; moodiness; narrowness of feeling; scarcity of contact; exaggerations (cf. misunderstanding love).

UNITY

UNITY IN DIVERSITY (Baha'u'llah)

Just as body, soul, and spirit do not merely stand alongside each other, so behavior is not merely a sum of the features of the actual and basic capabilities: Man has the ability to integrate the elements of his personality into a functional unit. This means that an actual capability is not something alien, something derived from without, but is a part of the personality itself. It was probably mastered up on the foundation of the capabilities. Its outward appearance is changeable, yet it is an essential part of one's personality. In other words, man cannot exist without order. Everyone has some kind of division of time and space. How these divisions mesh with socially desirable punctuality and orderliness is a question of how one adapts to their environment. Furthermore, unity of the personality means that changes in individual aspects can produce changes in the total personality.

I believe that a person who gains insight into the causes of his pedantry will also be able to develop a new attitude toward his frugality. One generally tends to first attribute unity of personality to an adult, and particularly to old people who are no longer viewed as sexual beings. Unity is thereby equated with maturity and wisdom. On the other hand, man seems to us to represent unity at every stage of his development: the infant, the toddler, the child, the adolescent in puberty, the older teenager, and the adult. Each can find at his stage of development his own identity, his own unchangeable unity. It is still possible, however, for a person to be susceptible to certain forms of loss of identity at various stages of his development. This means he is susceptible to certain disorders.

But the fact that identity can be disturbed is no reason to give up on a person's identity at a particular stage of his development. If we take the primary capabilities, which we understand as the prerequisites for emotional relationships, and instead of viewing them as individual capabilities, we integrate them into the course of closer interpersonal communication; an ideal model of the developmental chain can be depicted:

Unknown capabilities, anxiety, aggression, imitation, faith, doubt, hope, trust – confidence, patience, certainty, love, and unity.

Both partners go through this developmental chain. But generally they do not take the same position at the same time, but go in phases. Faith, doubt, and hope in one person can correspond to the unknown capabilities in the other. Certainty in one person can correspond to another person's doubt. The relationship between the partners in terms of the developmental chain can prevent conflicts, but when the phases are out of sync in a way that produces conflict, the situation can lead to dissonance. One partner, for instance, can react to his companion's messiness with aggression and doubt. Or someone's anxieties may produce a sense of hopelessness in another person. Or conflict-laden imitation may destroy the love between two people.

Disorders and Conflicts

Loss of unity; career as life goal; sexuality as life goal; religion as life goal; one-sidedness; prejudices; inferiority complex; inhibitions; conspicuous behavior.

ANXIETY, AGGRESSION, AND IMITATION AS POTENTIAL SOURCES OF CONFLICT

ANXIETY IS THE EXPENDITURE OF ENERGY WITHOUT A GOAL.

We have regarded anxiety, aggression, and imitation as necessary developmental steps. This does not mean that they are always necessary. Often they prove to be sources of disorders and limitations to one's individual happiness. Aggressive contents or those that are marked by anxiety or imitation express themselves in thoughts, verbalization, and action. We must keep in mind that here we are evaluating anxiety, aggression, and imitation as the condition for and the result of disorders in interpersonal relationships and psychological processes. They relate to the behavioral categories of the secondary capabilities, as well as to the emotional categories of the primary capabilities.

In Thought and Dream

For two years a 9-year-old boy has been dreaming that his mother is a witch or demon. The boy seems moody and dreamy, has problems in school, and can't seem to concentrate. He also complains of stomach trouble and headaches.

In terms of content, his anxious dreams can be traced back to his mother's behavior. She was particularly concerned with ambition, orderliness, and obedience in the boy. She dominated almost every situation where these actual capabilities were involved. He experienced her expansive behavior, which seemed to swallow up the child, as a demonic force. He transformed this force into visual images in his dreams.

In dreams we deal with conflicts that are associated with the actual capabilities. This is thus a process that is linked to our ability to think in terms of images. In the case of unresolved conflicts the contents of anxiety, aggression, and imitation occupy the center of our thoughts. We are preoccupied almost exclusively with the things that are disturbing us. The protective function is obvious: One doesn't have anxiety (or aggression). Rather, the anxiety controls the person. The anxiety or aggression in one's thoughts or experiences is not always directed against the outward source of the problem, the child, the friend, the wife, or the social force. The aggression can also find its target in the person himself:

I drive as crazy as I want to. If I have an accident my wife can consider herself responsible. Why doesn't she understand me and treat me with as much consideration as my mother always did.

Or:

If I've got a headache now, it's because my son is so messy. I might die of heart failure, and it'll be all his fault.

This «polite aggression» directed inward results in a defusing of the external conflict situation. This kind of aggression often puts the victim under considerable suffering. The suffering becomes all the stronger in that these ideals are outside one's conscious control and seem to run by themselves automatically. Their most extreme form is found in the thoughts one has about suicide: *What will happen when I'm not around anymore.* Because this kind of thinking brings a certain amount of satisfaction in that it «punishes» others for their insensitivity, this manoeuvre of «building sandcastles» eventually becomes dangerous. By constantly being preoccupied with the idea of punishing others - but really hurting himself - a person develops an entire program for himself. When there is provocation, even of a minor nature, the program can then run in the form of irrational action, even going as far as suicide. In many cases this reaction is influenced by an appropriate model who, as far as possible, gives the entire action a heroic tinge.

In Speech
Understatements and Exaggerations:
To get attention I build up a story or downplay it as needed. I often call my husband and tell him I said something to someone that isn't true. I tell

him this so he won't tell the person the opposite sometime. (34-year-old housewife)

Promises:
If you pass in school this year you'll get a new bike. But when the child does pass: Well, yeah, you passed all right, but not with flying colors. You didn't really do well enough to deserve a bike. (28-year-old engineer, speaking of his relationship with his father)

White Lies:
When my husband is home in the evening he doesn't even want to be disturbed by a phone call. But when the phone rings I become curious and answer it, because maybe the call is for me. But if it's someone who wants to speak with my husband I have to tell the caller that my husband isn't at home. If I don't do that, he complains that I am incapable of providing him with a nice quiet evening. (35-year-old secretary)

Threats and Curses:
When I've worked all day and my husband comes home and flops down on the couch, I threaten him that I'll let the kids go hungry and not give them baths, because I need the rest more than he does. (32-year-old housewife)

Rumors and Gossip, Both Positive and Negative:
I carefully say positive things until I know the opinions of the person I'm talking with. Once I find out that he doesn't like a certain person, I always say something negative about that person, too. (42-year-old housewife) *You look so pale today. I once had an uncle who was also pale like that, and it turned out that he had cancer. But hopefully it won't be such a serious thing with you.* (56-year-old widow)
You have such darling children. What a shame they run around alone on the streets so much. (62-year-old retired woman)

Teasing and Jokes:
Look at that girl with the flaming red hair. She looks like a witch. (7-year old boy)

I can never tease someone about how they look, because I was teased so much as a child. The thought of it still upsets me. (22-year-old Office clerk)

Irony and Cynicism:
Well aren't you good with your hands! (Mother speaking to her 5-year-old daughter, who had just broken a coffee cup)
God is dead; the funeral will be the day after tomorrow. Religion helps people hate each other. (51-year-old attorney)

Talking to Oneself:
They just come, mess up the place, and eat our food, and I have to clean the place up. (28-year-old housewife talking about guests her husband had invited to the house)

Griping:
I gripe constantly about everything. Mostly I gripe to my kids and my mother about how they mess up the house... (37-year-old housewife)
I really get upset about how unfair my boss is, and I gripe a lot. (32-year-old secretary)

Swearing:
I swear to God I don't know anything about it... I give you my word, what I'm saying is no exaggeration... (from a therapy group for youths)

Expectations:
How cheap! They bring such piddling little birthday presents for our child. (34-year-old mother)
There you see what my work means to my boss. Look at what he gives my colleagues for their birthday. And then look at what I get. (24-year-old secretary)
My brother is my mother's little darling. She always favors him over me. (8-year-old boy)

In Actions

Anxiety, aggression, and imitation take on a new appearance in concrete behavior. In thoughts and speech they remain on an abstract level, but in action they suddenly become concrete and produce results of their own. Aggression in upbringing has a unique position. Socially it is expressed as isolation from a minority group («Don't play with those dirty kids!»); in discrimination («Foreigners are stupid and dishonest»); in destruction of personal property («After me, the deluge»); in acts of violence, criminality, and crimes of affluence; in pogroms (acts of violence against masses, group egotism, and war); in wide gaps between workers and employers, extending all the way to slavery and work camps; and in legalized and sanctioned persecution. In the *personal* realm anxiety, aggression, and imitation appear, in addition to their open forms, in the three escape reactions: into loneliness, into activity, and into illness.

The three reactions are characterized by the fact that one tries to avoid a conflictual area. One wants to avoid certain demands and tensions by withdrawing into one's shell or into an area one can control. A personal little world is built to counteract reality.

Escape into Loneliness
Children in a situation like this prefer to play by themselves. They become loners and often develop a vivid imagination, which finds considerable support in television.

The child's preoccupation with himself is revealed in such acts as picking his nose, playing with himself, sucking his thumb and biting his nails. By manipulating his own body he tries to make up for his lack of contact with other people. His aggressions are turned inward against himself. This is why eating problems often occur in connection with the «escape into loneliness.» For one thing, food means substitute satisfaction. Gluttony becomes conspicuous. Or in another situation the child will refuse to eat, and thereby punish the other person. Constipation is another kind of refusal. In this case the child refuses to relinquish his bowel movement.

The child's desire for care and attention is often expressed by an act that is very unpleasant and disturbing for the parents. What we are talking about here is bed-wetting, a phenomenon that depth psychology has aptly termed «crying down below.»

Pronounced masochistic traits can develop from the person's retreat into himself. Children pull out their hair, bite their lips, and tend to injure themselves or have accidents with noticeable frequency, It is precisely here that the hidden concern for escape into loneliness becomes clear: through retreat and passivity the person shows his need for attention, love, and patience. If the cry for help, which the escape really is, is not understood over a long period of time, reactions tend to develop.

In puberty the lack of contact develops into a tendency to masturbate frequently. This, however, can also be viewed as a transitional occurrence. The escape into loneliness continues: In adulthood, the eccentric and loner appears on the scene. He pulls back from social activities and spends his free time almost exclusively with gardening, playing with his dog, collecting stamps, watching TV, participating in «individual» sports like hiking alone, or in solitary alcoholism. Passive self-manipulation, of which drug dependency is the most conspicuous example, is also a type of escape. Through drugs, anxiety and inhibitions find their expression.

Escape into Activity

The escape into activity is an escape forward. A child that seeks this way out appears to be busy and interested in many things. He tries to reach goals associated with the realm of accomplishment or with the realm of social interaction. In the foreground there is always some form of success and recognition. The location of the activities can be a social setting. The child constantly needs friends and playmates around him. Through them he develops a capability for organization and the talent for dealing with social situations. If he doesn't take a leading role in the play, or is unable to achieve one, he tends to become a spoilsport or troublemaker, often displaying aggressive behavior. Similarly, the child can develop strong dependencies on his friends and seem unable to get along without them. Another area of activities is that of achievement in various desired behavioral fields. A child can practice kicking a football every day for weeks, or demonstrate tremendous training discipline in swimming or other sports. Or he becomes very preoccupied with books dealing with a certain subject, becomes a bookworm, or even learns passages by heart. While sociability is a reward in itself, in these activities I have just cited there is a particular reward from success. A 3-year-old child who practiced soccer received praise not only from his father, a professional player, but also from the neighbors. Their encouraging words («You'll be a great soccer player some day.») Simply strengthened his resolve to keep at it.

In such cases there is an obvious need for attention. At the same time there is often a tendency toward exclusivity, which can be viewed as a typical sign of escape. Only the *one* area occupies the center stage. Only the *one* area brings success. Another activity will be neglected and lose importance. The «bookworm» has no understanding for or interest in sports. For him they are a waste of time. The «sports enthusiast» underestimates the importance of applying himself in school. In terms of the actual capabilities, there is an imbalance here in favor of the secondary capabilities; the primary capabilities are neglected. *Neatness is an important part of life. Emotions are a lot of nonsense.*

Escape into activity always has the character of being on the offensive. Conflicts are brought out into the open. Aggression is directed outward as well. Here we find the active, loud, defiant person the troublemaker; the guy who does it better; the spoilsport; the one with ambitions. When inner tensions are strong the aggression is often played out and is expressed, depending on the situation, in an attack on certain people and things, as an active manipulation of something alien. There is a tendency toward sadism, with corresponding pleasure.

In adolescence the most conspicuous escapes are activities involving violence, and the «crimes of affluence.» The opposite sex is viewed as an object. As far as sexual activity is concerned, the achievement motive is clearly in operation.

The quiet types, those who plunge into political, business, or scientific talks with great fanaticism, should also be mentioned here.

In adults we find the successful type, the scholarly type, the managerial type. In the various fields the achievement motive is developed to its most extreme, often creating an imbalance. The connection between achievement and emotionalism is particularly striking in those cases where a man who was focussed on success drops his wife after he has achieved the success he was pursuing. Here achievement is the means by which one receives different kinds of attention and self-confirmation, even in the sexual realm.

Escape into Illness
This is based mostly on learning experiences. Here imitation plays a central role. The imitation is learned according to this pattern: The child, suffering from a cold, is mothered and pampered by the mother or other person. Previously the child might have felt put down because of the mother's career, because of sibling rivalry, or because the mother insisted on neatness and obedience. Now the child makes an important discovery: When you're sick, the annoyances stop; you get some peace and quiet, and aside from that, you are on center stage, finally getting the attention you've wanted for so long. The child makes use of this discovery whenever he is faced with a tough situation: mother scolds him, he's afraid of an important test at school, company that he doesn't like is coming for or a visit, or he has to visit people he'd rather avoid. In these cases the escape into illness promises to be a way out of the dilemma. The child decides to get sick.

Imitating other people comes about in this way: A child discovers that when there are disagreements in the family, the mother withdraws because of migraine headaches. Her husband then leaves her alone, or even takes care of her. The kids have to look after things in the house because «Mom is under the weather.» This discovery becomes a model for subsequent behavior. The child makes an association that is in large part unconscious: *When I get in a tough spot and have problems I can't solve, or face unpleasant situations, then I'll get sick (just like Mom), and can count on getting attention from other people.* In the course of the child's development this pattern of reaction becomes a natural thing for the child; after a while one no longer knows how this behavior got started, or how it really operates. The child is taken from one doctor to the next, gets all sorts of prescriptions, etc., but finds no real improvement. The adult maintains the pattern, for he has learned just what he can gain from it.

Anxiety, aggression, and imitation are like signals. They point to a facet of a person's character where there is imbalance or lack of differentiation. There is a certain limitation in the person's ego. These signals are indications of a loss of unity, and hence of opportunity.

The absence of anxiety and aggression is not the essence of health. Rather, health is the ability to deal with and process these anxieties and aggressions. The goal of parenting and of retraining is not the elimination or the acting out of anxieties and aggressions. Attention must be given to the lack of differentiation in the area of the primary and secondary capabilities.

Secondary Capabilities

The Girl with the Red Velvet Dress

A girl once wore a red velvet dress that made her very happy. She took care of the dress as if it were her own body. If she found the slightest speck of dust on its hem, she hurriedly brushed it away. Once when tears fell on the dress, she sucked them up with her mouth. The dress had a powerful effect on the other children; they always wanted to be near the girl with the beautiful dress. Her playmates tried to touch the dress, and were very proud when they were able to do so. One day while she was playing, the girl slipped and fell down. She knocked her head on the stones of the sidewalk, and thorns tore her dress. The girl paid no heed to the wound on her head. She looked only at the rip in her dress and cried. (After P. Etessami)

We act just like this girl when we are in the company of other people. In our culture we have developed a series of actual capabilities that, like our clothing we treasure and wear proudly, even if they cause us some suffering.

Punctuality

THE ONLY TIME YOU WERE EVER ON TIME WAS WHEN YOU WERE BORN.

Definition
With this term we mean the strict adherence to a division of time that we have agreed upon, or that is expected of us.

Situations Involving Punctuality:
He often gets to the office late.
She takes her time getting supper on the table.
I feed my baby every four hours, right to the minute.
I'm a slave to my clock.

We're never late.
Out of courtesy to those patients scheduled after you, please be on time, and please notify us promptly if you cannot attend.
By law you are required to appear on time.
My schedule is so hectic that it's giving me heart trouble.

Development

For the fulfilment of his basic needs an infant is dependent in large part on his surroundings. The schedule for his feedings and diaper changes determines his first divisions of time: While psychoanalysis views toilet training as the child's first cultural achievement, we give this designation to his punctuality. The child's adaptation of his needs to his mother's attention is his first major accomplishment in the realm of culturalization. The following basic experiences can influence the development of his personality:

- At the first sign that the child wants something, the mother fulfils his desires. To a certain extent she is overly punctual. But under conditions like these the child does not learn to develop patience. He does not learn how to wait.

- The child's desires are fulfilled after some delay; people keep the child waiting. Depending on the strength of the desires, the child can become resigned (this is the case with quiet children without strong drives) or stubborn and aggressive (as when children are lively, with strong demands).
- The mother fulfils the child's demands sporadically. This leads to inconsistency and changeability later on. As far as punctuality is concerned, the person will sometimes seem to be overly punctual: at other times he ignores all schedules and appointments. His expectations can also be unpredictable. This all leads to insecurity: *You scold me because I was late today. But yesterday and the day before you didn't say a word.*

Significance and Results

It is typical of many people that they get very upset if they find they'll be late for an appointment. We could call this active punctuality. Passive punctuality, however, is even more of an emotional matter. People in this category find it particularly maddening when they have to wait for other people. Other people's lack of punctuality can cause them to lose faith in those people. They don't want to have anything to do with them, because they are always late. On the other hand, some people's pedantic punctuality and high expectations of others can get on people's nerves. Punctuality thereby becomes a means of punishing people, and further, a means of self punishment.

Examples

I expect other people to be right on time because I have no patience and cannot stand waiting. When I have to wait, I get so mad that I really blow up when the person finally arrives. (33-year-old mother of two, suffering from headaches and heart pains)

When I get home and find that supper isn't ready, I don't even want to know why. I just slam the door behind me and go to bed. But I can't get to sleep. (39-year-old architect, stomach ailments)

My son's lack of punctuality is driving me up the wall. But I don't dare say anything. Then I get severe pains in my stomach. (32-year-old mother of three children)

In my husband's family they always ate together at a certain time. But in our house everyone ate when he wanted to. I have a very different sense of time to my husband. This causes a lot of friction between us. (29-year-old teacher, repulsed by sex, also suffering from sleep disorders)

Situation (What is under discussion)	Actual behavior (How I reacted)	Ideal behavior (How I could have reacted in a better way)
Melissa gets home from school quite late. Her supper is still on the stove.	Mother: *As punishment you don't get any supper. I've tried to be kind, but that doesn't seem to work. So now I'll lay down the law.*	Mother: *It can happen. But now of course you have half an hour less for television, before you have to start your homework. Because we really want to stick to that schedule.*
Jeffrey got up too late. He's afraid he'll be late if he takes time for breakfast. It wouldn't be the first time.	Jeffrey: *Mom, can you drive me to school? Otherwise I'll be late if I go ahead and have breakfast first.* Mother: *Yeah, I'll do it fast.* (She's thinking: What must the teacher think of us if Jeffrey is late again.)	Mother: *I'm sorry, but you have only yourself to blame. You'll have to make a choice. Either you skip breakfast, or you get to school late.*
The father has promised to take the kids rowing after dinner on Sunday.	Father arrives an hour later than he had agreed. He says, *Now it's getting too late. It's not worth our going rowing any more today.* When the mother asks why he was late he replies, *I really wanted to get here on time, but I was having brunch with some friends and didn't want to tell them I had to leave.*	The father's friends at brunch: *What, you want to go already? You can't do that to us.* The father: *I'd really like to stay, but this time I promised my kids I'd take them rowing. That's why I don't want to be late.*
Judy was invited to a party. It was agreed that she'd be home by 10 p.m. She gets in at 11:30.	11:30. Her parents are still up. Father: *That's the last time you go to a party. I've really had enough.*	Mother: *If you had called, we'd have probably not said no. It's not a question of principle. We simply want to be able to depend on each other.* (Parents had discussed the matter)
Mrs. and Mr. F. would like to go to a play. Fifteen minutes before the play is due to start, Mrs. F. is still putting on her makeup. And then she has to get dressed.	Husband: *Your damned poking around is going to ruin the whole evening for me. You're always late. We won't make it to the play tonight. And you can just forget about that little trip we were going to take this weekend.*	Husband: *If I can help you in any way, just say the word. Otherwise we'll be late. The next time I'll remind you earlier that were going out. That way we'll have more time to get ready.*

Disorders and Conflicts
Excessive punctuality; unrealistic expectations that others will be on time; expectant fears; time pressure; constant fear of not finishing something despite strong exertion of will; lack of punctuality; unreliability; breach of trust; social conflicts; aggression; difficulty in concentrating; stress; inner unrest; stomach and intestinal problems; coronary and circulation problems.

CLEANLINESS

BEFORE WE GO OUT WALKING I TAKE A CLOTHES BRUSH AND CLEAN OFF THE ENTIRE FAMILY.

Definition
Here we mean cleanliness as far as our bodies, clothes, daily objects, household, and environment are concerned.

Situation Involving Cleanliness:
I just can't get my boy to take a bath.
My husband has body odor because he doesn't shower every day.
My wife's a fanatic about cleaning the house.
When Frankie comes home from school he looks like a pig.
Keep your city clean.
Your husband makes a good impression. He always looks so well groomed.

Development
As psychoanalysis has shown, parental attitudes toward the young child's cleanliness are of major significance. Erikson, for instance, saw correlations between early toilet training and subsequent aggression. In psychotherapy there are correlations between toilet training and individual compulsive acts such as the compulsion to bathe. Toilet training and the parent's model affect the individual's attitude to dirt, cleanliness, and even interpersonal contact *(Don't play with those dirty kids...).*

Significance and Results

Cleanliness has first of all a protective function. Parents who forbid their kids to play in the dirt do so to protect them from illness and infection. They know about germs; children don't.

We have to make a distinction between this protective function and the anxious attitude that is correlated with the lack of cleanliness: A child who puts his dirty finger in his mouth causes his mother to panic. She fears the child could become sick in the next few days. An anxious attitude like this, however, prevents the child from becoming familiar with his body and his environment, of which dirt is also a part. Since the sex organs and the excretory organs lie close to each other, their location, in connection with a strong emphasis on cleanliness and with a lack of sex education, can contribute to a rejection of sexual activity.

Examples

If our floor isn't clean enough to eat off of, my husband gets furious. His mother was always cleaning the house, and now he expects that of me, too. (35-year-old housewife, infection of the large intestine)

Whenever I went to the bathroom I'd have to wash my hands for three hours. We had to keep terribly clean in our house when we were kids. My father would have even liked to polish the snails. (35-year-old man, chronic constipation)

When we go on a picnic in the woods, Mary throws empty cans and garbage around. This makes me furious, though it doesn't bother my wife at all. We've very often had arguments about this. (41-year-old man, marital problems)

Yesterday I screamed at Lydia «How often have I told you not to come in so dirty. It always looks like a pigpen in our home!» As a child I also had to look clean as a whistle when I went outside. (40-year-old mother, constant headaches, no organic cause found)

My husband always has such bad breath; I simply can't sleep with him. He takes out his bad moods on the kids. His mother was a real slob too. (27- year old woman, lack of interest in sex)

You can't depend on anybody, you have to do everything yourself. I've given up on my cleaning lady, because she only half does things. The dirt would pile up in the corners... (52-year-old housewife, headaches, no organic cause found)

Situation	Actual behavior	Ideal behavior
After playing outside Linda comes into the house with her dirty shoes on and then sits down at the table without washing her hands.	Mother screams at Linda: *How often have I told you, you shouldn't get so dirty outside. This place always looks like a pigpen. I'm not going to let you play outside any more.*	Mother: *I like it when you play outside so nicely. You know what? Why don't you take off your shoes outside the door and put them next to the other dirty ones out there. And now go wash your hands. I made some good spaghetti.*
Matthew drops some food on his trousers while he's eating lunch.	Mother: *Can't you watch what you're doing? Do you think we get free cleaning when we take your trousers in?*	Mother: *Well, you did pretty well all this time. A little stain now and then doesn't hurt. But if you'd use a napkin we wouldn't have to take your trousers to the cleaners.*
The husband repeatedly comes home from work dirty. His fingernails are black and his face is covered with dust. He doesn't really feel like getting cleaned up before he goes to bed.	At first the wife says nothing in the evening, only later in bed, when her husband starts to become amorous, does she begin to complain about a headache, pains in her back, and that she is tired. She withdraws to the edge of her side of the bed.	The wife: *Have you noticed how dirty you are? How about if I give you a nice manicure, and then we take a shower together?*

Disorders and Conflicts

Ritualized cleanliness; excessive sensitivity; compulsive washing; anxiety; lack of cleanliness; aggression; breach of trust; difficulty in establishing contacts; sexual disorders; self-hatred; wetting one's pants; bowel movements in one's pants; eczema; allergies.

ORDERLINESS

ORDERLINESS IS HALF OF LIFE

Definition

Orderliness is expressed in the spatial relationship between things; nothing hinders the functioning of other things, and everything can be found without wasting time.

Situations Involving Orderliness:
My daughter's room looks like it's been hit by a tornado.
My husband certainly didn't invent the practice of cleaning up a room. At the office he's very proper. At home he's an absolute slob.
The apartment seems sterile and uninhabited.
She leaves everything lying around.
A church service follows an ancient sacred rite or order.
From outside, okay, but inside, what a mess! Just don't open the cupboards.
The company is well organized.

Development

Even the most disorganized child has his sense of order. In this context we mean the ability to organize and structure his perceptions and his environment.

Through the model presented by the parents and in the immediate environment, the child acquires the sense of order prevailing in the population group.

Tidiness develops according to the developmental stage of the child. The seeming lack of order in a child who leaves his toys scattered around or even takes them apart can be viewed as a stage of his development toward orderliness.

Significance and Results

Orderliness is linked to a whole series of actual capabilities: punctuality is an orderliness of time; politeness and honesty are an ordering of interpersonal relations. Ambition is orderliness in terms of one's dedication to work. Since orderliness deals with one's experiences and their organization, not just with external elements, this actual capability is a particularly emotional one. A compulsive man, for instance a man whose compulsive orderliness is a way of protecting himself can fall apart if something is changed in his orderly world. If messiness is consistently punished and the strictest orderliness is rewarded, anxiety, compulsions, and aggression can develop, frequently accompanied by psychosomatic problems: Messiness can get on a person's nerves, but so can pedantry.

Examples

*Whenever I didn't clean up my room I heard «I don't love you any more.»
I panicked when I heard that. Today I'm terribly fussy. This causes a lot of
conflict with my husband and kids.* (39-year-old woman with chronic
constipation and sleep disorders)

*If I didn't clean out his school bag and see that he had the things he needed
for the next day, I guarantee you my boy would take the wrong schoolbooks,
or even none at all. I'd rather not even know what would happen to him in
school then. I'd like to spare him that.* (28-year-old mother, whose 8-year-
old son was not self-reliant and was prone to temper tantrums)

*In my grandparents' house every piece of advice came with words from
the Bible. «The good Lord sees everything,» whether we left food on our plates,
didn't finish our sandwiches, or didn't hang up our clothes. These were all sins,
and we'd be punished for them. Today I can't stand to hear anything about
religion.* (48-year-old architect, suffering from depression)

*After I discovered that my secretary had filed important documents that
weren't yet taken care of, I'd really had enough of her. When I see all the stuff
piled up on her desk I get a strong urge to push it all off the table.* (45-year-old
manager with heart problems; no organic cause found)

Situation	Actual behavior	Ideal behavior
8-year-old Matthew doesn't empty out his school bag.	His mother cleans it out and packs up the books and papers he'll need for the next day.	Mother reminds Matthew that he didn't empty out his bag. But instead of doing it herself, she gives him the opportunity to have his own experiences with messiness.
The desk in Peggy's room is covered with glue and bits of paper she'd been cutting.	Her mother says in a loud voice: *What will Daddy say when he sees your messy desk. And besides, you haven't done your homework, your hands are all dirty, and yesterday you were an hour late in getting home...* She gives Peggy a spanking.	Mother: *You always make your bed so nicely. Could you also clean off your desk a little?*
The medicine cabinet, which it is the wife's job to tidy up, is not in order.	Husband: *I'm at my wit's end with your lack of order. I have to spend hours looking for my medicine, and when I find the right container, I see that your hormone pills are in it, not my prescription.*	The husband informs his wife of the mess in the cabinet and asks: *When would you have time so we could clean it out together? I need your help so we both know where to find things.*
The boss is very upset about the mess on his secretary's deck.	The boss complains to another employee about how useless the secretary is.	The boss takes time to explain his system to his secretary, and to say why he likes things a particular way. They agree to discuss any problems that may arise.

Disorders and Conflicts
Pedantry; fussiness; compulsion to control things; lack of orderliness; carelessness; sloppiness; aggression; breach of trust; problems in school; conflicts at work; guilt feelings; anxiety; headaches.

OBEDIENCE

IF I SAY IT'S RED THEN IT'S RED, EVEN IF IT'S TEN LAYERS OF BLUE ON BLUE.

Definition
Here we mean the adherence to request, regulations, and orders from outside authorities. Obedience is particularly demanded and given in

75

reference to various qualities which are associated with content (such as orderliness, punctuality, etc.)

Situations Involving Obedience:
You have to break a child's will.
Children must eat what is served them.
A good spanking never hurt anybody.
You can't be a master while you're still an apprentice.
What the parents say goes, because they are God's representatives. Obedience is one of the pillars of the military and is a basic principle of the legal order. Whoever doesn't want to listen must feel the road.

Development
Obedience is taught either through punishment or threat of punishment, or through reward for carrying out orders. A person has three alternatives: He can identify with the authority, adopt its views and behaviors, and expect others to do the same.

Second, he can resign himself to it. This is often the cause of behavioral disorders like inhibitions in making friends, anxiety, and bed-wetting, or of psychosomatic symptoms like headaches, stomach, and intestinal problems.

Lastly, he can revolt, unleashing his aggression against either the authority or a weak scapegoat.

An adult's relationship to obedience can mirror his confrontation with parental authority.

Significance and Results
Obedience, which is built on the principles of reward and punishment, is one - but not the sole - factor in holding people together. Obedience guarantees the functioning of a group or society.

Unconditional obedience, however, can lead to conflicts when laws and authorities no longer meet the needs of the times. It limits one's independence to think and to act. If the obedience is determined by rigidly held authorities or laws, anxiety and aggression develop whenever something new occurs.

Disobedience in the form of rebellion against authority contains a creative force. But the danger exists that the disobedience, with its revolt, can go beyond its goal and put the cart before the horse.

Obedience can also be practiced in the tension between desire and anxiety. Two forms can be observed: Outwardly a person is obedient and subservient; but inwardly, or as far as others are concerned, the person can be arrogant and bold. Or: Outwardly a person appears to be disobedient, open, and rebellious. This disobedience, however, is coupled to an inner dependency; the disobedience, in fact, is an expression of this dependence.

Examples

My mother demanded absolute obedience from me. She justified this by saying she was my mother, what God wanted her to be, and that I would bring God's wrath down upon myself if I didn't obey. Inwardly I revolted, but still gave in. Everywhere I looked I saw God lurking like a policeman. (22-year-old student with anxiety, irregular heartbeat, and excessive sweating)

Whenever we visited relatives, she would say for example: «When Mom says yes, the answer is...?» And I had to reply, yes. And «When Mom says no, the answer is...» And I had to say, No. She would then look at me triumphantly, as if she had just completed a successful circus act. And I got my lump of sugar in the form of a hearty kiss, which turned my stomach. I never dared say a word. (19-year-old boy, addicted to drugs)

I can still remember what my mother used to say: «If I didn't spell things out for you in the smallest detail, nothing would turn out right. Even then you have trouble. You prove that to me again and again.» – Even today my husband still has to digest everything for me first. (33-year-old housewife with depression and anxiety)

Situation	Actual behavior	Ideal behavior
Elizabeth doesn't feel like practicing her piano lessons.	Mother: *If you don't practice now, I won't take you ice skating tonight and you won't get any dessert.*	Mother: *I can understand that you don't want to practice. You'll get over it, I'm sure. But if you continue to feel the way you do now, we'll have to cancel your lessons. We don't want to force you into anything.*
Frank wants to play longer.	Father: *Now get moving. I'll teach you how to obey me.* He spanks Frank. *A couple of spankings didn't hurt me either.*	Father: *Frank, you can play for five more minutes, and then come to supper.* – After five minutes the father goes to the children's room or calls: *Frank, time to eat. Come on now, please.* (By giving him the previous warning the father sees that Frank is not abruptly torn away from his playing.)
Carol set the breakfast table today. As the mother comes out of the bathroom she notices Carol's «surprise»	Mother: *I've told you a hundred times that we use the plain dishes on weekdays, but you used the good china. Hurry and change it.*	Mother: *I'm really surprised. I'm really pleased that you set the table. Dad will be happy too, when he hears of this. You wanted to make it extra nice today, with the good china and all. You know, we usually use the other china for weekdays.*
Hank has his rock music blasting till all hours of the night.	Mother says to father: *For heaven's sake, tell that boy to turn it down. It's driving me crazy.* Father: *Now you know that a boy has to have some freedom. We've got to simply put up with it.*	The next day the father says to Hank: *I can understand that you like to play your stereo real loud* *How would it be if we'd agree on a set time for that? You could play it as loud as you want after school and then turn it down when Mom gets home from work. We'd then make exceptions, for instance, when you have friends over in the evening.*

Situation	Actual behavior	Ideal behavior
The car is the favorite child in the household. The husband lets his wife drive it only when he's right there beside her. One day, to get some errands taken care of faster she takes the car by herself.	Husband: *I'm just glad you didn't wreck it. From now on, you can drive the car only if you're willing to keep it clean too.*	Husband: *Before you drive to town by yourself again, let's practice a bit. And I think we should always decide in advance when one of us wants to use it.*
John is supposed to paint the garage instead of going to the football game. He's not happy about that.	Father: *If you don't learn to control your contrariness, you'll never amount to anything. I don't want to hear another word. Now get to work.*	Father: *Actually you're right. You can still paint the garage tomorrow.*

Disorders and Conflicts
Demand for blind obedience; draconian strictness; belief in authority; autonomy of command; crisis of authority; physical punishment, disobedience; anxiety; aggression; defiance; mistreatment; nail biting; bed-wetting; difficulty in adapting to situations; marital conflict.

POLITENESS

THE MOTTO IN OUR HOUSE WAS: WHAT WILL PEOPLE SAY!

Definition
Politeness can best be illustrated with its extreme forms: super friendliness, subservience, or flattery on the one hand, and unsparing and hurtful disregard on the other. Differentiation analysis interprets politeness as the inhibition of aggression directed against society.

Situations Involving Politeness:
Harry's behavior toward his friends leaves a lot to be desired.
My husband's way of expressing himself really disgusts me.
I could care less what people think of us.
I'm friendly because I require too much love. You should always be kind to strangers.
He always makes a mess of things.

She's like a bull in a china shop.
Politeness is the virtue of kings.
Diplomacy is another word for lying. Going to church is part of being proper.
Children should be seen and not heard.
When my husband and I go for a walk he's always several feet ahead of me;
as I trail along I feel like a servant.

Development

In acquiring a sense of politeness, a child learns from a model (usually the parents) or from his own success (his own behavior). The parental reaction to seemingly impolite behavior by their children is particularly important. More than the other actual capabilities, politeness is determined by the culture and the social level.

Significance and Results

Politeness is the adherence to the forms and rules of social contact. Certain game rules must be followed. An excessive demand for politeness can mean that aggressive impulses must be denied or suppressed. This excessive demand is the reflection of insecurity and problems of self-esteem. Politeness always corresponds to honesty: They always stand in opposition to each other. At first polite behavior is applauded: the environment reacts to it positively. But if politeness is bought at the too high price of denying basic drives, it can turn into aggression that is usually directed inward.

It makes my husband very happy when I act as if I got along perfectly with my mother-in-law. But afterwards I'm angry with myself that I let myself get caught in the trap and didn't say what was on my mind. Then I have to go to bed because I've gotten a bad headache. (36-year-old housewife)

Rule of thumb for politeness: What would you say if someone treated you the same way you treat that person?

Examples

My mother has no idea of manners or propriety. It was particularly bad because I always had to eat with her at the place where she worked. She was a cleaning lady. We would eat with the men she worked for. I'd sit there and break out in a cold sweat, wondering just what she'd do. She had never learned how to use a knife and fork. Today good manners are terribly important to me. My yardstick is: What would people say? (39-year-old mother with stomach and intestinal problems)

My mother put a lot of emphasis on manners. I was a well-behaved child. But that all changed when I started college. My new behavior caused a lot of violent arguments at home. One time my mother even said «You're going to put me into an early grave.» Nowadays people don't want to have anything to do with me, because I can be so mean. I'm totally isolated. (23-year-old female student with trouble making friends, no interest in sex)

Situation	Actual behavior	Ideal behavior
n the kitchen.	*Hey, give me that slice of bread.*	*Would you please pass the bread?*
In the bathroom.	*If you don't hurry up, you're really going to get it.*	*Please hurry a bit with your shower. Breakfast will be ready in a few minutes.*
In the children's room.	*Your room looks like a pigpen.*	*Do you find that your room is tidy?*
When the husband changed clothes he just threw his things on the bedroom floor.	*Do you think I clean up this place just so the lord of the manor can mess it up again?*	*I'd really appreciate it if you'd put your dirty clothes in the hamper.*
The wife is doing her spring-cleaning.	*The father says to the mother: You're driving me up the wall with your constant cleaning!*	*I like it when the house is clean too, but don't you think it is enough to just go over the house twice a week?*
The secretary, on behalf of her boss, has to turn down a colleague's request for vacation days.«	*To the colleague: It's not my fault that your request has been denied.*	*The boss has denied your request.*
Double entry book-keeping.» (Polite, but not honest)	*Secretary to the boss: You're right. I'd do it that way myself.*	*I have a different opinion, of course. But you must decide.*
A neighbor calls Mrs. M. to see if she could baby-sit her daughter for a few hours.	*Mrs. M. says to the neighbor: Of course, just bring Peggy on over. But the neighbor barely leaves Mrs. M's house, and Mrs. M. complains, That woman dumps her daughter off on me every chance she gets.*	*Unfortunately this is a bad time for me. I was just getting ready to go to the store. An hour from now I'd be glad to look after her.*

81

Situation	Actual behavior	Ideal behavior
The mother wants her child to be polite to the lady neighbor.	*You have to be nice all the time. Otherwise God will be angry with you.*	*It makes Mrs. Miller happy when you're nice to her. And that helps the two of you get along better.*

Disorders and Conflicts
Excessive politeness; flattery; unrealistic expectations of politeness; ritualized courtesies; inability to say no; rudeness; egotism; lack of tact; insolence; hidden and open aggression; lack of security in social situations; anxiety; insufficient ability to assert one's will; guilt feelings; headaches; stomach - intestine problems; heart trouble; tendency toward alcoholism.

HONESTY

MY CHILD LIES LIKE A CARPET.

Definition
We define an honest person as one who expresses his opinion openly; a dishonest person, on the other hand, is one who reacts guardedly or with white lies. Differentiation analysis includes truthfulness and veracity in the category of honesty. In a partnership honesty is equated with fidelity; in social communication we label it as openness and integrity.

Situations Involving Honesty:
Truthfulness is not one of my daughter's strengths when she is dealing with her father.
Our son Carl wears his heart on his sleeve.
At home Sally is never one to hide her opinions; but in school her teacher has to drag them out of her.
My wife is not very outspoken when it comes to saying what's really on her mind.
At work it is wise not to say everything you think.
I have to tell the lady next door everything I hear; otherwise she doesn't give me a moment's peace.
I'm always concerned about avoiding confrontation.
My only flaw is that I'm just too honest.

Development

At the age when a child starts talking and begins to spend time with playmates, the child cannot yet make a clear distinction between his own perception and reality. This lack of differentiation makes it necessary that the people around the child show understanding and a willingness to deal with the world of the child's experiences. If the adult does not understand the child's «logic of experience» and punishes it as «lies» in order to teach the child to be honest, the child can actually learn to become dishonest. The child learns to be afraid to tell the truth; he learns to conceal his opinions. Furthermore, by not paying attention to the child's normal behavior, the parent can spur the child on to dishonesty. To get the attention of the parent, the child will start to tell exciting stories and thereby put himself on the center stage. Parents also teach their children dishonest behavior when they ask them to tell little lies: *If someone calls, tell them I'm not at home!* This kind of behavior becomes a model. One should also be aware that dishonesty simply encourages more of the same. Lying is seldom punished; indeed, it is more frequently rewarded in that it helps a person, at least provisionally, to avoid an unpleasant situation.

Significance and Results

Honesty and politeness are closely related: *Because I was too polite I didn't give my honest opinion.* Or: *I'm just too honest, and other people consider that impolite.* While honesty can be viewed as an inhibition of aggression, honesty often has the characteristics of aggressive behavior: telling someone his opinion without any «adornment;» telling someone some-thing right to his face; confronting someone with something.

Overly emphasized honesty can also be interpreted as rudeness, frequently leading to conflicts in interpersonal relationships, especially when one of the partners, feeling insulted, simply pulls back. Dishonesty, the opposite extreme, produces only temporary advantages. It often leads to complicated structures of lies that the person can't get out of. This represents a field of conflict that is laden with tension.

We find the extremes of honesty-dishonesty and super honesty in: nagging, vicious gossip, exaggerations, underestimations, and teasing. In relation to the person doing them, we find a guilty conscience, inner unrest, and psychosomatic disorders.

Examples

Whoever lies once can never be believed again, even when he tells the truth. My mother always said this to me, and eventually I thought to myself. Well, I can go ahead and lie since no one will believe me anyway. (34-year-old civil servant with problems in his professional life)

    My father was determined to beat honesty into us. But instead he forced us to lie. (21-year-old female student with problems in establishing contact with others)

    My father always told the naked truth and caused a lot of sorrow by expressing his opinions that way. As a result I learned to say what others want to hear, but inside I'm mad at myself. (48-year-old housewife with stomach and intestinal problems)

    I've had headaches and stomach trouble since I found out my husband was having an affair. He was able to keep it a secret from me for years. In other matters, too, he was not open with me. The kids had to suffer under the tension that existed between the two of us. (45-year-old housewife)

Situation	Actual behavior	Ideal behavior
Andy is two hours late in getting home from school. He says, *The teacher kept us there longer today.*	Mother: *That's a damned lie.*	Mother: *Well, that's rather unusual. If you had to stay in after school, or did something else, please tell me about it. It's just a shame that well have to warm up your supper again.*
Bobby took a dollar out of his mother's grocery money.	Mother: *You little thief. I'll never be able to trust you again.*	Mother: *I don't think it's right that you took the money. I even feel sad about it. Tell me what you wanted to do with the money. Wouldn't it have been better if you had asked me for it? Besides, I don't take money from your billfold, and I expect the same from you.*
Melissa would like a bigger allowance. She says she needs more money for school.	Father: *You just blow the money on useless junk.*	Father: *Could you bring the receipt? Whenever you want to buy other things, we'll talk about it, okay?*

Situation	Actual behavior	Ideal behavior
Mrs. B's girlfriend invites her to supper, but Mrs. B has a French class that evening.	Mrs. B: *I'm sorry I can't come, I'd really like to, but I'm not feeling well.*	Mrs. B: *I can't come, although I'd really like to. I have a French class tonight. How would it be if we were to meet Saturday evening?*
Mrs. L finds out that her husband had an affair on one of his business trips.	Big fight at home. All hell breaks loose. A divorce attorney is hired.	Wife: *As you can imagine, I'm not overjoyed to hear about this: But I would like to know if this was just a one-time thing. I think we should make use of this crisis and discuss openly what we treasure in each other and what we should work on in our marriage.*

Disorders and Conflicts

Fanaticism about honesty; strong drive for validation; vanity; excessive expectations of oneself and others; dishonesty; lack of integrity; infidelity; deceitful pretensions; lack of discernment between fantasy and reality; social conflicts; anxiety; aggression; headaches; heart and circulatory trouble.

JUSTICE

THE OTHERS ALWAYS GET PREFERENTIAL TREATMENT:

Definition

One considers a certain treatment as unfair if it is determined by personal likes or dislikes rather than by objective considerations. The feeling of being treated unfairly arises when one has been expecting impartial treatment.

Situations Involving Justice:

When I get home late you punish me. But if Martin is not on time, nothing happens.
He always bought all sort of expensive things for himself, but I had to be satisfied with cheaper stuff.
She is of the opinion that I have to earn the money and she can spend it.

*How can God be considered just when his representatives here (the priests)
are so unfair?*
*When my husband's mother comes he's all smiles. But when my mother comes,
you ought to see the face he makes!*
I lost the case only because my opponent had a better attorney.
He got a better grade than I did only because he comes from an academic family.

Development

The justice and injustice that a person experiences colors his impression of
the world. Everyone has a sense of justice. It develops due to the uniqueness
of the individual and to the level of his development. The following saying
addresses this uniqueness: *Treating two people the same way means that
one of them is treated unfairly.* With reference to the level of development
this means *not letting a 5-year-old boy stay up as late as a 15-year-old one.*
The way the parents treat a child, and how fair they are to him and his
siblings, determines the child's individual relationship to justice. The way
the parents treat each other can become the child's model for his own
relationship with a partner later on. Unfair treatment is the root of the
deepest prejudices against other people, and also against other religions.

Significance and Results

Just as fairness can produce feelings of trust and hope, so injustice can
lead to rebellion, desperation, resignation, and hopelessness. Justice
affects the expectations one has about one's future. In terms of content,
justice can be related to various behavioral areas: punctuality (Steve
finds it fair that his brother has to be at home the same time as he does),
cleanliness (Helen finds it unfair that her mom makes her get out of
bed because she hasn't brushed her teeth), ambition (Maggie is furious
because she has to sit and work on her homework while her brother is
already outside playing). As in the case of parenting, partnerships show
a fluctuation back and forth between the extremes of justice and love.

Examples

*When she did her Christmas shopping my mother always made sure that all
the gifts had the same monetary value. That was always a problem in our
house, because it meant that we always had to give gifts that equalled what*

we got. At the time I found this «fairness» to be a compulsion. It was such a degrading «exchange.» Today I can't give anyone a gift without imagining that I'm obliging the other person to give me something equal in return. (36-year-old housewife with headaches and sleep disorders)

My mother's inferiority complex kept her from being fair. Whenever other kids hit me, they were mostly kids from «better homes,» and they were always simply in the right. My mother always said, «They probably knew why they did that. Who can guess what you were really up to.» (23-year-old student), with depression, anxiety, and difficulty in making friends)

Whenever something went wrong in our house, the immediate opinion was: You were the one, because who else could have done it? This unfairness really hurt me. Recently I came to realize that I've been doing the same thing with my kids. Except that my kids defend themselves, not like how I reacted back then. I still let a lot of things eat away at me. (27-year-old housewife with stomach and intestine disorders)

Johnny (age 9) came to me a few days ago and said, «Carrie only needs to cough and you go running to her. But you never have time to play with me.» I replied, «Carrie behaves differently than you do. You could learn a thing or two from her. Just take a look at her room, and then see how yours looks!» (41-year-old housewife)

Situation	Actual behavior	Ideal behavior
Patty to her mother: *You don't love, me any more. You always hold Bobby so much, but not me.*	Mother: *You know that's not true. I treat the two of you the same. After all, I have to be fair.*	Mother picks up Patty: *Patty, you know I love both of you very much. Neither of you should get the short end of the stick.*
12-year-old Wally to his father: *I always have to look after Kathy (age 2). I never get to play outside with Stevie.*	Father: *You should be happy that you have a little sister. You're always complaining. I don't think you really like her. You should be ashamed of yourself.*	Father: *You know that for the next few weeks that can't be helped, till Mom gets home from the hospital. But you really should have time for play. Let's think about how we can arrange that.*
Mrs. F. has enough to do with three children and a house to take care of.	*Mr. F. to his wife: Look at our lady neighbor. She has a job, takes care of the house, and still always looks splendid.*	Mr. F. to his wife: *I'm amazed at what our lady neighbor accomplishes. But I think the upbringing of our little kids is more important that your earning money. If you feel like working again later on, we'll try to find something that's right for you.*
The husband frequently goes out with his colleagues from work. His wife doesn't think that this is fair.	The wife keeps quiet, doesn't come out of the kitchen all evening, and goes to bed early.	Wife: *I don't like being alone all evening long. How would it be if we would have friends over some time? And you and I could also do something together some evening.*
7-year-old Melissa to her mother: You always take sides with Janie when we fight. Then I'm the one who started it. You do that on purpose.	Mother: *You're older and should be ashamed of yourself, always picking on little Janie. I have to protect her from you.*	Mother: *No, Melissa, it's not always your fault, you know that. Sometimes things get to me. Let me make a suggestion: From now on you two battle things yourselves. I won't interfere. You're already very careful that you don't hurt Janie. If the two of you can't agree on something, then both of you come to me, okay?*

Disorders and Conflicts

Being a stickler about justice; self-righteousness; being overly sensitive; feeling of being weak; depression; unfairness; retaliation social injustice; individual and collective aggression.

AMBITION - ACHIEVEMENT

SUCCESS IS 10% INSPIRATION AND 90% PERSPIRATION.

Definition
We understand the term «ambition» as the willingness to stick to a very taxing and bring activity for a shorter or longer period of time in order to achieve a definite goal. Ambition is a criterion of social success.

Situations Involving Ambition:
The gods made sweat a prerequisite for success.
In school our boy doesn't exert himself at all.
She works up a storm when it comes to taking care of the house, but she doesn't lift a finger for me.
It's his ambition to be self-employed.
The Germans are hard working and thorough.
God didn't create us to be do-nothings.
By shirking his dunes he steals time from God.
Idleness is the devil's workshop.
You are measured by what you accomplish.
I had to sweat too, till I got it done.
All day long I'm working under the gun.

Development
In a child's development play is the preparatory step for learning ambition and accomplishment. Through play the child learns to know his environment and his own limits. By playing alone and with parents, playmates, animals, plants, and objects around him, he develops a relationship to himself and to his surroundings.

Depending on the shape of this relationship, ambition can later develop into dedication to a particular task. To accomplish this, the child, while playing, must be able to deal with himself and with his playmates, as he perceives them. Parents and relatives influence the child when they load the child down with a lot of toys or with various alternatives, when they prescribe the child's play down to the smallest detail, or when they have little patience for the child's attempts at independent play.

In school ambition is demanded with more serious appeals. The child may then renounce certain activities and turn to ones that more easily satisfy his needs. It's therefore easier for the child to be industrious if he finds the task satisfying in itself. Success is, of course, closely linked with ambition, but touches on other factors as well. The actual capabilities, orderliness, punctuality, cleanliness, politeness, etc. play an important role in these regards.

When parents require accomplishments from their child, they should always remain aware of the uniqueness of their child's capabilities.

Significance and Results
We don't need to go into detail about the consequences of laziness - as an escape from demands placed upon us. These are generally well known to everyone. Ambition, however, can create problems of its own i.e. when ambition, achievement, and success become the isolated measuring stick for the quality of a personality. Imbalanced observations such as these ignore the primary capabilities like patience, confidence, and hope.

The results of ambition can be competitive struggle, fear of defeat, the feeling of absolute inferiority, presumptuous perfection, and problems of self-esteem.

«Positive» attitudes toward ambition can be found in the modest person who is afraid of changing jobs; in the worker who sacrifices everything; in the one who keeps striving; in the one who aims for success; and in the «quarterly» worker who works at peak efficiency only when enough work is piled on him.

Examples
Sometimes I have the feeling that I am utterly lazy. But that's only when it comes to studying. Then I feel that everything is over my head. At times like that I'm totally apathetic, and just crawl in bed. When I get the urge to clean house, though, that never happens. My mother worked like a dog all her life, and work came to be her purpose in life. But only physical labor. As far as she's concerned, there is no other kind of work. She's proud of the fact that she's a real workhorse. (22-year-old female student with learning problems and fatigue)

A mother reports: *When my husband says to our son, «You did your homework well,» he starts making faces as if we were really coming down on him hard. The child simply doesn't want to do anything he's supposed to do. It doesn't do any good to scold. I just can't get him to do anything. He's on the go the whole day, but not when it comes to doing his homework.* (28-year-old mother with difficulties in raising her child)

My mother loved things tidy; that's why I wasn't allowed to play in the living room. Apparently I took on her excessive love for orderliness. Because when I think about it today, nothing I ever did was playful. I always dusted and swept the room where I kept my dolls. The doll clothes were washed every day. The dolls got their hair combed every day. I only wanted things that were pretty and good. (35-year-old mother of three, suffering from fear of the future)

Situation	Actual behavior	Ideal behavior
Four-year-old Tommy wants to go to the store for his mother.	Mother: *You can't do that. You're too little.*	Mother: *Well, that idea makes me very happy. You know what, I'll write everything down on a piece of paper, and you give it to the lady in the store. I know you can do that.*
Grandma comes to visit every week. Every time, she brings Jennifer a toy. Jennifer plays with it for half an hour, but then wants a different one. If she doesn't get one, she starts crying.	Mother to Grandma: *That's really nice of you. Jennifer will like it.* But in reality the mother is angry. She thinks to herself: *I really ought to ask Grandma to bring Jennifer a gift only for her birthday and at Christmas. But my mother would be so hurt if I said that. I can't hurt her that way.*	Mother says to Grandma before her next visit: *I know you love Jennifer and like to make her happy. But Jennifer has enough toys for now. But she needs other things. Please talk it over with us the next time you want to give her something.*
David is working on a modal kit that is really complicated for him. Finally he throws it down. *I just can't do it.*	Father: *You never finish anything. Give it here; I'll do it myself.* Or: *If you start something, finish it. Now just sit here and work on it till you get it figured out.* Or: *If you can't finish it, just drop it and try something else.*	Father: *That really is a hard model. But don't you want to give it another try?* He gives his son a little help, but lets him continue on his own so that he'll develop confidence in himself.

Situation	Actual behavior	Ideal behavior
Anne feels totally destroyed. In the last few days she's been having trouble in her French class.	Mother: *Now sit down and stay there till you get it right!*	Mother: *You've been talking about nothing but school. Go outside and play a while. Afterwards you'll see that you can do the French homework a lot easier*
Mr. B. has a very responsible position. He comes home late every evening. His kids hardly ever see him except on Sunday. He has practically no time to play with them, because on the weekend he takes care of a lot of personal correspondence.	Wife: *Do you live for your work, or for the kids and me; You can just choose right now!*	Wife: *I know how demanding your work is, and we are proud of what you've achieved. Can we somehow help you so that you have some time for the kids and for me? We want to try to overcome this problem together.*

Disorders and Conflicts

Escape into work; excessive striving; compulsion to accomplish things; stress; too many demands; fear of failure; boredom with civilization; mental blocks about work; laziness; escape into loneliness and illness; competitive struggle; envy; aggression depression; anxiety; heart trouble; tendency to have stomach trouble; headaches; tendency toward alcoholism and drug dependency.

FRUGALITY

IF YOU SAVE SOMETHING, YOU'VE GOT SOMETHING. IF YOU'VE GOT SOMETHING, THEN YOU ARE SOMETHING!

Definition

With this term we mean handling money and things in an economic way. This is entirely compatible with generosity, but is less associated with the extremes of being wasteful or stingy.

Situations Involving Frugality:
My son throws his money out the window with both hands.
I get angry with my husband because he turns every penny over in his hands ten times before he'll spend it for anything in the house.

*Sometimes I buy something on impulse and I'm angry with myself afterwards
for throwing my money away like that.*

*At work he is lavish when it comes to spending money on friends and co-
workers. But you ought to see what he's like at home. There he seems to want
to save every penny.*

*My mother-in-law gives a lot of money to church. But when my husband was
a little boy he had to wear hand-me-downs.*

*I could really do without my tenant. He leaves the lights burning till all hours
of the night.*

*Every time my secretary has to jot down a note, she takes a clean piece of paper.
That really upsets me.*

Development

We learn to hang on to things and to share. In a narrower sense of the
term, frugality has to do with whether we hold on to something or let
it go. Holding on can become stinginess. Letting go can grow into an
addiction to throwing money away.

Psychoanalysis has tried to relate toilet training to frugality. The
child carries out the basic functions of thrift, namely holding and giving,
as he learns to delay his bowel movements as long as is desired. In this
sense stinginess corresponds to the rigid «holding on» when a person
is constipated. The addiction to spending money is like uncontrollable
diarrhea. Frugality can also be traced to early eating habits. The child just
can't get enough food down his throat. In learning to deal with money
the child must first learn the value of money. He learns this best through
expending energy and time to accomplish something. In addition the
child can become thrifty through practice. Here models are important.
Giving the child an allowance is one way for him to practice being thrifty.

Significance and Results

In its extreme forms of stinginess and waste, frugality aims at the
following: *Independence:* By being in control of money and things, a
person tries to be independent of others.

Power: One acquires more and more things so as to have power over
others. The idea of having power is often enough in itself.

Substitute for love: A person tries to buy friends, emotional attention, and love. A neglected child tries to make himself loved with toys and candy. Adults who need to feel more important try to win their friends recognition by being very generous towards them. For someone who needs love, a fur coat is the price for the love he expects to get in return.

Examples

My husband says we have to save on electricity. A 40-watt bulb is just as good as a 60-watt one. He learned that from his mother, who was sometimes downright stingy. But on the other hand he lavishes all sorts of toys on our kids. (33- year-old mother, disinterested in sex)

I sacrificed everything for my kids. I literally starved so they would have a better life. I didn't treat myself to anything. But they frittered the money away on silly things. Now it's too late for me. (56-year-old woman with depression and heart trouble)

Situation	Actual behavior	Ideal behavior
The mother doesn't treat herself to anything. She sacrifices every penny to give her kids the things they want.	Cindy and Tom: *We need money for ice skates.* Mother: *Okay, but that means I'll have to give up the idea of a subscription to the theater this season.*	In the family group the children learn that every member of the family has a right to a piece of the financial pie. Father: *Mom needs money for her free time, too.* Step by step the family decides how to allocate the money.
The daughter asks for a bigger allowance.	The father refuses without giving a reason: *For Pete's sake. You just make do with what you get.*	Father: *First why don't we talk about why you need a bigger allowance, and then we can decide.*
The son has already spent his whole month's allowance by the middle of the month. Now he asks for an advance.	Mother: *If you didn't spend so much money on junk you'd have enough. I won't hear another word about it.*	Mother: *You know you can spend your allowance any way you want, and that we don't check up on you. But you should learn to watch how you spend it. How would it be if you'd set up a budget every month?*

Situation	Actual behavior	Ideal behavior
When her first child was born, the wife gave up a good job, where she had earned well. Now she is dependent on her husband.	Husband: *When I come home tired from work, I should expect to find the house in order. After all, I'm the only breadwinner in the family.*	Husband: *Since you quit your job, you definitely have less money at your disposal. Right now I don't earn enough for the two of us to have a lot of spending money. Hopefully that will all change when the company gives us our next raises.*

Disorders and Conflicts

Excessive frugality; stinginess; money as a means to power; waste; overestimation of one's importance; tremendous need to feel important; fraud; passive expectation; naïve optimism; irresponsibility; anxiety about life; depression; hopelessness; inner unrest; guilt feelings.

DEPENDABILITY - EXACTNESS - CONSCIENTIOUSNESS

IT'S NO WONDER THAT I HAVE NO PATIENCE WITH THIS MESS.

Definition

We speak of dependability when we can rely on a person. Even in our absence we can count on him to handle an agreed upon task and we know he won't disappoint us.

Exactness means that a job is carried out as described. The greater the exactness, the less likely it is that there will be errors. Conscientiousness presupposes an inner measure for precision, care, and accuracy. One speaks of conscientiousness when an accomplishment meets this inner standard and is thus consistent with «conscience.»

Situations Involving Dependability:
My son is already a man of principle, just like his father.
My wife gives in to her every whim, and swings back and forth like a reed in the wind. One minute she says one thing; the next minute it's an entirely different story.

My perfectionism at the office is so bad that I go over the inventory list five or six times. Sometimes I'm still there at 11 o'clock at night.

I barely come away from confession and I start wondering if I really confessed everything. So I go right back and get in line again. And by the time it's my turn, I've thought of another sin I had forgotten, or else I make up one that I perhaps did.

Now that I know what people are really like, I only trust my dog.

Once he's promised something, he sticks to it, even if the situation has changed completely.

Safe only when used according to directions.

Development

As the definition indicates, dependability, precision, and conscientiousness are three complex behavioral areas that develop in the child-rearing situation. One must always ask in relation to which actual capabilities were these three characteristics developed and required. A person's dependability usually reflects the attitude of the important people in his development:

Just leave it, I'll take care of it later.

You'll really catch it if you are late again.

Take your toys somewhere else and let me have some peace and quiet.

Significance and Results

Dependability and trustworthiness belong to those qualities that are of fundamental importance for interpersonal relationships. They create an atmosphere of security, friendship, and freedom. The opposites of dependability are rigid adherence to a promise or an old habit (often confused with loyalty), and the unreliability that the partner would label unpredictability and weakness of character. Similarly, exactness can go off into two opposite extremes: At the one end of the scale there is compulsive pedantry- related to such concepts as thoroughness, scrupulousness, perfectionism, and brooding. A good representative of this is someone who is a stickler for principles.

At the other end of the scale we find thoughtless «carelessness,» where exactness can fluctuate depending on the person's mood.

Examples

At work my mother was always a dependable, conscientious employee. She felt a great responsibility to the foreigners working there, and her very existence centered on her being a good worker. At home she didn't need to impress anybody, because she could get my attention in other ways, or at least try to. Since she could do with me what she wanted, she could go back on her word, and I couldn't do a thing about it. She was simply stronger than I was. I noticed this and acted the same way later on. My husband put up with it until our marriage finally fell apart. (36-year-old divorcee)

It's terrible with Mary. She can't finish any assignment, any task. Everything is half done. Who does she get that from? My husband and I aren't like that at all! [Comment: The father tyrannizes the family with his pedantry.] (10-year-old girl, unable to concentrate, with learning problems, aggression, bed-wetting)

How often have I told Bobby that people just can't rely on him, and that he'll never amount to anything if he keeps going this way. But it doesn't do any good. In fact, he just keeps getting worse. (12-year-old boy who is «disobedient.» The boy never does what his parents say.)

My mother was a perfect example of precision. She punished any deviation from the norms that she set. When I went to the store I was always told what brand of margarine I should get, etc. If I accidentally bought a different kind, even at the same price, I was sent back to the store to exchange it, because she wanted brand A, which «tasted much better» while the other stuff just couldn't be enjoyed. As I grew up I just became the opposite kind of person. There were times when I've been an absolute slob. My husband didn't like that one bit. (44-year-old woman with marital problems)

Situation	Actual behavior	Ideal behavior
Michael copied a text. He made a lot of mistakes, just because he was in too big a hurry. Several sentences are missing.	Mother: You *keep writing that text till you do it without a mistake, even if you have to sit there and do it all evening!*	Mother: *You made a number of errors with some of the words. Correct the mistakes and write in the sentences you left out. Then we'll go over it again together.*
Dr. M. has a new secretary who is not working up to his expectations.	Dr. M: *My previous secretary didn't make mistakes like these.*	Dr. M: *You know, you have to get used to working in a new area like this. That means you have to pay particular attention to your work. Here's an example of how a good document should be written. If you have a question or a suggestion, be sure to see me. I'll check your work again after a while.*
Various business friends call Mr. S. at home. His wife takes these calls, but by the time her husband gets home in the evening she's forgotten a good part of them.	Mr. S: *With your carelessness and forgetfulness you're going to ruin me. That phone call was very important for me.*	Mr. S: It's a pity you forgot who called. How would it be if we'd put a note pad and ballpoint pen next to the phone. Then you could write down who called and what he wanted. This wouldn't put any strain on your memory, and besides, it would be a good example for our kids.

Conflicts and Disorders

Excessive precision; perfectionism and fussiness; inflexibility; lack of precision; unreliability; superficiality; breach of trust; fear of failure; social conflicts; inner insecurity; disappointments; excessive demands; depression; guilt feelings; insomnia.

CHAPTER III:
MISUNDERSTANDINGS IN PARENTING
PARTNERSHIP AND PSYCHOTHERAPY

MISUNDERSTANDINGS

ABOUT THE CROW AND THE PEACOCK

In the palace park, a black crow perched on the branches of an orange tree. Down on the well-tended lawn, a peacock marched around proudly. The crow screeched, «How can one even permit such a strange bird to enter this park? He walks around as arrogantly as if he were the sultan himself. And with those downright ugly feet! And his feathers such a horrible shade of blue! I would never wear a color like that. He drags his tail around like a fox.» The crow stopped and waited silently for a reply. The peacock did not say anything for a while, but then he began to speak with a melancholy smile, «I don't think your assertions correspond to reality. The bad things you say about me rest on misunderstandings. You say I'm arrogant, because I hold my head up so that my shoulder feathers stick out and a double chin disfigures my neck. In reality I'm anything but arrogant. I know my ugly features; and I know my feet are wrinkled and like leather. This actually bothers me so much that I hold my head erect in order not to see my ugly feet. You see only my ugly parts. You close your eyes to my fine points and to my beauty. Haven't you noticed that? What you call ugly is exactly what people admire in me. Why don't you see me as I am?» (After P. Etessami)

We don't judge our partners and their behavior objectively. Instead, our perceptions differ from one person to the next, depending on our experiences, the depth of the emotional relationship, and the expectations we have of the particular person. Misunderstandings are the result of the subjectivity with which we perceive our partners. But it's hard to recognize that these are misunderstandings, even when we are the ones affected by them. Quite often we just have a vague feeling that something is wrong. We start to ask ourselves questions:

Did I understand my partner right?
Did I make myself clear in what I said?
Why wasn't he able to understand me correctly?
How did these misunderstandings come about?
Will it really hurt me if I admit I misunderstood?
If my partner makes an effort to understand me, will I be willing to make some compromises?

In the following pages we want to try to illustrate typical misunderstandings that occur again and again in interpersonal relationships. Under the heading *Comment* we summarize the misunderstanding under discussion. In addition we use a brief motto to capsulize the important distinctions. This motto, under the heading *Antidote*, can be used in the event of a conflict. At such times the antidote can remind you: I don't have to act the way I am right now. I can do it differently.

IF PARENTS WERE WELL RAISED, ONE COULD GIVE BIRTH TO WELL RAISED CHILDREN. *(Goethe)*

THE GOAL AND CONTENT OF PARENTING

Misunderstanding: *If you have something, then you are something.*
From the time I was a child I was drilled to be an achiever. As far back as I can remember, my parents saw to it that I worked hard. Even as a young child I was given a lot of tasks to do. Before I started school I already knew how to read and write, and got homework assignments from my parents every day. My mother paid special attention to my handwriting. If something didn't go right, she'd go for hours without saying a word to me. Although I was one of the best in my class, I was tired of school. But I could never show that I felt that way, because then there would have been trouble at home. Now I'm a successful attorney. I like my work very much, but I have no ties to other

people. I'm not close to my kids either. I hate having free time... I've reached my goal. It's important for my parents and for me that I'm an academic...

From this report by a 42-year-old lawyer we find more than an extreme example of an imbalanced upbringing: In today's society an achievement orientation is considered the standard that every individual has to submit to. A strong emphasis on ambition, as we find it in the example of the attorney, occurs in numerous families, even in reference to the other secondary capabilities like orderliness, cleanliness, punctuality, and politeness. All of these secondary capabilities were learned, just as the contents of anatomy, physiology, and physics can be learned in the course of one's formal education.

But a person cannot learn to love himself and a partner in the same sense. Love is the result of a development that began in early childhood and was shaped by the interaction with the persons closest to him. If scientific knowledge and social norms are acquired through schooling, the experience of emotional relationships has an impact on personal development, particularly on character formation. It is possible to consciously pose and answer the question of the goal of upbringing, but mostly this question is dealt with on an unconscious level. A person raises his child according to his own experiences, without really considering whether these experiences are also valid for the child's capabilities, the times he lives in, or the necessity of his development.

MY PARENTS WERE NEVER IN AGREEMENT

My parents were never in agreement on how to raise their kids. They actually had opposite ideas. For my mother freedom was the key element, although from time to time she could also get excited about obedience and orderliness. But she never raised us in a systematic way. As far as morals were concerned, I had the impression that she was watching over us, even though she never set rigid rules. As for my father, he wanted strict obedience and submission at all times. But we resisted him on this. It's hard to say what goal my father set for us. I can imagine he wanted us to be decent girls and to get married. I felt that my mother just wanted us girls to marry well and to be happy. (33-year-old mother of two, problems in upbringing)

AT ALL COSTS WE WERE SUPPOSED TO BECOME DECENT PEOPLE

At first my mother had only one goal, to make an orderly and decent woman out of me. Her motto was, «If you have something, then you are something.» The people in our town looked up to us, but that was because we owned the most land. I was also supposed to become a «pretty, strong, healthy woman,» because where we came from life revolved around eating and work from morning till night. Even today all my relatives think I'm skinny and ugly, as if we didn't have enough to eat. (34-year-old housewife with heart and stomach trouble)

Misunderstanding in the goal and content of parenting, stems from confusing training with upbringing. This misunderstanding is a serious one because the «educators» are not usually aware of it. Suddenly they are faced with the results of this misunderstanding, and don't know what to do about it.

Disorders and Conflicts
Imbalance; too few demands and expectations; too many expectations; desperation; escape into work; escape into loneliness; escape into illness

> *Comment*
> A person doesn't just need information in the sense of training. He also needs an emotional basis for mastering his education. Of course, a purely factual education can build character, but the educator then looses control of it, and it becomes the source of conflicts, confrontations, and disorders. Conscious upbringing means more than knowing the contents; there must also be an awareness of the goal:
> Why and for whom am I raising my child?
> For myself? For himself? For mankind?
>
> *Antidote*
> Learn to distinguish between training and upbringing

THERE IS A DIFFERENCE BETWEEN A PERSON WHO HAS HIS BELOVED AT HIS SIDE, AND A PERSON WHO WAITS AND LONGS FOR HER ARRIVAL. (Saadi)

THE RELATIVITY OF VALUES

Misunderstanding: *I expect my family to be clean and neat. By that I mean they have to be exactly as clean and neat as I want.*

When my kids and my husband help me around the house, for instance with hanging out the wash, I check to be sure they do it just the way I do. If they don't, I criticize them and then hang it the way I want. And then I complain that I have to do everything myself. I work under the assumption that they all know how I like things. When I'd clean house, I often destroyed something the kids were building, because I didn't think it was important. Only when I'd see their reaction, would I know that it was important to them. (35-year-old mother of two)

Different conditions in our lives, families, and cultures lead to different development. In this process society is the chief transmitter of the norms by which we evaluate and judge certain behaviors. Various societies have standards that can change with time. This relativity has become especially important today, since there does not seem to be any general binding criteria for evaluating the correctness of a standard. The relativity of our day is found in the orientation crisis that exists in child rearing. Here we are not speaking simply of the influence that parents and teachers have on a child from the time he's born until he is out of school. We are, talking about something much more complex, something that deals with the person's total development as an individual and a member of a group. Just as cultures can differ, we can find differences in people within a single culture. Thus, people can be divided into interest groups, family groups, generational groups, and sexes. And then there are differences between individuals. A good example of this is the situation in the following family, where there is really a triangle in operation:

The father insists on punctuality and neatness in the household, and gets very upset over his wife and children's messiness. But he's not so strict when it comes to honesty in his marriage. He imagines how it would be to have a mistress. It would not be at all hard for him to find reasons to justify his behavior. The wife is the epitome of neatness and cleanliness. She can't stand to have a speck of dust on the furniture. Manners are also important to her. If the child doesn't say a proper «hellos,» when company comes, she becomes angry or withdraws from the child. Because she also places a lot of importance on honesty, there is growing tension between her and her husband. And out of this tension there can develop conflicts and problems. Let's look at the two people more closely. The man works for the welfare of his family, earns money, enjoys sports, and is concerned about his children.

He figures that he has done what he should, and this enables him to feel he has the right to cheat on his wife. The wife devotes herself to her home and expects complete devotion from her husband and children. She believes that complete honesty without compromise is the foundation of every marriage. Here we can clearly see that the partners have definite ideas that cause them to see some things very sharply, but to be almost blind to other things. One can well imagine that communication and understanding between them is practically impossible, because they have such different opinions. The results of all this are aggression against each other and against the kids, and anxiety that is directed inward. Dishonesty and pedantry, however, are no privileges of men (and being a fanatic about cleanliness is not peculiar to women).

In this family there were also similar problems in understanding between the mother and the 8-year-old daughter. It aggravates the mother that the girl doesn't like to take a bath, that she neglects her homework, and that she doesn't keep her room cleaned up. The daughter, on the other hand, finds her mother overly nervous and sometimes even repulsive. They both have different concepts of *neatness, cleanliness,* and *industriousness.* The father blames the mother for the daughter's messiness and poor performance in school. He thinks he's entirely innocent in this matter. The mother, however, sees him as the cause of the problems. She feels he doesn't show enough interest in the girl's schoolwork. Let's look at some more examples:

MY HUSBAND NEEDS HIS REST

When my husband gets home from work he gets cleaned up, eats, and then sits down in front of the TV. There's not even a thought given to the possibility of our going out somewhere. But I have to get out of there after having taken care of the kids the whole day. *(37-year-old housewife, mother of three)*

THE CHILDREN'S ROOM AND A PLAYGROUND ARE TWO DIFFERENT THINGS

I like to have my house perfectly neat. Then I feel comfortable and cozy in my home. But my children are just the opposite. They drag all sorts of rocks, sticks, and boxes into the apartment, and use them to build a cabin or something. But my sense of order rebels against this, because I think people should distinguish between a children's room and a playground. I feel especially uncomfortable about all this because we recently got new wallpaper. (26-year-old housewife who came for psychotherapeutic treatment because her youngest son stutters)

As we have seen, the attitudes and ideas about certain areas of life are critically important for our interaction with other people. Misunderstandings about the relativity of values are particularly crucial in the relationship between parents and child.

CHILDREN PLAY BY OTHER RULES THAN ADULTS

The father who gives his son - and really himself - a toy train for the child's birthday expects the boy to play with it just the way he would. But the child can't do that. He has to experience the train in his own way. If this opportunity is taken away from him, the train and the whole situation surrounding it will remain something alien to the child. He'll either turn away from the toy and act indifferently toward it - which the parents frequently interpret as ingratitude. Or the train will become something frightening and threatening for him. He might dream about being run over by a train. Or he can dream that the train becomes a vicious animal that is running after him.

Dreams like this are a form of psychic processing. The child can become familiar with the train only after he has been able to grasp its meaning. But to grasp it, he has to do more than simply play with it according to the rules, as is customary for adults. What's involved here is the child's total activity. The train is taken apart and examined; its insides are removed; the wheels are taken off. Here the child is following his interests. He wants to know what makes the train move and what makes it emit steam. This is a form of curiosity, an urge to explore. The child is attempting to understand the world and how it works.

If the adults do not see this as a part of the child's development, they interpret it as sheer destructiveness on the part of the child. If we applied this criticism to adults, it might look this way: A man is sitting in a restaurant eating a delicacy. Another man sits down near him and watches carefully as he cuts his meat into tiny pieces, picks each one up with his fork, lifts it to his mouth, and slowly chews it. White watching every movement of this ritual the man begins to speak. He criticizes the man: «Doesn't it occur to you that you're cutting the meat and the salad into such tiny pieces that you can't even taste them? You are simply destroying, ruining this wonderful food on your plate.» As our guest slowly loses his appetite, the man keeps talking about a destructive eating phase, aggressive impulses, and so on. As absurd as this scene may seem, it is much like the example of the child with the new train. Maybe our gourmet had never thought of viewing the actions of chewing, swallowing, and digesting food as acts of destruction, even though that is what they really are. We can also assume that destruction is not the chief reason for eating. It is probably very rare that a patient complains that his teeth or his stomach no longer have enough destructive power. But this very destruction is necessary for the growth and maintenance of the organism. Regardless of what we eat - rice, potatoes, meat, vegetables, fruit - they are all physically destroyed and chemically processed in our mouths, stomachs and intestines. To a certain extent they become our own flesh and blood. To put it in terms of imagery: When we eat a pork chop we don't want pork protein in our muscles. We want our own protein. This is why we have to break the food up into tiny pieces until we can build our own protein from it. We should keep this image in mind when we think of the mastery steps that every child must take. The child takes his world apart - either in reality, as in the case of his toy train - or in his imagination. He breaks it down into the smallest parts possible so that he can then construct a world that he understands and feels comfortable with. This experience forms the basis for his relationship to his environment, but the process by which this is achieved stands in contrast to the values and order system that want to keep the «nest» stable. And it is here, in this contrast that conflicts can develop.

The relativity of values is even more evident when adults give the child a toy that they think is very valuable and worthwhile. The child, however, may prefer a toy that has a far less monetary value. Similarly, various attitudes to the same object can lead to misunderstanding within a family:

A 32-year-old mother has considerable problems with her in-laws, who, for years, have been lavishing toys on her child: *I don't know where to go with all the toys. They never think of giving my child something practical like clothes. It's driving me crazy.* An analysis revealed that the father-in-law had been off to war while his own son was a young boy. Having missing out on this period of his son's life, he had tried to make up for it by giving presents to his grandson. Toys thus have a different meaning for the grandfather and for the mother. For the former they are an exoneration: for the latter, a burden.

The various ways a child evaluates something can be misinterpreted by the educator as impoliteness, ingratitude, petulance, and aggression.

Release from the Hospital

Two boys almost the same age, hospitalized for appendectomies, showed completely different behavior after a week in the hospital. The one was very cooperative and seemed quite satisfied with the atmosphere there. When any mention was made of his being released, he let it be understood that he'd rather remain there. The other boy grew more impatient with every passing day. He constantly asked the nurses and the doctor. *How long do I have to stay here? When can I go home?* The nurses found him downright impudent. The doctor interpreted his behavior as aggressiveness. There were very different circumstances in the different behaviors of the two boys. The first boy came from a broken home. His mother, who had a job, had very little time for him. This is why he liked the attention he got at the hospital, and why he wanted the situation to continue. The other boy, though, had a good relationship with his parents. He liked to swim, and his swimming club was going to have a tournament in his hometown in the next few days. He absolutely didn't want to miss out on it.

Because of the differences in the children's experiences and in the doctor – nurse – patient situation, the same event, release from the hospital, produced two entirely different reactions.

Disorders and Conflicts
Meddling; fixations; inflexibility; conflicts with partners; expectations; disappointments; anxiety; aggression; isolation; escape into work; desperation; mental blocks and lack of willpower; helplessness; mania; nagging; the feeling of not being understood.

Comment
Age, sex, personal experience, education, social class, social environment, philosophical or religious belief, political opinions, and the general atmosphere in a particular situation determine differences in value systems. There are various standards for measuring values: They can be measured by monetary value; by their rarity, by their usefulness; by their prestige; or by the feelings they evoke. The actual capabilities can function as these kinds of measure. Differences in measures are the main cause of misunderstandings and interpersonal conflicts. Such conflicts are particularly frequent when people have rigid standards they refuse to change. This leads to trouble when they are confronted by people who have other values. Other problems can arise when the values within a society are influx. We feel helpless when confronted by this situation; often we can do nothing but release our aggressions.

Antidote
Learn to distinguish between absolute and relative values.

EVERY AGE HAS US OWN PROBLEMS, EVERY SOUL ITS OWN LONGINGS. (Baha'u'llah)

Nossrat Peseschkian, M.D.

THE DIMENSION OF TIME AND THE IMAGE OF MAN

Misunderstanding: *I'm at a total loss with modern ways of raising children.* In the past fifty years social conditions have undergone a lot of changes. People have been only partially aware of this process. People who have hung on to old ideas have been left behind, thus creating an image of man that no longer fits the times. This leads to misunderstandings. If one compares our contemporary social conditions with those of earlier times, a development through the following three processes can be seen.

Population Growth
At the time of Christ approximately *200* million people inhabited the earth. *By 1950* it was about *3* billion. For *1990* there are estimates of *6* billion; for the year *2030, 12* billion; by the year *2070* it is expected to have doubled again to *24* billion, etc. (Niemöller, *1968).* This process is not simply a matter of quantitative increase. It is closely associated with a number of problems that are becoming more and more important to us. Questions like hunger, the environment, and socio-economic relations play a role here. According to United Nations estimates, *57%* of the population in *1950* was undernourished. While *1.3* billion people had enough to eat at that time, another *1.7* billion were hungry. By the end of this century there will be a total of *7* billion people. This represents an increase from *3* billion to *7* billion in a fifty-year period from *1950* to the year *2000.* In addition, experts predict that the population will be increasing at a much faster rate than production. This prediction, in fact, is already proving to be true, which means that by *1999* the percentage of the population that is undernourished will no longer be *57%,* but *75 %,* a total of *5.6* billion people. In other words, for every person who has enough to eat there will be three people who don't. (Quoted from Niemöller, *1968).* This quantitative development will usher in structural changes.

Urbanization
This process is clearly related to the increase in population. Until a few generations ago most of the world's population was rural. But then there was a drastic change in many parts of the world. In the USA three-fourths of the population now lives in large cities or metropolitan areas. This trend can be seen almost everywhere in the world, albeit at

different rates of change. Only recently have people become sensitive to the psychological implications of urbanization. The consequences of this change threaten to increase at enormous rates.

Urbanization creates a whole set of problems for parenting and interpersonal relationships. Improvements in hygiene have become quite widespread, but this has often led to a rather sterile environment. The child who grew up in the country could use the barnyard as his playground. But in the modern city the child is limited to his parents' apartment. This environment limits his developmental possibilities and sets the scene for new conflicts. Finding a playground is in many cases either nothing more than a theoretical question, or leads to even worse alternatives. The population density of the city results in more intense relations with the social environment, but this intensity is at the same time a potential source of conflict. If in earlier times the extended family was responsible for raising the children, this function seems to fall to the neighbors today. The mother of a nine-year-old complains, *I'm having problems with my neighbors because of my son. They think I should watch him more and be more of a disciplinarian. It really bothers me that they want to interfere. They nag at my boy and tell him he has no business being out on the street. But he knows I've given him permission to do that. Because he doesn't cozy up to people right away, they don't like him. If someone finds a scrap of paper on his lawn, of course it was my son who did it. These problems with the neighbors are driving me crazy. I cried all afternoon because they are treating my boy so unfairly.*

Differentiation

Scientific progress in connection with social and economic developments ushered in the process of differentiation. This concept coincides to some extent with the division of labor. In earlier times one person functioned as leader, priest, judge, and doctor. Today we find that the various functions are largely separated from each other and are highly specialized. Many occupational groups today are defined by a limited number of hand operations. This is certainly the case with the worker on the assembly line.

As differentiation increased there developed distinctions between types of work, careers, social tasks, sciences, and administrative institutions.

We find a similar differentiation within the family. In predominantly traditional societies the extended family was the main form. Here several generations were represented. Today the nuclear family is dominant. Generally only the parents and children live together. Grandparents no longer have the role they once did; in many cases they have only a partial function, for instance as babysitters. By dividing up the role of the family members, a number of institutions now play a greater role in raising the children. This already starts when the baby is born at the hospital and is taken care of by nurses. Then the child is raised in part by the father, mother, grandparents, babysitter, kindergarten teacher, school, college, women's support group, etc. This differentiation in the parenting process is not necessarily bad, but it does create its own problems that must be addressed. Given the changes that have taken place in society, parenting can no longer be carried out the way it once was. If a person thinks it can still be done as in earlier times, he is simply deluding himself. Modern times, after all, have created new conditions that affect human development, even if we choose to close our eyes to this fact.

Disorders and Conflicts
Fear of change; tendency to maintain a familiar condition; inflexibility; imitative tendencies; generation conflicts; dependency on the opinions of others; denial and suppression of individual and collective past; escape into the world of fantasy; fear of the future

Comment
To a great extent a person's social group and the larger society are subject to the dimension of time. This means that society's demands and expectations change in the manner described above (population increase, urbanization, differentiation). The environment is thus itself dependent on time. The changes in the environment do not leave society and its people untouched. Role expectations, both those imposed by others and those imposed by the individual himself, change with the changing needs of the environment. If a person today were to act like the hunters and food gatherers of mankind's earliest times, he would be faced with conflicts that stem from a shift in the dimension of time.

Antidote
Learn to unite the past, present, and future.

THE MILK MUST BE GIVEN IN THE RIGHT AMOUNT. IT IS THE MILK WHICH STRENGTHENS THE INFANT SO THAT LATER ON HE CAN DIGEST SOLID FOODS. (Baha'u'llah)

DEVELOPMENT

Misunderstanding: *My son keeps reminding me that he's not a baby any more.*

NOT EVERYTHING AT ONCE
The mullah, a preacher, entered a hall where he wanted to give a sermon. The hall was empty except for a young groom seated in the front row. The mullah, pondering whether to speak or not, finally said to the groom, «You are the only one here. Do you think I should speak or not?» The groom said to him: «Master, I am but a simple man and do not understand these things. But, if I came into the stables and saw that all the horses had run off and only one remained, then I would feed it nevertheless.»

The mullah took this to heart and began to preach. He spoke for over two hours. After that, he felt elated and wanted his audience to confirm how great his sermon had been. He asked, «How did you like my sermon?» The groom answered, «I told you already that I am a simple man and do not understand these things very well. However, if I came into the stables and found all the horses gone except one I would feed it, but I would not give it all the whole fodder I had.» (Persian Story)

The story of the Mullah and the groom illustrates the problem in raising children. You either give too little or too much at one time. You let the child stay as he is, or you smother him with attention. In both cases the child's development is misconstrued.

MY SON ACTS LIKE A BABY
I pick up my son, hug him, and talk to him as if he were only three, even though he's seven already. There he reminds me that he's not a baby any more, but a big boy. When I'm in a bad mood or when he makes me mad I scold him and say he's acting like a baby. (34-year-old mother)

Nothing can change the fact that a person remains his parents' child all his life. This is a natural and unavoidable circumstance. But quite often there is something else behind it: Even long after the child has grown up, his parents may still treat him as a child. Parents like to ignore the increasing independence that their children show as they develop. Every person needs time for his development. He needs it for his physical maturation, for his psychological differentiation, and for his development as a social being. In turn, it is expected that he also grants other people the time they need. All disorders in parenting can be traced back to the adoption of roles or to role expectations that did not correspond to the particular time. Too many demands, too few demands, and inconsistency are the central causes. They tend to show up when the development of the child, the educator, and society intermingle. Now the effects multiply; and causes that seem secondary suddenly escalate into drastic potentials for conflict.

TOO FEW DEMANDS

My mother gives me advice on everything from kitchen equipment to doctors, and gets very upset if I don't follow her suggestions. She tries to treat me the same way she did twenty-five years ago. (32-year-old mother of two children)

Here we find some connections that are typical for the case of too few demands placed on an individual; the mother does not hold expectations that correspond to the capabilities of the daughter. The following case can serve as another example: A 35-year-old divorcee lives with her mother. Although the daughter is quite intelligent, the mother acts as if she were dealing with a seven-year-old. The mother bombards her daughter with all sorts of regulations: *Have you gone to the bathroom? Here's a Kleenex. Blow your nose. Wear the flowered dress. Be home by seven o'clock. Why do you feel you have to work? We've got enough money. You've got it good living here with me. Why should we need other people around?*

If the daughter tries to break out of this situation from time to time, for instance by getting a job or trying to make friends, her mother stops it by accusing her «child» of being aggressive and discourteous. The mother also reacts by developing heart trouble *(I'll have a heart attack because of you).*

This forces the daughter to turn to her mother again and to drop her attempt at liberating herself. It should be noted that the daughter's divorce had come about at the mother's urgings.

TOO MANY DEMANDS

A six-year-old child who had been enrolled in school one and a half years too early by mistake, proved to be doing poorly. A licensed teacher then documented that the child was *underdeveloped for his age due to low intelligence.* But an examination of this finding showed that the child was actually well developed for his age, and that the teacher had judged him not according to his real age, but according to the average age of his classmates. Making great demands does not necessarily mean a child will fare badly. Placing high expectations on him will just as likely cause him to live up to those expectations and to develop precocious behavior:

My son is a genius: The five-year-old son of a couple, where the mother was working and the father doing graduate work in political science, was supposed to be taken by his father to kindergarten every morning. But quite often the father studied till all hours of the night and wanted to sleep the next morning. So, without his wife knowing about it, the man would give the boy medication so he would sleep till eleven. Then both would get up, and as a substitute for kindergarten, the father would play with the boy. He tried to teach him all about technical, political, and philosophical things. To win even more of his father's love and attention, the boy began to learn this material rapidly and to behave in a way that his father expected him to. The boy acted «reasonable», was reserved when in the company of others, had little contact with children of his own age, and developed strong inhibitions that eventually led to behavioral disorders.

Inconsistency

A child's capabilities are challenged unequally. The child might be expected to do things, which at his age are impossible for him. If the teacher notices this, he might feel sorry for the child and give him an easier assignment. The next time the child is faced with a tough problem he faces a conflict of self-esteem. The teacher, by continually giving him an easier task, actually teaches the child an inappropriate solution. The child comes to expect that others will solve hard problems for him. As a result, the child does not develop a consistent strategy for dealing with things; he doesn't learn to grapple with a problem for a long period of time. *If I wasn't getting anywhere with a particular game, my mother would say, «Well, just do something else.»*

Disorders and Conflicts
Too many demands; too few demands; impatience; alternating between desire and anxiety; too high expectations; disappointments; resignation; emotional dependence; striving for self-reliance; the problems of breaking away.

Comment
Raising a child in accordance with his age means that one satisfies his needs according to the stage of his own development.

Antidote
Learn to give the child what he needs at his particular stage of development.

YOUNG PEOPLE BUFFER LESS FROM THEIR OWN FOLLY THAN FROM THE WISDOM OF THEIR ELDERS. (Vauvenargues)

IDENTITY CRISIS

Misunderstanding: *I don't know who I am!*
The personality and self-concept of an individual develop step by step over time, in accordance with his capabilities and possibilities. These capabilities are differentiated further through their confrontation with the environment. A person thus does not remain the same. Even if certain traits are hardly subject to change, one repeatedly makes new discoveries regarding oneself. A person can discover capabilities and limitations that he didn't know existed or didn't want to know about. Capabilities and attitudes change. The child learns to develop his senses, even though they are already there in their entirety. He learns the behavioral norms; his fantasy unfolds; his understanding becomes differentiated; his original relationship with his mother extends to others in his family and his social group. Each stage in his development has its own problems and conflicts. We call these *developmental crises*. If these developmental crises are dealt with, if they are worked through as *stages of identity*, the personality can unfold in harmony with its development.

At various times in a person's life, he will be faced with a number of problems at once. As he experiences this situation he may come to say, *I don't know who I am.* Puberty is a time when this is likely to happen. The adolescent is no longer a child, but not yet an adult. He is faced with experiences that shake his very core. These are the problems of sexuality, problems that now emerge for the first time. But other questions also become critical: what he will become later on, what profession he will take up, how he should deal with his environment. A number of roles, sometimes contradictory ones, are expected of the adolescent, and he is faced with the task of integrating them into his personality. In his transition to adulthood certain expectations are placed on him that he adopts as his own. These are three main things that we expect in an adult: equality, freedom, and responsibility.

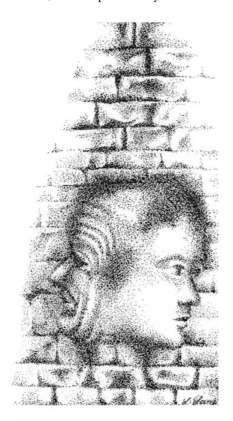

Equality

The adolescent, having been treated as a child previously, is now, at least to some extent, treated by adults as an equal. He himself demands this equality. Conflicting attitudes to the adolescent's rights leads to tension in his upbringing. Equality ultimately means: One is prepared to give and to take, to speak and to listen, to criticize and to be criticized. Equality is thus understood as a kind of balance, which is not automatically achieved. It can be acquired only through confronting the environment.

Freedom

External freedom covers all personal, economic, and technical possibilities that the adolescent had no access to until now. Now he can stay up as long as he wants. He can spend his time with people he finds interesting. He can buy things without first asking for permission. The following example illustrates the opposite of this kind of external freedom: A mother relates: *Recently, when my in-laws visited us for the first time since we got married five years ago, I dared to use a very pretty pink table cloth instead of a white one. It was a catastrophe.*

A 17-year-old girl tells about how her father acts. *I couldn't even dare buy the littlest thing for my room unless he first approved it. Except for last semester, I've been taking painting classes for several years, and am pretty good at it. I even had one of my paintings exhibited once. I'm mentioning this because I think it shows that I don't have bad taste. Anyway, one time I put a picture by Picasso over my bed. I meant it only to be temporary. But my father was so insulted by it that I took it down after a few days.*

Inner freedom has to do with planning how the individual areas of external freedom are valued and assessed. On the basis of his previous experience, a person will thus decide what his goals are, what area he will operate in, and what he will turn his energies to. An adolescent who has just been given this kind of freedom is much like a person who has suddenly come into a lot of money. If he hasn't learned how to handle money, the money won't do him any good. In fact, it can do a lot of harm. Inner freedom is thus the freedom to make choices.

Responsibility

This is the opposite of passive tolerance. A person can regard another person as an equal and grant him his freedom, thus demonstrating tolerance toward that person. But this tolerance is frequently a sign of indifference. Active tolerance can only develop when a person feels a sense of responsibility, when he accepts the obligatory nature of freedom and equality. Active tolerance involves the ability to identify with the other person and to recognize his capabilities, and through them, the uniqueness of his personality. It means accepting him as he is.

Equality, freedom, and responsibility are tasks that the adolescent cannot fulfill from one day to the next.

In three months I turn eighteen. Then I can do what I want.

Legal freedom exists for every adolescent, whether the parents desire it or not. But how this freedom is used will depend on how the parents and the parenting situation have functioned since the child was very young. If the adolescent hasn't been given opportunities to handle adult responsibilities, he will be much like the person who has known water only through washing his hands and is suddenly tossed into the ocean. Whether he can swim is a matter of luck more than anything else. For the person entrusted with raising a child, the task is to further the child's development by giving him the opportunity to deal with problems and tasks.

The three adult characteristics mentioned above take on concrete shape in a person's relationship to himself, to his partner, to his fellow men, to social groups, and ultimately to things that he does not know and can never know. Since a person can develop in all areas, not just in a particular one, imbalances in his development could become the source of developmental disorders.

I DON'T HAVE ANY ENERGY LEFT

A 17-year-old boy buffers from apathy, disinterest in work, inhibitions, and sleep disorders. He complains that he can't concentrate any more, and that school is an unbearable torture for him. He has absolutely no energy for the demands that school places on him. An analysis of how he spends his day reveals that most of this energy is focused on his relationship with his 16- year-old girlfriend. He spends three or four hours a day with her, thinks about her all night long, and can't get her out of his mind during the day. As a result, he has no energy for himself, his parents, for other people, or for school.

Here is a diagram that shows how energy can be divided over several areas:

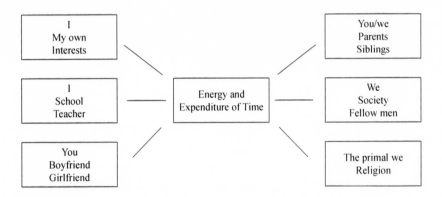

In the case described above, the adolescent estimated that he expended his energies in these areas as follows:

Own interests	5%
School	5%
Girlfriend	85%
Parents	1%
Fellow men	3%
Religion	1%

The boy did not have a lack of energy; he was not lazy or weak. Rather, he showed an imbalance in how he divided his energies among the various areas of his life.

It is very important how energies are channeled and directed in the various developmental stages of the individual. Heavy emphasis on certain areas and neglect of others can produce potential conflicts in how the person deals with his world. The people close to the person will be confronted with the results of this development, but they will, as a rule, not have insight into the conditions that led to it. Identity is not found in withdrawing from the outside world. It comes through openness to and expansion into all realms of social experience.

Disorders and Conflicts

Identity crisis; insecurity; inability to make decisions; lack of personal guidelines; lack of an inner compass; anxiety; escape into sexuality, into social interaction, or into clubs and parties; disappointments; lack of energy; self-criticism; depression; too many demands; too few demands.

Comment
Parents, educators, and others close to the child are faced with the important task of making it easier for the child, the adolescent, or the partner to deal with his identity crises at the various stages of his development. The prerequisite for this is a sense of trust between the two «parties.» With this trust as a base, one can deepen one's understanding of the problems confronting the other person. Only then can one support that person in his development in the various areas.

Antidote
Learn to distinguish between lack of energy and the mischanneling of energy.

ON THIS DAY WE WILL GIVE YOUR EYES THE POWER TO MAKE DISTINCTIONS. (Moḥammed)

MAN - ANIMAL

Misunderstanding: *The previous development of man seems to me to need no other explanation than that of animals.* (S. Freud)

Freud's assertion that despite all his efforts he could find nothing in man that was not also in animals, is more than the idle opinion of a scientist. It is not based on facts. Rather it sets forth a view of man that defies and despises man: It defies religion's assertions that man is the crowning glory of creation. It despises man in the light of his individual and collective difficulties. The question of whether the same rules apply to man as to animals is of important practical rather than theoretical significance.

The question revolves around how man is to be regarded, how he can and must be treated, which developmental possibilities can be expected, and which ones must be written off. The question of man vs. animal thus abounds with consequences for parenting, for the relationship to man in general, and for psychotherapy.

To characterize the relationship between man and animal, it is more worthwhile to compare the three functional areas of body, environment, and time, than it is to make global comparisons.

Body

The body is the principal element that man and animal have in common. Indeed, human anatomy and the anatomy of an animal, as well as the way their organs function, show a striking similarity. This similarity can lead a person into making the mistake of thinking that the two are equal. This is an oversimplification; it neglects peculiarities and typical differences.

In comparison with animals, man has a much more sophisticated brain organization, as is evident from the greater size and finer structure of the cerebrum. In addition to this, man has a capability that can be interpreted as the spiritual counterpart of the brain's differentiation: An animal lives through his body; man does this, too, but he is also able to experience his body. He can distance himself from his body and make it the object of his thought. He is not simply influenced by his body; he can also affect it in turn. When an animal is sick it must rely mostly on the functions and self-healing properties of the organism. This is the case with man as well. But he can also actively and consciously take control of his body. Through the power of his thoughts, expectations, wishes, and conflicts he exerts an influence on his bodily functions and on how these are experienced. We find examples of this in the psychosomatic and somatopsychic realm: Hunger makes a person restless. Heart trouble gives him anxiety. But on the reverse side: Excitement increases his pulse rate and blood pressure. Depression is associated with a lowering of the blood pressure. As these examples show, thoughts are at the center of these processes: *I will experience what I expect. My thoughts affect my body.*

Environment

The environmental dimension concerns man's relationship to his total surroundings. This includes his relationship to a partner or to a social group, to animals and plants, and to all the things in the world.

While an animal, by birth, can only react by instinct, man acquires greater latitude through socialization, and through about social behavior. The environment can develop his capabilities. These capabilities include the traits and unique qualities of the individual. When looked at in terms of content, they are mainly the primary and secondary capabilities. An animal may very well display a certain behavior involving cleanliness, thrift, orderliness, and even industriousness. These capabilities are of an instinctive nature. As a social being, man has, in principle, access to individual actual capabilities. Only in the course of his socialization are they developed, expanded, unfolded, and refined through his learning experiences. The significance of primary and secondary capabilities in the social relationships point out a basic difference between man and animal. In animals instinct mechanism function as a basis for social life. The rules of social behavior are quasi inbred the animal. But in human beings, social rules must be learned and followed. The structure of the actual capabilities and their values is transmitted from one generation to the next as the content of that society's traditions. The primary and secondary capabilities are socialization patterns; as such they are also the content of interpersonal communication and individual experience.

Time
Unlike animals, man has conscious access to the categories «past», «present» and «future». Man's ability to meet the demands of life is linked to the sharpness with which he perceives these categories and is able to put them to use.

The cave dwellers of prehistoric times had to develop a sense of time in order to dominate the physically superior animal world around them. Indeed, man's success in his struggle for survival is largely due to his ability to keep future goals and needs in mind, and to use the experiences of the past to take actions in the present that will lead to the accomplishment of those goals for the future. Only with this ability was he assured of dominance over his rivals in the animal kingdom. This enabled him to master the entire world and to use its bounty to satisfy his needs.

Unlike an animal, man can consciously look back at his own experiences and at those of other people. By building on his collective past, he can advance beyond his historic level.

Disorders and Conflicts
Identity crisis; overestimation of one's self; fear of failure; inferiority complexes; loss of unity; egotism; dependency on friends and things; tendency to be crude, rough, and cruel to animals; excessive love for animals (as for instance, when one prefers to walk one's dog rather than go strolling with the wife); inability to accept or show love within the family; «strong» personalities who endure all sorts of things and show neither consideration nor sympathy as they go all out to achieve their goals; inability to withstand outside influences.

Comment
By equating man and animal, one bestows on man only the ability to act instinctively, as if he were motivated only by innate drives. In this view of man, social norms function only to suppress those drives that are destructive and threatening to society. But man shows significant differences compared with animals in the three areas, of body, environment, and time. Man does not need to be trained like an animal. His drives do not need to be suppressed. Instead, it is a question of differentiation.

Antidote
Learn to distinguish between experiences through the body and experiencing the body itself.

I WILL VISIT THE INIQUITIES OF THE FATHERS UPON THE CHILDREN TO THE THIRD AND THE FOURTH GENERATION. (Old Testament)

INBORN - ACQUIRED

Misunderstanding: I didn't have to teach my son to be neat. He had that quality right from the time he was born.

...As a child I was always told that I got my stubbornness from my Aunt Tilly. She never got married, and I would end up the same way. My good qualities, like my athletic and musical talents, I had gotten from Grandma and Grandpa. In attributing my qualities to various people, they always

looked at our close relatives, particularly the ones we had a good understanding with at that particular moment. Only if it were a negative quality, would they say it cam from outside the family; it came from the girlfriends I hung around with. If my parents couldn't find anyone to blame it on, they said I was just God's way of punishing my mother and Grandma...

MY DAUGHTER WAS BORN MESSY

My 12-year-old daughter was messy from the time she was born. I always had trouble with her. Now she's even doing badly in school. No one can put up with her messiness. She's just the opposite of her 9-year-old brother. He was a tidy child right from birth. Is it possible to make something out of a child who has always been messy? When asked how she had dealt with her daughter's messiness the mother replied: *I scolded her a lot, and once in a while I had to spank her. I didn't have to teach my son to be neat. He was that way right from the start...* (34-year-old mother having trouble raising her children)

What the mother regards as «inborn» is really the result of attitudes and different practices in raising children. It turned out that there was a simple explanation for the difference between the son's and daughter's neatness. The boy's positive sense of orderliness was due to learned behavior. He had been able to witness, almost on a regular basis, how his older sister was punished for not living up to her mother's sense of orderliness. To avoid this punishment, and to spare himself the loss of his mother's love, he learned from his sister's example. By watching her, he came to understand the causes of her trouble with her mother, namely her messiness, and he resolved to be as neat as his mother wanted. Examples like this show that apparently «inborn» behavior actually comes about as the result of definite influences in the child's educational environment.

In a different report a 34-year-old mother of two whose former husband suffered from depression writes: *I suffered from the terrible fear that my children would inherit their father's illness. I was especially concerned about my oldest son. I attributed his unpredictable behavior and his temper tantrums to my husband.*

The question of whether something is inborn or acquired strikes home for a lot of parents, educators, and spouses. The word «inborn» is automatically associated with a compelling, hopeless development that cannot be changed. The word «acquired» on the other hand, evokes the feeling that one can change what has been acquired, that environmental factors are important, and that ultimately there is hope for improvement.

The idea that behavior is acquired repeatedly poses new problems for parents, educators, and others close to the child. The idea of inborn behavior, however, seems to draw the curtain on any hope of change.

YOU CAN'T DO ANYTHING ABOUT IT ANYWAY

Among my relatives I always found somebody with a trait that my children had inherited. I consoled myself with the idea that everything is inborn or inherited... (43-year-old housewife)

The ideology of inheritance in the above case becomes a rationalization and an excuse. But the woman's assertion by no means diminishes the importance of scientific research in genetics.

In argumentation like that of the woman in the above example, there is a tendency to overlook the importance of the environment in general and the child-rearing process in particular. The Grand Mogul Akbar, who lived about 700 years ago, wanted to know that man's innate language was. To find an answer to this question he had a number of infants separated from their parents and raised in such a way that their caretakers provided them with the necessary food and care, but did not speak with them or show them any personal attention. The results were shocking. When the children were released they did not speak a language and were unable to learn one. They were no longer educable; even the attempt to train them for military service proved unsuccessful (Stokvis, 1965)

Friedrich von Hohenstaufen conducted a similar experiment. A group of children, raised without language or sign of personal attention, proved to be susceptible to disease and died after a relatively short time (Mitscherlich, 1967).

These results occurred again, recently in a similar form. Three groups of children from approximately the same social class were compared with each other. The first group comprised children from normal family situations. The second group was made up of the children of female prison inmates. These children had been able to visit their mothers for about two hours each day. In the third group were children from orphanages.

In this group only the most basic needs had been met. The children in this third group showed the highest death rate, subsequently displayed the most conspicuous social behavior, and had the lowest intelligence scores of all three groups. The children from normal families had the highest intelligence, scored best in tests of physical well-being, and proved to be the least susceptible to emotional disorders (cf. Spitz, 1960, 1967; Bowlby, 1952). From these experiments one can draw an obvious conclusion: Upbringing determines the development of a human being.

Harlow and Clark conducted experiments with rhesus monkeys. These animals have a common evolutionary background with man. In many respects their development is much like that of a human being in his first year of life (Schmidbauer, 1972): «Aggressiveness in the rhesus monkey is, in the case of a normal animal, curtailed by emotional ties as well as by fear. If these animals are isolated in their early development, only their fear will keep them from being aggressive. The result of this is a so-called ambivalent behavior: Anxiety is coupled with a ferocity that has no regard for anything. While the normal rhesus monkey will take sides with a weaker one and will lavish a lot of attention on his offspring, the «damaged» monkey will act like a bike rider who mows down anything and everyone in his path».

Margaret Mead (1970) and Erikson (1971) showed that transmitted norms are not immutable and generally valid standards, but that they depend on the prevailing social and cultural conditions. Mead poses the question, «Which factors in the child's upbringing are responsible for the fact that the child is gentle, content, warm-hearted, trusting, and not aggressive, ambitious or reckless?» She then gives this answer: «There is a very fine and clear connection between the way a child is fed, put to sleep, disciplined, taught to discipline himself, cuddled, punished and encouraged, and how he eventually turns out to be as an adult.»

Erikson confirms the basic findings of these studies with the results of investigations he carried out among the Sioux and Yurok Indians. In particular he looked at toilet training and feeding rituals in connection with the rather aggressive-resigned character of the Sioux and the compulsive orderly and clean behavior of the more peace-loving Yuroks. Erikson carried this comparison over to Western societies: «As we will see, there are cultures where the parents ignore anal behavior and leave it to the older children to take the toddlers behind a bush, so that the children's desire to take care of the matter eventually coincides with their desire to imitate the parents. Our Western civilization, however, has decided to take the matter more seriously. This depends, though, on the spread of middle class morals and of the ego ideal of a mechanized body. It is simply assumed that early and rigorous toilet training not only makes the atmosphere in the home more decent; it is also considered absolutely necessary for instilling a sense of orderliness and punctuality. Later on we will discuss whether this is true or not. Without a doubt, there is among our neurotic people today a type of compulsive person who has more mechanical punctuality and frugality in matters of both affection and his feces than is either good for him or is in the long-term interests of society. In many segments of our society, toilet training has become one of the most difficult aspects of parenting» (1971).

Studies with twins most clearly show the relationship between heredity and environment. Whenever twins were raised in different families or under different socio-economic conditions, there were, as a rule, significant differences in behavior despite some noticeable features that the two had in common. This is best illustrated in the anecdote about the identical twins who grew up in separate environments and took on completely different behaviors. The one became a criminologist, the other a criminal.

Many behavioral norms that are assumed to be innate are actually the result of influences in early childhood. We see this illustrated in an example from the animal world. The tiger hunts and kills his prey. Behavioral research has proven that hunting is inborn in the tiger, but killing the victim, is first taught by the mother tiger. From this we can draw a further conclusion: A behavior that one sees as a unified process is really made up of various partial behaviors that can each have a different origin. In man, who has only a limited instinctual nature, the relationship between «inborn» and «acquired,» as it involves individual behaviors, must be even more complex.

Disorders and Conflicts
Self-alienation; too many demands; too few demands; the feeling of having missed out on things; jealousy; hatred; envy; denial; gigantic

expectations; disappointments; pessimistic outlook; sceptical, mistrustful, and negative personalities.

Comment
Every person is born with a multitude of capabilities. Which ones develop and which remain undeveloped, ultimately depend on either the constructive or a repressing influence from environment in which one is brought up.

Antidote
Learn to distinguish between inborn and acquired.

AN EDUCATOR'S WORK IS LIKE THAT OF A GARDENER WHO TAKES CARE OF DIFFERENT KINDS OF PLANTS. (Abdu'l-Baha)

UNIQUENESS

Misunderstanding: *I expect my husband to have those qualities I like in other men.*

An educator's work is like that of a gardener who takes care of different plants. One plant likes a lot of sunshine, while the other likes cool shade. The one likes the riverbank and the other likes the barren mountaintop. While the one grows best in sandy soil, the other in rich loam. Each must have the care that is best suited for it. Otherwise it will not reach its complete perfection. (Abdu'l-Baha)

I HOLD UP TO MY CHILDREN WHAT OTHER CHILDREN DO BETTER

If I'm mad about something I'll say to my daughter for example, «Look at your brother, how nice and quiet he plays with his blocks. You fumble around like a five-year-old.» To my son I'll say, «Your sister is only six, but already she has stayed by herself and also gone to the store for me. You're still a baby, hanging on to my coattails.» At every opportunity I held up to my children what other children do better. I did that so long, that eventually they started to hate the kids I used as an example. (32-year-old mother)

A man complains, *«Why can't my current wife be like my departed wife?»* Typical for these examples is that the person is not recognized in his uniqueness. The attempt is made to compare him or her to other people. This attempt, for the most part, seems legitimate when it involves individual capabilities. Our civilization's achievement system, which operates from first grade up through a person's career, tests on this comparability. This alone should give us cause to consider its implications. Daily experience shows that people, despite their many similarities, differ from each other in countless details. These differences occur in the areas of the body, the environment, and time.

Uniqueness and Body

Despite all the regularities that the sciences of anatomy, physiology, pharmacology, and biochemistry have discovered in the structure arid function of the human body, these sciences are confronted again and again by the significance of the individual's uniqueness. This uniqueness is shown most of all in variations from the norm - variations that, however, do not fall into the category of illness.

The individual's physical uniqueness is particularly noticeable in the doctor's office, when it is a matter of prescribing the proper medication for the patient. It has been shown repeatedly that people react to medicine in different ways. A particular branch of medicine, «pharma-psychology» deals with individual reactions to medication. This field of study has proven that individuals react to medication in paradoxical ways (Eysenck). It can be drawn from this the conclusion that the type and amount of medication must be determined on an individual basis. Individual differences are also found in metabolism and nourishment. While some people are strongly affected by coffee and can't sleep if they have a cup in the evening, other people can enjoy coffee without having it disturb their sleep. The human nervous system also shows the uniqueness of the individual. The human brain differs so widely in its structure, mass, and weight that it can be said that no two people have brains that are alike. This anatomical fact is reflected in the differences in how people experience the world. Studies on the sense of feel, on sensitivity to warm and cold, and on sensitivity to pain all demonstrate that each individual has his own reaction to various stimuli.

In other words, everybody experiences the world in his own way. If a person is different from others, if a child walks at an earlier age, eats less, needs more sleep, this is not necessarily a sign of abnormality or illness. More likely it is a sign of his individuality. It is then up to the environment to shape, encourage, and support that individuality.

Uniqueness and Environment

The variational possibilities of the individual body and senses are vastly increased when one also takes into consideration the influence of the environment. The environment works on a person every day and every night. The way the parents treat their child, how much patience they have with him, the child's position in the family - firstborn, middle child, or baby - all affect the child's development. Kindergarten, school, and playmates also play a role. Later on he is influenced by job opportunities, his choice of a career, his experience with partners, the forms of his interpersonal relationships, his religion, and his convictions.

The different development of a person is based on the one hand on the uniqueness of his capabilities, and on the other hand on the influence of his environment:

Some children start asking questions earlier than others do. Some develop a greater perseverance and intensity in asking questions; others ask fewer questions.

Some children are more interested in fairy tales and are ready at an earlier age to listen to them.

Some children develop a vivid imagination; others stay more on a realistic level.

There are some children who develop stronger ties to one of their parents at a particular phase of their development.

One child likes to play with his siblings; another prefers to play alone; the third enjoys being with playmates.

Uniqueness and Time

Body and environment, in turn, are dependent on another factor, namely time. Body and environment are not static areas. They are undergoing constant change. The uniqueness of the body must therefore always be seen in connection with time. As our examples of uniqueness show, it always depends on the person's stage of development. But the concept of uniqueness should not serve to disregard or conceal all the developments that could possibly occur. This is why human development can only be understood when one compares its uniqueness with the expected course of development as described by developmental psychology and physiology.

Uniqueness means happening only once, dependent on time. If a child tells a lie, his parents' reaction to it will determine how it affects the child's development. If the child's behavior is viewed in terms of the time dimension, one will recognize his uniqueness: Tomorrow, the day after, or the next year the child may show completely different behavior in a different environmental situation. If the child's uniqueness is not correctly interpreted, if the situation is given tremendous weight, one ends up confusing the concrete, situational behavior of the child with the essence of the child. So we see that a person can view another's conspicuous behavior in different ways. A disappointment, for example, doesn't necessarily have to be experienced as such. It can just as easily lead to an expansion of one's perceptions. The ability to go beyond the present moment also means that a person can accept someone who he dislikes or even hates. Man has the flexibility to react to a situation in a way that puts the old situation in a new light.

Even if many events and experiences persist, man has only a limited time in which the capabilities can be developed. For the development of his body as well as of the actual and basic capabilities there is only a certain amount of time available (finiteness). If the time is up, a person has a lot of trouble making up for the lost time; in some instances it is impossible for him to make it up on his own. To take an example from the realm of the body: Only up to a certain age can the coordination of the eye movements be developed automatically. After that the disorder can be taken care of only through surgery. And here is an example from the environment: If a child is not given the opportunity to play he can become a troublemaker or a recluse. Here again, the child can generally only be helped by another person, for instance through play therapy administered by a therapist.

The possibilities for change in human behavior are relatively great compared with what used to be considered unchangeable. A child is not doomed to be what he is at this moment. The same holds true for physical sufferings as well as for mental disorders. But the opportunities for change are limited by time.

Since every person is unique in terms of his body and his experience of his surroundings, it is problematic, to say the least, to take a conclusion about oneself and apply it to another person. This is true for statements like, *Getting whipped didn't hurt me one bit, so why should it hurt my child?* (42-year-old attorney)

My parents didn't have any time for me. But I made something of myself anyway. I just don't understand why it should be that because I didn't have time for my son; I am blamed for his problems. (45-year-old contractor)
I took the medicine that worked so well for me, and gave it to my girlfriend. (32-year-old housewife)

All the men in our family became engineers. I don't understand why our youngest boy wants to study art. (44-year-old engineer)

It is important that we recognize the special and individual strengths and capabilities of our partner. Here it is not a question of his being able to compete with others in his age group, or even to be the best when it comes to a particular capability. Rather, it is important that we recognize and support his capabilities independent of any such comparisons. Some people are more talented in practical things, while others have more abstract talents. Some have great organizational skills; others are more artistic. There are plenty of opportunities for everyone to develop their own special skills.

Beyond all this, we can't close our eyes to our own weaknesses or to the weaknesses of others. Only through the awareness of weaknesses is it possible to change them. If a child has no interest in school, or if his performance in maths drops off, the main cause does not necessarily have to be lack of attention and concentration. The child could have an eye problem. Perhaps he can't clearly see what's written on the board. Criticizing him will only make matters worse. If the problem were diagnosed correctly, as in the above example, getting glasses for the child would solve the problem. If the problem is not recognized, the situation can lead to a desperate competitive struggle, not just to resignation: One wants to accomplish as much as the others, but doesn't have the prerequisites for it. The result can be a flurry of activity to equalize the performance. Other results can be aggressiveness toward the fellow classmates, envy, grudges, jealousy, and eventually permanent disappointment.

Similar results occur when there is hearing trouble, metabolic disorders, or organic disturbances of the brain. In school, the possibility of congenital alexia, which can be corrected through appropriate training, should be considered.

Personal activity and one's individual effort are important for the uniqueness of the individual. He is not just the product of his body and his environment. He creates himself at every moment.

Disorders and Conflicts
Inability to make decisions; identity crisis; loss of self-esteem; self-hatred; jealousy; rivalry; contact disorders, mistrust; identification; projection; feelings of inferiority; disappointments; aggression; resignation.

Comment
If a person compares his partner with other people, it isn't enough to look at only one capability. It is important to include the uniqueness of the person and the conditions under which that uniqueness is seen in various areas: If you treat everybody the same, you are really treating them unequally.

Antidote
Learn to distinguish between uniqueness and uniformity.

IN THE MORNING I LAUGHED WITH JOY; BUT WHY I NOW WEEP IN THE GLOW OF THE EVENING, I DO NOT KNOW MYSELF. (Hafis)

THE UNCONSCIOUS

Misunderstanding: *I don't know everything about myself.*
Mr. and Mrs. B. came for psychotherapy because they were having marital problems. Mr. B. was 42, Mrs. B. 34. Both had professional backgrounds. They complained of family tensions in the past few years, even though they had a good marriage otherwise. In their report they spoke again and again of problems with their children, and in these discussions their 9-year-old son played a central role. As the youngest

of three children, and really the «baby of the family» he had developed a very intense relationship with the mother. Because of his scientific work the father had had little time for the boy in the last few years. When the father and the son were together, the boy bombarded him with a lot of wishes that the father could not fulfill and did not want to. But if the boy didn't get his way he'd go running to his mother to complain to her, *Daddy makes me mad...* The mother defended the child and tried to make up for the father's rejection by paying special attention to the child. Her behavior became a kind of reward. After a while the mother became the boy's advocate, and had a number of open disagreements with the father. This produced the following mechanism: I provoke my father until he says no. Then I turn to my mother. She takes my side and spends a lot of time with me. This gives me an advantage over the other kids in our family.

Neither the child nor the parents were consciously aware of what was going on here. The process was driving a wedge between the parents and the child. Only when they discovered what was happening were they able to draw some conclusions and institute changes that relieved the tension within the family.

A large part of our mental functioning and interpersonal relationships is dictated by attitudes and behaviors whose origins and motives are unknown to us. From them develop unintentional reactions and processes whose results had not been anticipated nor desired by the parties involved.

The function of the *unconscious* can be illustrated with this example: When we have eaten, a number of bodily processes and metabolic events start to take place. Although they occur, we are not conscious of them unless a disorder develops, signaled to us by pain or discomfort. The same holds true for interpersonal relationships. How often do we catch ourselves doing something we hadn't meant to do? Even though, for instance, we know that spanking is not the best way to raise children, and that impatience will make us only more upset, we often lose control of ourselves at the slightest cause, and discard the principles that we know are right. Later on we are angry with ourselves: *Sometimes I do something that is contrary to my principles and that I regret afterwards. Even though I vow every day that I'm going to be nice to my daughter, I find that I get angry with her, scream at her, and say bad things...*

The actual capabilities play an important role as the content of the unconscious. Imbalances in the pattern of the actual capabilities are usually looked upon as being very obvious, and this is why we are often not conscious of them. But they have a strong emotional component and to some extent live lives of their own, eventually affecting our relationships with other people. Experiences that would lead to a confrontation between our own affective actual capabilities and our environment can be suppressed. They simply disappear from our consciousness. We don't remember them even though they are still stored in some area of our memory. We call this process *repression*. Experiences that we have not processed develop their own dynamics and reappear from time to time in a more or less open form in our dreams, thoughts, or speech and actions.

The Annoying Mother

A 17-year-old girl suffers from inhibitions and lack of human contact. The family situation is marked by the fact that everyone tries to avoid open tension. There are never loud arguments, although there are certainly a good number of problems between the family members. The father pays more attention to his mother, who lives with them, than he does to his own wife. The wife uses this as a reason to complain to her daughter every evening when her husband goes upstairs to be with his mother. The daughter listens to these complaints at the supper table and during the evening. The wife talks about nothing, but her husband and mother-in-law. This has become a ritual that is carried out every evening. The daughter would like to take up some other activity and go out for a change. She wants to do this even more, now that she has a boyfriend. Only the idea of her mother sitting alone in the kitchen all evening makes it impossible for her to do what she really wants. The girl suppressed her honesty, which was undoubtedly very aggressive, because she was afraid of feeling guilty, of having a lot of blame placed on her. Even her open desire to go away was enough to cause her to feel guilty. In accordance, the girl acted obediently and politely toward her mother, suppressing her own wishes, and, hence, the areas of openness and honesty.

What we have here is a conflict between politeness (submitting to something as a kind of defense) and honesty (self-assertion as a threat to one's self-esteem because it would lead to guilt feelings). This conflict is for the most part unconscious. And just as in this conflict between politeness and honesty, there can be complications between other actual capabilities because they have such a strong unconscious affective force.

MY LITTLE WORLD

A father complains about his 18-year-old daughter, who has become aggressive and defiant. The father was a rather reserved man who devoted his interests and energies only to his family. When the girl began to emancipate herself, the family's closed circle was broken. The father saw this as a threat to his world, because he was suspicious of other people. While his relationship with his family («thou») had been well developed, it turned out that his relationship to the rest of the world («we») was incomplete and unstable.

A protective function that generally works unconsciously plays itself out in such a way that man takes problems that he can't solve in one area, and transfers them to other areas:

MY POOR KIDS

My husband is sometimes very rude to me. But I don't dare say anything to him about it because he might throw a fit. So I take my anger out on my kids. Afterwards I feel bad and apologize to them. (43-year-old working mother)

I ALWAYS SAW MY DIVORCED HUSBAND IN OLIVER

I used to holler at my son Oliver and punish him for the littlest things, and couldn't understand why I was doing that. Today I know why. Oliver looks very much like my former husband. I thought my son's father was very ugly, and I transferred this feeling of ugliness to my son and renounced him.

I COULD NEVER DEAL WITH THIS KIND OF WOMAN

My mother could never assert herself with her mother–in–law, and we kids were the same way till we grew up. It has occurred to me that I've never been able to deal with women like her. I've never been able to assert myself with them.

Disorders and conflicts

Repressions; rationalization; deceptive maneuvers; failures; symbolic dreams; inner resistance; over-compensation; misunderstandings, and social conflicts.

Comment
The potential conflict in the unconscious is of a paradoxical nature in that a certain screen is set up, but behind this screen conflicts can fester until they eventually break out. This happens because the screen actually keeps the person from processing the conflict. Besides the protective function that is in operation in the repression mechanism, there are other functions that can lead to further misunderstandings.

Antidote
Learn to distinguish between the conscious and the unconscious.

IF EVERYONE KNEW EVERYTHING ABOUT OTHER PEOPLE, HE WOULD READILY AND EASILY FORGIVE THEM. *(Hafis)*

IDENTIFICATION - PROJECTION

Misunderstanding: *There's nothing else I can do but secretly go in front of the mirror and dance Swan Lake.*

An Eastern merchant owned a parrot. One day the bird knocked over an oil flask. The merchant became very angry and hit the parrot on the back of the head. From that time on, the parrot, who had previously appeared to be very intelligent, could not talk anymore. He lost the feathers on his head and soon became bald. One day, as he was sitting on the bookshelf in his master's place of business, a bald headed customer entered the shop. The sight of the man made the parrot very excited. Flapping his wings, he jumped around, squawked, and, to everyone's surprise, finally regained his speech and said, «Did you, too, knock down an oil flask and get hit on the back of the head so that you don't have any hair anymore?» (After J. Rumi)

This story demonstrates how we consciously or unconsciously transfer earlier experiences, encouragements, and disappointments to other situations, and even to other people. The process of projection is psychologically represented this way:

We have a desire or need. To bring this wish into reality we act accordingly. We call the wish or need the motivation for our behavior. Out of this motivation, this driving force, the behavior develops:

Motivation → Behavior

Now when we observe other people and their behavior, we think that they are driven by the same motivations that would move us in a similar case. We thus assume a definite link between the behavior and the motivation, and conclude from the action a certain intention:

Motivation ← Behavior

Of course, this method can lead us to make conclusions that really do correspond to what is motivating the person. But there is also a danger of error: Every ball is round, but not everything that is round is a ball.

YOU LOOK LIKE A MONKEY

A nine-year-old boy called the five-year-old daughter of their guests a monkey. The girl's mother was immediately insulted, because she misunderstood the compliment that was at the heart of this assertion. The boy was very interested in a TV show where a monkey played the main role. He was very enthusiastic about this monkey, and the girl's lively behavior reminded him of it. When the boy said the girl looked like a monkey he really meant, «I like you.» If the girl's mother had ever uttered the word monkey, she no doubt meant it as a reprimand. She attributed the same meaning to the boy, although for him the word had taken on the character of a compliment.

In a similar way children might call their mother a cow, for instance, or their father a horse, without understanding that these expressions could be interpreted as insults. Then they would be punished and labeled as impolite children. The mother, who treats her children to hot chocolate, is equated with a cow that gives milk. The father, whose work hardly ever lets him spend time at home, is, in the child's fantasy, very much like a workhorse. Why shouldn't the child say what he really thinks? After all, that is what he's learned honesty to be.

Transferring a conclusion about yourself to another person might help you understand that person better, but it could just as easily lead to misunderstandings.

IF YOU GET PREGNANT, OUT YOU GO

The 17-year-old daughter had received permission to stay at a party till midnight. It got to 12:30, and the girl wasn't yet home. The father was already asleep, but the mother was pacing the floor. Eventually she woke up her husband. *Look, it's going on one, and Sandy isn't home yet.* Both parents became upset, and as a result the mother blamed the father, because he had given the girl permission to go to the party. The girl finally showed up around 1:30, and immediately her parents jumped on her: *We can't depend on you. You've taken advantage of our generosity. That's the last time something like this will happen. Lord knows who you've been messing around with. If you get pregnant, out you go...*

The parents transferred their worries, aggressive ideas, and wishes onto their daughter's behavior, without really questioning her motives. What was the real reason why she got home so late? The roads had been very icy that night, and the fellow who had hosted the party had decided to walk her home rather than risk driving on the ice. The weather had also knocked out the telephone service, so there was no way of contacting Sandy's parents. In parenting, the misunderstanding between identification and projection is expressed in two typical forms. *My child should achieve what I achieved; he should take me as a role model.* In terms of depth psychology this statement goes something like this:

Why should my child have it better than I did?
Recently I was witness to a dispute. Two adults were having a lively discussion about how to raise children. Off to the side stood a shy little boy biting his nails. The one man - apparently the boy's father - said

with great conviction, after the argument had gone on for some time, *«My great-grandfather was raised this way. It didn't do him any harm. My grandfather was raised this way, and so was I. This kind of upbringing didn't hurt us at all. We all turned out to be decent, industrious, and orderly men. And my grandfather even lived to be more than 80. I don't see why this kind of upbringing should hurt my boy. Later on he'll be grateful when he thinks about the spankings he gets now.»*

This view represents a type of upbringing where one person confuses his own capabilities and qualities with those of another person. From his own needs and wishes he creates expectations that the other person should live up to. If these expectations are not fulfilled, there is a sense of disappointment: *You do not deserve the trust that I put in you.*

ACTUALLY I ALWAYS WANTED TO BE A CHEMIST

For as long as I can remember, I wanted to be a chemist. I was very interested in the chemical elements and the processes that they can generate. Even when I was a child I played around with chemicals. I was especially fascinated with the structure of molecules. I still know the table of elements by heart. But my father wanted me to be a doctor. You see, he's a successful doctor with a lot of patients. But I have no desire to work with patients. There is often a lot of aggravation with them. Chemicals appeal to me more than people do. I don't have a real profession now. I've changed jobs 22 times. (28-year-old patient who had been under treatment for schizophrenia for several years)

MY CHILD SHOULD HAVE IT DIFFERENT THAN I DID... MY CHILD SHOULD HAVE IT EASIER

Depth psychology interprets this statement as hardly anything but: *My child should achieve what I didn't.* Here we find that the adults transfer unfulfilled wishes, unsatisfied needs, and unlived experiences onto their children. The difference between the level of development reached by the parent and the son's level is intentionally overlooked, with the result being that these expectations place too many demands on the child. It is in this sense that we can understand the statement of a little girl who had been raised in an antiauthoritarian way. The girl says, *Oh Mommy, do I have to play what I want to again today?* The opposite would be: *Mommy, do I have to play what you want me to play again today?*

In this situation the educator distorts the practices he enjoyed in his upbringing and tries to use them to make up for lingering unfulfilled wishes by having them fulfilled in his partner or children:

With my kids I've always done the exact opposite. I mean, I took my parents' way of doing things, but I just turned them around 180 degrees. (41-year-old banker)

I've always tried to set a good example for my children because I don't want my children to have to go through what I went through. I've gone to the other extreme and wanted-in fact, I still kind of want- everything to be 100% perfect. (38-year-old manager)

At first I treated my child in a very traditional way. For example, whenever he'd play outside I'd be at the window all the time, calling after him. I couldn't concentrate on my work at all (like Mother). Or I'd drag the little fellow off the bus because other people behind us wanted to get off too, and I was afraid they'd make comments about my boy being too slow. Or I'd fly off the handle if he spilled his milk - he was a real pro at that. Or I reacted instinctively to crumbs on the table or on the floor. But it's right that I then made a complete turnaround. Suddenly there was a lot of rebelliousness in me, without it I wouldn't have survived. I had been furious with my mother for years. But then I became an adherent of antiauthoritarian parenting. My fanaticism for neatness and cleanliness turned into utter sloppiness. (36-year-old housewife, mother of three)

In most cases, however, the projected wishes do not match the developmental level and possibilities of the partner, because these wishes often assume certain capabilities that must be developed step by step. Here one seems to be putting the cart before the horse. Through the projection of one's wishes and through the demand to identify with the, the partner, but also oneself, is subjected to too many expectations. *From the time I was a child I wanted more than anything else to become a ballet dancer. When my daughter was born it was already obvious to me that she would go into ballet. When she finally got to be three and a half I enrolled her in dance class. My dream seemed to be fulfilled. But my daughter had other ideas. She didn't like ballet, and after two years I had to take her out of the class. I was heartbroken. There was nothing left for me to do but secretly stand in front of the mirror and dance Swan Lake.* (28-year-old mother of two)

Children don't just see what their parents see; through identification they also experience it in a similar way. Everyone can recreate the experience that he found in the behavior and attitudes typical to friends or relatives. But in many cases the model actualizes itself. The person does not think, speak, and act as he would on the basis of his own convictions, but as the model would have done in similar circumstances.

Although I know that every child needs his own free space, I get terribly upset with how messy my daughter is; I find I'm acting just like my mother did with me. It really bothers me that I use the very same words and arguments as my mother did...

Here there is a tradition of symptoms and prejudice. The parental attitudes towards objects in the environment become automatic for the child, the only possible way to act. They become second nature, thereby possibly blocking access to the person's real nature.

◆ *Identification,* as an inner mechanism, takes place unnoticed for the large part. As probably the most socially important form of learning, it represents a necessary prerequisite for the development of the personality. If the identification model is not appropriately integrated, that is, if it is adopted rigidly and not further developed in harmony with the development of the personality, there can eventually be disorders, conflicts, and confrontations. This all rests on the fact that no distinction has been made between a person's own personality and the behavioral patterns of his model.

To be able to imagine what another person is thinking or feeling, we must be able to step into his shoes. This process is known as projection.

◆ *Projection* is the transferral of conscious and unconscious expectations and also one's own personality features onto the external world and onto one's social partners. People who succumb to the misunderstanding of projection see in other people those qualities that they refuse to see in themselves. One sees the thorn in the other guy's eye, but not the log in one's own.

The misunderstanding of projection can thus be labeled systematic dishonesty toward oneself and injustice toward one's partner. The aggressive person is an example of this: If you ask him why he attacks other people, why he is rude and dishonest toward them, why he hurts them and complains about them, he will reply that he has to defend himself, that all of them are so cruel and so powerful, and that the world is very unjust.

Disorders and Conflicts

Excessive tendency to imitate others; excessive expectations; desire for security; identity crisis; renunciation of a model; idealization; prejudice; disappointments; mood fluctuations; hopelessness; doubt; criticism of oneself and others.

Comment
Not everyone with a baldhead has tipped over an oil flank. To avoid misunderstandings: Don't use your own experience to make assumptions about others. Ask about their motivations.

Antidote
Learn to distinguish between your own motives and those that are alien to you.

WHOEVER MISTRUSTS EVERYONE USUALLY WATCHES OUT FOR HIMSELF THE LEAST OF ALL *(Graff)*

GENERALIZATION

Misunderstanding: *Children only disturb things.*
The crow in our introductory fable had seen only the peacock's ugly feet. Compared to this impression, all of the peacock's positive features were ignored. The ugly feet - and there is even reason for argument about the concept of ugliness - were generalized, thereby concealing the other «good» qualities.

We are able to understand our world partly because of the ability to apply one experience to another, and to act the same way in similar circumstances. To learn and to take control of our environment we must be able to make generalizations. Without them, our experiences and perceptions would disintegrate into countless events with no apparent link to each other. Only through generalization are we able to compile and summarize our perceptions, to form principal concepts, and finally, to think abstractly. But this ability itself can be considered a basic type of misunderstanding. By transferring our own experiences, there is a danger of making a false assumption. If a child touches a hot stove, he'll avoid touching other stoves for a long time, regardless of whether they were hot or cold. Here we see the protective function that generalization has always had. But this protective function is linked with the danger of viewing an event only from the perspective of one or more experiences, and thus of misinterpreting it. Just because the stove was hot once does not mean that it has to be hot now, or at some time in the future. In our relationships to ourselves and to others we tend to make generalizations. We use one experience to make a conclusion about someone's qualities; or we apply certain qualities to other qualities; or we judge an entire person on the basis of a few observations.

I'M A FAILURE

The fact that I'm having problems with my kids makes me feel that I'm a failure, that I'm absolutely good for nothing. (24-year-old mother of two)

LIFE DOESN'T HAVE MEANING ANY MORE

When I have a headache, I don't want to hear about anything. I'm no longer open or receptive and don't even want to go on living. Nothing has meaning for me. (37-year-old graphic designer)

MY SON IS A TERRIBLE CHILD

When my child comes to me, dependent, quiet, and without aggression, then I think he's the dearest child imaginable. At those times I love him totally and don't understand how I can sometimes be so hard on him. I feel very guilty then, and try to make up for it. But on those days when he is down right belligerent, aggressive, and stubborn, I think to myself that I have a really awful child. (28-year-old mother of an 8-year-old child. The child was being treated for aggressive behavior.)

WHY DO I DESERVE SUCH A SON?

I think politeness is very important. When my son throws a tantrum at home and uses all sorts of ugly words, I see him as a very primitive person. And I have to ask myself what I did to deserve such a son. (46-year-old father of a 16-year-old boy; generation conflicts)

I CAN'T STAND A BEER BELLY

I simply can't stand it when someone has a beer belly, for instance my ex-husband. I find it so repulsive, I can hardly, bring myself to establish contact with him: It's like that every time I meet someone like my previous husband. I'm immediately turned off by someone like that.

WHEN I SEE THESE LONGHAIRED GUYS!

I used to go to a lot of events with my husband. On these occasions it often happened that a famous professor, for instance, would give a talk. Usually some young fellows are sitting in the corner, longhaired, sloppy, and acting like little snots. I'm immediately opposed to these guys, and expect them to make aggressive comments to the speaker, which usually does happen. It never occurred to me to think about why these young people act the way they do. I'm completely prejudiced against them. Inside I get terribly upset over them, to the point of feeling physically ill, and would just love to go up to them and give them a piece of my mind. But instead I do what I always do: I keep it all bottled up inside, and no one has the foggiest idea of what is going on inside me. It's struck me often that I hate every form of aggression in people, although I struggle with that so much myself. I think it comes from the fact that I grew up in a very aggressive atmosphere. (63-year-old housewife)

Hatred towards groups, races, and peoples stems in principle from the misunderstanding of generalizations: *You've never had time for me. You've never been nice to me. You always keep me waiting. The rich are exploiters; the poor are failures; the Swiss are very clean; the Bavarians drink; the Scots are stingy; politicians are crooked; doctors only want to earn a lot of money; men are after only one thing; women are all devious.*

The mechanism of generalization proves to be the most all-encompassing when it is used as a statement about all people:

I distrust everyone. Because my parents got a divorce, I don't trust anyone. (8-year-old schoolgirl)

Individual experiences can be generalized to such an extent that they touch on the entire kind of experience and on the relationship of God. An apparently good relationship to God, or the total renunciation of God is found here. If there is a good God, how can there be so much injustice in the world?

Disorders and Conflicts

Generalizations, prejudices; unfairness to oneself and to others; fixations; exaggerated expectations; too many demands; too few demands; disappointment; desperation, anxiety; aggression; social isolation.

Comment
In the case of generalizations it is typical that one area is emphasized to the neglect of others. Generalizing causes a narrowing of one's field of vision.

Antidote
Learn to distinguish between the part and the whole.

IF OUR UNDERSTANDING DOES NOT DIFFERENTIATE BETWEEN DOGMAS, SUPERSTITION, AND PREJUDICE ON THE ONE HAND, AND TRUTH ON THE OTHER, WE CAN NEVER REACH OUR GOAL. *(Abdu'l-Baha)*

PREJUDICE

Misunderstanding: *I can't stand redheads*
A mother says to her 15-year-old daughter when the girl comes home an hour late one evening: *You don't need to offer an explanation, I wouldn't believe it anyway.* The mother confronts her daughter's tardiness with her mind made up in advance. She sees disobedience, defiance, unreliability and a breach of trust in her daughter's conduct. The girl is given no opportunity to explain what happened. Naturally the daughter could tell a white lie and deceive her mother. But the other possibility is not considered. The daughter can feel rejected and misunderstood and also feel there has been a breach of trust: *I can say what I want, but Mother has other ideas.* So a vicious circle is formed, blocking any chance for resolving the conflict.

Prejudice is probably the most common misunderstanding in social interactions. An attitude acquired through certain experiences is transferred to others by generalization, identification, and projection. Even if the attitude was valid at the time it originated, this does not mean it is valid now. Prejudice is thus a judgment that was made before the facts were examined; it has a strong affective component.

THE RED-HAIRED GIRL

A girl was supposed to be admitted into a therapy group made up of children aged nine to twelve. The group was asked if they would accept a new member. Of the seven in the group, three said no. An analysis of their reasons resulted in this: One boy, so he said, had had some bad experiences with girls. A girl had once hit him for no cause when he had accidentally bumped into her in the schoolyard and spilled the milk she happened to be holding.

The second member of the group was disturbed by the girl's red hair. Her grandmother had once had a servant girl with red hair; being jealous of her, the grandmother had openly spoken against the servant girl in the granddaughter's presence (association with strong affective component).

The third objector, a boy, did not want a girl admitted to the group because he had a sister whom his mother preferred over him.

Our judgments, prejudices, and attitudes cannot be traced back simply to conscious personal experiences. Rather, they are based on impulses, stimuli, and unconscious motives which were mainly programmed into us during a stage that we have almost no access to as adults

FOREIGN WORKERS, IN MY OPINION, WERE A NECESSARY EVIL

Until recently I considered foreign workers as nothing more than a necessary evil, I always told my kids that, too. Today I realize that that was prejudice on my part. Here's what made me change my mind. One night I found myself Standing beside my car along the highway. My car had broken down, so I was trying to flog down a car so I could get help. But all the cars just whizzed, right by. Finally someone stopped. As soon as he started to talk, I knew he was a foreigner, and from the way he was dressed, I figured he was a foreign worker. At first he tried to figure out what was wrong with the car. But after an hour he suggested I have the car towed. He said his car wasn't powerful enough to give me a tow. So he drove me to the nearest large town, which was almost 15 miles away. He lived in that town, so we went to one of his friends who worked in a garage, and he got the guy out of bed. Here I saw for the first time just how crowded those foreign workers have to live. The wife made us some coffee, and then we drove back to where my car was. By now it was two o'clock in the morning. After about 15 minutes my car was running again. The two refused to accept any money. I invited them to my house. I must say, I have slowly changed my opinion, starting that night. I began to realize that I had had no good reasons to dislike the foreign workers. Now I wanted to really look into the matter, so I started gathering as much information as I could find. (35-year-old manager)

Prejudices associated with interpersonal behavior deal with the actual capabilities. They are built up as expectations about individual primary and secondary capabilities. A prejudice does not have to be associated with negative qualities. It is just as possible to have positive expectations without having gone to the trouble of examining the validity of those expectations. Without such an examination the result is either too many demands, or too few.

A child's previous success was sufficient cause for the father to rule out the possibility of failure later on. When the child's performance in school dropped off, the father felt terribly disappointed. His opinion of his child made a complete turnaround: *I've always known that nothing good happens if a person rests on his laurels. Now I'm also thinking about taking my child out of that school. He has demonstrated that he's stupid.*

Whether they are positive or negative, prejudices rest mainly on a generalizing, limited field of vision. One particular actual capability will be separated from the rest and will be looked at independent of the entire personality. Expectations, attitudes, and ideas are then linked to this one capability.

You've always been messy, and will never change.
You can never again believe a person who has told a lie.
You've always let me down; so don't even try to make an excuse.

I've read it myself, and it's true.
I know for myself what is right and what is wrong.

Prejudices never show a tendency to correct themselves. Instead, they are likely to move on into other prejudices, or to make a complete reversal. A person would rather change the world than revise his prejudice. Why is it so hard to reduce prejudice? Often the people don't realize that they are prejudiced. To avoid having to put the prejudice to the test or to seriously examine it, these people automatically do everything they can to avoid those situations that would challenge their ideas. But how can a person ever know if he has succumbed to an error (in the form of prejudice) if he never puts himself in a position where this error could come to light? Or, to go back to our original examples, how can a person claim that his child is dishonest, his partner disloyal, without giving that individual a chance to defend himself? How can we know if we are prejudiced or not, if we aren't willing to face people with different ideas and qualities, and if we aren't willing to deal with them?

Disorders and Conflicts
Injustice; discrimination; aggression; guilt feelings; imbalance; fanaticism; racial hatred; self-hatred; social failings; poor judgment; fear of the truth.

Comment
A prejudice is an untimely judgment, usually with a heavy emotional component. Many interpersonal conflicts are based on prejudice. In many cases problems in raising children are not due to fate or inherent evil. Rather they are the result of the vicious circle of prejudice.

Antidote
Learn to distinguish between judgment and prejudice.

IT IS OBVIOUS THAT THE FUTURE GENERATION DEPENDS ON THE MOTHERS OF TODAY. *(Abdu'l-Baha)*

MAN AND WIFE

Misunderstanding: *Oh dear, just a girl!*
Being a woman was a punishment to me. A woman: inferior, loyal, emotional, stupid, weak, suffering because of what men are like, dependent. Man: good, unfaithful, objective, intelligent, strong, risk-taking, imperturbable, independent. From this I concluded that for me the most important thing was to act like a man. (23-year-old female student)

There's hardly a more emotional subject than the relationship between man and woman. At the same time, there is hardly an area that is more weighted down with prejudice. The misunderstanding of man - woman does not just play a role in the current confrontations within one's marriage or job. It also has implications for parenting.

Educational, influence goes beyond such matters as preparation for life, social behavior, aggression, and intelligence. It is also a chief factor in developing role behavior, particularly in terms of sex roles. Is, for example, the care of young children a «typically feminine» instinct?

Female adult rats were placed in front of a nest occupied by baby rats who had no mother. The adult rat immediately began to feed and take care of the little ones. Male rats, when placed in front of the same nest, did not at first take care of the young. But after they became aware of the young, they treated them very much like the females had done.

From the United States comes this report of an experiment: An American couple brought their 17-month son in for a normal circumcision, to be done with an electric instrument. Through improper use of the instrument the child's penis and testicles were cut off. The parents didn't know what to do. What kind of future would their boy have? Psychiatrists and psychologists advised them to raise the child as a girl. The parents took this advice and altered their parenting procedures. They dressed the boy in girl's clothes, let his hair grow long, and told their two older boys that they had made a mistake. «It's a little girl, not a boy.» After three years the parents found that their «girl» was really acting like a girl. While the boys played with their cars in the sandbox and got dirty in the process, the «girl» played with dolls and kept neat and «clean.» The brothers tended to be protective of their «sister,» and tried to do all sorts of favors for «her.» Seldom was there rivalry between «her» and the boys. She acted completely like a girl.

The child begins his «cultural education,» via his parents, on the day he is born. Who hasn't noticed first hand how differently people react - friends, relatives, and parents themselves - when they hear that the new baby is a boy or a girl. *Ah, a little girl. - What, a boy to keep the family name going? Congratulations!* It has been confirmed by experiments that male babies are more active and restless than females, they get angry more easily, cry more, sleep less, and demand more attention from the mother. But this can be interpreted in different ways:

It may be the result of «innate characteristics.»

It may be the result of different treatment of the babies by the psychologists doing the study, or, more likely, by the parents, who, because of obvious sex stereotypes, act differently with male babies and female babies. It may be the result of an interaction between innate and acquired factors. The last of the three above interpretations seems to be the most accurate, as judged by previous scientific research. But emphasis on innate sex differences served as a defense of existing prejudices: *Women's brains weigh less than men's do. Women are women because they don't have a penis. They are deficient beings. Women are less practical than men. Women live for only three things: the kitchen, the kids, the church. Women are not able to assert themselves the way men are. Men are better at organizing things than women are.*

Little things that often seem humorous can point to fixed ideas about women... *That must be a woman driver... That's no work for a woman... You can't expect that of your sister... That's just women's gossip.* Role divisions within the family most clearly reveal the relationship between man and woman: The husband has to work, while the woman just stays at home. This relationship alone is a model. The children will learn: Father is busy in the world outside; mother is responsible for things within the family.

Therapist: *Have you ever talked with your husband about his taking over a part of the housework and helping raise the children, like a division of labor?*

Patient: *No, my husband couldn't even imagine something like that. He's busy enough with his job.*

These kinds of attitude often lead to the raising of the children falling into the mother's domain, while the father's role becomes that of the authority who metes out rewards or punishment. He makes an appearance only when things go wrong.

My father went on business trips a lot. Whenever he got home my mother would tell him all the bad things I did, and I'd get spanked for them then. Now my relationship to my father is not at all good... (36-year-old employee)

The fact that the mother usually has a central role in the children's upbringing is often used by the husband as an excuse for leaving the entire responsibility in his wife's hands. This is like «Heads, I win; tails, you lose.» If everything goes well, the father feels it proves he made the right move; if things go badly, he can blame his wife. As a result of this, many women feel that they are carrying too heavy an emotional burden. Some then develop physical and psychological problems, or look for an escape in their work. There they expect to be treated more fairly.

In my case there is escape into work. Sometimes I get upset about everything. Then I simply have to clean the house, although I know that it is nonsense. When that happens I know that I'm getting depressed, but I can't do anything about it. I take medication, but the depression lasts for three weeks or so. (35-year-old sales clerk)

Basically I like to work. If things were different I would feel useless. And I'm also of the opinion that work is a good antidote for too much emotionalism. This is why I like to keep busy. When I'm working I don't run the danger of having to deal so much with the confusion of my feelings. (44-year-old business woman)

I took the initiative and had a strong desire to get a job. I felt I wasn't doing well as a housewife and mother. I had a lot of trouble with my child and didn't feel competent to be a good mother. By having a job I could give the responsibility for the child to someone else (my mother–in–law). I thought the child would get more love and attention this way. I also thought that my relationship with my child would improve if I didn't spend so much time with him, and I tried to look forward to seeing him again in the evening. There were also other reasons why I wanted to work, for instance, to get some recognition in a career, to be with other people, to never let myself get sloppy, to leave the house looking well groomed every morning, and to earn my own money. (29-year-old secretary, conflicts with mother-in-law, sleep disorders)

The parental expectations about the sex role of their child can have a decisive influence on his future. Choice of career and education are also affected by the influence of sex stereotypes.

Disorders and Conflicts

Imbalanced division of roles; «fate of the housewife»; too many demands; too few demands; separation anxiety; children as one's life goal; marriage as a security institution; belief in authority; bondage; anxiety; aggression; mental problems; emotional reactions; envy of the other sex; generation crises; submission; crises of emancipation.

Comment
When women enjoy the same educational advantages as men, the results will show that both man and women have similar capabilities and are equally suited to education. Then one will learn to treat women as equals.

Antidote
Learn to distinguish between sex as a result of nature and sex roles as a product of upbringing.

THROUGH I SPEAK WITH THE TONGUES OF MEN AND OF ANGELS, AND HAVE NOT CHARITY, I AM BECOME AS SOUNDING BRASS, OR A TINKLING CYMBAL.
(I Corinthians 13:1)

JUSTICE - LOVE

Misunderstanding: *It serves you right that you cut your finger.*
The principle of justice weighs one achievement against another; it is a basic principle of parenting, where the individual actual capabilities and accomplishments are in the foreground. But justice remains impersonal, blind to the uniqueness of a person.

I work for you outside the home so you can take care of me and the kids at home. You don't have any time for me, so from now on I won't have time for you, either.

Or.

You don't have time for me, so I'll find someone who does.
You had a successful day at work and you've taken good care of us, so I'll be especially nice to you.

155

Because you did so well in school, you can go to the movie tonight.
You were so nice to our company tonight that you can stay up late tonight and watch television.

Equality and comparability are very important for justice. This realization was a basic principle in law, as we see in such an early document as the code of Hamurabi (1986-1728 B.C.): «Punishment brings protection and expands the insight of the people and is a means of preventing the repetition of the crime.» Justice that has been raised to a principle, still dominant in our legal systems, determines the form of parenting in many instances.

I'LL TREAT YOU THE WAY YOU TREAT ME

It was Sunday morning and I wanted to lie around in bed a little longer, because it was only 7 a.m. and I don't like to get up so early on Sundays. Then my little boy came into the room and spoiled my good mood, I was pretty crabby toward him and said, «If you don't show me some consideration, even though I still need rest, I won't go swimming with you.» I'll treat you the way you treat me.

When people try to establish justice with their partners, they create a vicious circle that leads from one injustice to another. This can turn a marriage into a hell on earth. While most people see justice as the epitome of consistency, it is really quite unstable. One's own value system, previously accepted ideas, and one's own wishes remain untouched by it, as the following socio-psychological example illustrates: The people in the experiment were witnesses to how a group of teenagers teased and tormented a boy who had apparently not done anything to them. The boy cried, but could not free himself from them.

The witnesses to this had no way of intervening. In their conflict between pity for the boy and their inability to help him, they solved the dilemma in their own way. Without realizing it, they began to view the boy differently. Although they had felt sorry for him initially, believing he was being treated unfairly, they began to see more and more unfavorable traits in him as time went on. Finally they were convinced that he was getting what he deserved, and that he was to blame for it. When the experiment ended the witnesses felt that their judgment was just as correct as it had been at the beginning. They were unaware of the apparent contradiction of their change of mind. This change in their opinion had a protective function. After all, they could not reconcile the fact that they felt sorry for him, but did nothing except stand by and watch him be tormented. Otherwise they would have had to intervene. In order to make the situation more bearable for themselves, to protect their own egos, and to avoid further guilt feelings, they simply turned the situation around: the victim, so they said, was himself the guilty one. (Lerner and Simmons, 1966)

The opposite of justice can be seen in these statements:

I'll always be on your side and give you everything I have, regardless of what you give me.

I trust in you and have high hopes for you.

These statements are statements of *love*. Love is a sign of positive emotional attention, and touches the entire person. One doesn't build on particular qualities, capabilities, and traits, but refers to the bearer of these qualities: *I love you because you are you.*

In many cases this attitude contains certain advantages for the relationship. Problems that crop up are not exploited; open conflicts are avoided.

In extreme cases love loses control over reality and is separated from the concrete situation. When the issue is fairness toward a child or partner, people have expectations, which are to be met in the present. When love is concerned, however, the expectations are directed toward an unknown time in the future. One patiently hopes that the love (sacrifice) given to the child or partner will find its reward through recognition from society or from God.

When my son is messy, I just don't see it.
My husband doesn't have a lot of time. I don't tell him that, because I don't want to hurt him.
Regardless of what he does, I love him.

If the principle of *justice* dominates the parenting situation, conflicts are dealt with in an active way: One criticizes. In its most extreme cases the principle of justice leads to such drastic acts as when children are beaten, adolescents are thrown out of their homes, friendships are broken apart, and marriages are terminated by divorce. One simply doesn't want to have anything more to do with the child because he didn't do what was expected of him: *You don't want to adapt, so, don't expect anything from us either.* If the principle of love is the dominating force, there is the danger that the opposite can occur: Conflicts are concealed behind a mask of patience and courtesy, without even the opportunity to let off steam from time to time. Since the conflicts are not dealt with step by step, there can be explosive outbreaks. People who react in this way keep everything bottled up inside themselves; often they are like devoted servants to their children. But at some point something happens that breaks the camel's back, going beyond anything they had ever expected. These people are unable to release their energy in small doses. They live by the rule of all or nothing. An otherwise placid mother loses control of herself and abuses her child for a minor mishap. A seemingly modest and harmless father kills his 6-year-old child because he didn't want to eat his supper. Up till then the father had never laid a hand on the boy. A mother abandons her family because her husband forgot their anniversary.

A person is not just either fair or loving. Justice and love are so intertwined that the partner in a conflict often doesn't really know what's going on. Let's imagine a marital row: The wife has forgotten to go to the bank to take care of a transaction for her husband. He's very angry about this and screams at her, «I just can't rely on you.» But even though he feels justified in making a statement like this, he right away regrets his outburst and thinks to himself, «I shouldn't have screamed at her like that.» When he sees his wife doing the dishes he puts on an apron, helps dry the dishes, and mutters, «I didn't really mean that.» On the other hand, love can become a form of strict justice, if the expectations of love and attention are not met. The difficult thing here is that the partner generally does not have any insight into the cause of the person's change of attitude. Angry silence keeps it from being revealed and understood.

Justice and love form the basis for close human interaction and child raising. But both can produce mental and social conflicts, if one of them is made an absolute while the other is devalued, or when both of them are no longer seen in connection with the dimension of time.

Disorders and Conflicts
Fanaticism about justice; hidden aggression; fear of making a decision; doing an injustice to someone; injustice; too high expectations; blindness to reality because of love; lovelessness; mental burdens; disappointments; marital conflict; psychosomatic disorders.

Comment
It is right to expect your partner to have a sense of justice. Indeed, your partner expects you to make this demand on him. But if he fails in this regard, it is necessary that you make a distinction between your partner himself and his particular shortcoming. That is: I love you as you are, even if you have erred on this particular point. I know you can learn from your mistakes, and I will learn from mine.

Antidote
Learn to distinguish between love and justice.

THESE DETAILS MAKE ME A LITTLE UNHAPPY. (W. James)

SEX

Misunderstanding: *People don't talk about that.*

Attitudes about sex are more than simply non-binding opinions that can be changed when better arguments prove to the contrary. They are much too closely tied with the person's feelings and have developed in his own personality.

As long-lasting attitudes, three prototypes can be set up. They reflect characteristic positions regarding the theme of sex.

The Silent One

He has identified with group and religious norms to such an extent that he does not want to question them. Even if sexuality presents a problem for him, he will still say, «People don't talk about that. It's something everybody has to deal with for himself; we have to accept that.» He tolerates sex as a necessary evil; in marriage he pays his tribute to tradition; intercourse serves only as a mean of procreation. His motto in marriage is: Fidelity till death. Sexual activity that goes beyond the officially recognized area, such as masturbation, is suppressed as much as possible, and is always accompanied by guilt feelings.

Here we find such disorders as fear of sexual activity or a strong sense of guilt. Frigidity and impotence are also major factors.

The Open One

In this group we find mostly people who have broken away from traditional norms. In contrast to the silent type, they consider it important to talk about sex as frequently and as intensively as possible, to have a lot of sexual experiences, and to demonstrate their openness to sex at every opportunity. Among their mottos we find «Sex is a part of human nature,» and «Sex is fun, and everything that's fun is okay.» This kind of person frequently views sex as a kind of achievement. The partner functions as the object of the sexual activity, much like in the Persian proverb: Every flower has a different fragrance.

Despite - or precisely because of - the demonstrated openness to sex, it often happens that sexual disorders occur in this group. Such disorders include fear of sexual failure, fear of close relationships, lack of discretion in choosing partners, and associated with it, too many mental and physical demands. Adultery and group sex are treated as questions of tradition and a mere social game, respectively. These things are discussed openly.

The Two-Faced Type

Here we often find the attitude that we call the double standard. We can distinguish three groups:

- A person appears to be the silent type, the strict moralist. But when he doesn't have to live up to his social role, he does as he pleases. At home he will be the upright, strict husband, but in the evening he'll tend to sneak out to a brothel. While he publicly decries masturbation, he will masturbate in front of pornographic pictures. While he claims he has no sexual needs, he secretly prefers certain perversions. In the company of others he makes it known that sex is not a problem for him, and that he has the proper distance to it. But at home, in his fantasies, he dreams of things he has denied himself previously. The wife who demands absolute fidelity from her husband and perhaps seems frigid toward him has a lover of her own. Social norms that are anti-sex seem to be recognized and adhered to; but sexuality finds an outlet in one's «secret life» or in one's fantasies.

- A person pretends to be open. He talks about everything and acts as if there were no limits to what he does. But despite this obvious behavior, a person in this category is burdened with inhibitions and guilt feelings that make it impossible for him to really experience sex freely. To friends and acquaintances he'll announce:

Last night I met a girl and two hours later I had her in the sack.
That woman over there seems to have caught your eye. I've already played around with her, or she wanted to, but I didn't really need it.

In reality these statements have no real basis. The same thing can be found among women: They flirt openly, but if a man responds to the come-on, he's rejected. Harmless conversations, when retold among

161

girlfriends, can be expanded and distorted into marriage proposals or stories of wild and passionate nights. Here again we find an adaptation to social norms, namely the need to achieve, in this case in the sexual arena. One pretends to be very open so as to hide one's inhibitions and anxieties.

- A person belittles sexual problems because, at his age, they are no longer central issues for him: *I don't understand why you make such a fuss over sex. It's not such a big deal. I'm doing quite well in coming to terms with my sexuality.*

What is not revealed here is that the problems that the person belittles now were difficult for him years before. Even if one recognizes that some people have indeed managed to suppress their sexuality, for most people it isn't that easy. Here we also find an aggressive attitude: *Sex is really a filthy business. I'd be ashamed if I were you. When we were young there wasn't such filth.* Disorders in the two-faced person usually appear as internal and external conflicts. Sometimes there are sexual problems that are not perceived as such; rather, they are transferred to such areas as job and fellow men. Difficulty in making decisions is very characteristic of this group: *When I get through with school, when I get a secure job, when I have more money, when the house is done, etc. it will be easier for us to decide things.*

If a person is married, he wishes he'd remained single and mourns his lost freedom. Unusual cases can be seen where two people get married, realize they can't live together, get a divorce, realize that they can't live without each other, and finally remain divorced but live together as if married.

Disorders and Conflicts
Sex as one's goal in life; hyper-sexuality; compulsive masturbation; sexual demoralization; perversion; aggressive sexuality; fear of sex; compulsive sexual achievement; disappointment; self-esteem problems.

Comment

Even if these three attitudes about sex are very widespread and we can find aspects of one or the other in ourselves, they are still other alternatives for us. We can identify with social and religious norms that seem appropriate and timely for us. These norms can be used as a standard of measure without at the same time becoming a sword of Damocles.

Antidote

Learn to distinguish between sexual honesty and double standards.

LOVE FIRST CALLS ITSELF INTIMACY. (Goethe)

SEX - SEXUALITY - LOVE

Misunderstanding: *We understand each other so well, why can't we love each other, too?*

In West Germany some 300 marriages end in divorce each day, and this figure is only the tip of the iceberg. It does not include people who are separated or who continue to live under the same roof. It also overlooks the children who suffer from having to grow up in a broken home. The statistics in other countries are no different. In Iran, for instance, with a population of 30 million, there are 105 divorces per day. Other countries show similar or even higher rates.

Behind marital conflicts there are a number of factors, including ones where sex, sexuality, and love play a decisive role. Just as young people feel threatened by religion, ritual, dogma and prejudice, so a lot of older people view sex as an attack on good manners, as a sign of moral decay, and as «something filthy.» In the case of the young people in the above example, there is a lack of differentiation between faith, religion, and church. In the case of the older people's views on sex there is a lack of differentiation between sex, sexuality, and love.

Sex

Under the term sex we include all the physiological, physical processes in connection with a sexual activity. Sex is not the act alone, but also what a person knows about them: the structure of the sex organs, their function, the physical events during sexual activity, the reproductive processes, and birth.

Sex education enables us to develop a meaningful understanding of the physical aspects of sex. Sex must be understood in terms of man's physical, mental, and spiritual nature. When parents say they have taught their children about sex, this usually means that they have informed their children about the physical basis. A healthy child will automatically ask questions about sex, insofar as the parents show an openness to questions of this type. The information that is given should match the developmental level of the child. And here it is important that individual items of information do not contradict each other over the course of time. (Gone are the days of the stork!)

Like hunger, thirst, food, drink, and sleep, sex is one of the realities of life. Through eating we learn that some foods are not digestible; one would never eat a rock. But in psychotherapeutic practice we find that, as far as sex is concerned, a lot of people try to eat something they can't digest. Others go on ascetic, self-tormenting diets, and then there are some who seem to overeat when it comes to sex.

Sex is closely linked to our sensory perceptions. Just the sight of a man or woman, a touch, a stroke of the hand can cause sexual arousal. Sex leads to arousal. A person loves someone because of physical appearance; because of hair color, physique, bust, smooth skin, beautiful eyes, slender legs, etc. But what happens when these things change, when the face gets wrinkles, the hair turns gray, the bust line starts to sag? What happens if the face is destroyed by an accident? What happens if the body is misshapen?

If physical attributes are the sole basis for the relationship, then there is suddenly no longer a basis for that relationship.

HER BODY WAS ALWAYS EXCITING FOR ME

Without a doubt I was excited and fascinated by her body. This is how I reacted, anyway. And then there was her striking profile. Second, her sense of ease, which always impressed me, as I was more inhibited. Third, my heightened sense of importance, because a lot of other guys wanted her too. So, she had a «choice.» (26-year-old divorced man)

I GO FOR DARK-HAIRED MEN

I've never been physically attracted to my husband, because he didn't live up to the image of what I wanted in a man. He was blond and blue eyed, and men with dark hair and dark eyes had always fascinated me. It also bothered me that he always wore glasses. There was nothing unusual about his sex organs. But as a young bride I was very upset when he'd run around the apartment with an erection. It upset me terribly. I found it simply awful. (28-year-old divorced employee)

In this instance it is not just a question of one's expectations about the other person's physical qualities. Also important here is one's relationship to one's own body. Some people accept their bodies without any trouble; but just as frequently some people develop a sense of fear or distrust about their bodies. As a rule these differing attitudes are the result of different experiences the people have had in their lives:

MY BODY IS MY ENEMY

I'm afraid of my own breasts. When I bathe I feel terrible. My heart starts pounding, and I'm always relieved when the job is over. My body is my enemy. It is consuming all my energy. I have such a fear of my body that I can't stand to see any part of it naked. I wash myself bit by bit so that I'm never completely naked. The same happens when I get dressed or undressed. It's a struggle that takes everything out of me. I couldn't sign up for a gym class, and taking medicine is almost impossible, too, because it is a part of body care. I haven't had sex for a long time, because it would mean I'd have to be naked. (28-year-old female employee with sexual disorders and depression)

Sexuality

While sex deals with physical characteristics, sexuality is associated with mental and behavioral features as well as with those that are linked with the personality.

MY LOVER IS COMPLETELY DIFFERENT THAN MY HUSBAND

For the past six months I have felt depressed and anxious. I've only been married for a year, but already I find myself going to bed at night hoping my husband doesn't want to have sex. Although I find him physically attractive, we aren't compatible. We are complete opposites. My husband is very exact. If we're in a hurry to go somewhere he'll stand around another ten minutes and make sure everything is okay. If we're leaving the apartment he'll double check (and then check again) to see that we have the right papers, the keys, etc. Or he'll check to see that his hair is combed, even though the next gust of wind will destroy his splendid mane anyway. When he does that I stand there and tremble with fury. When I come home in the evening I am asked how much money I still have and how much I spent. That drives me up the wall. Sometimes I miss his not helping me with my coat, his offering me light, things like that. Three months ago I got involved with another man. He's a lot different to my husband. When I take out a cigarette he lights it for me. He helps me with my coat and he pours coffee for me. When I'm supposed to do something for him he'll ask, «Would you please...Could you...?» He's more superficial than my husband, not so terribly exact. If there's a bill that's not right, he'll say, «We'll take care of this later on» and he puts it aside. Even when he gets a written request he'll tear it up as he says, «We never received that... » When I was young we didn't take things so seriously in our house either. My mother disregarded a lot of things. She was very generous when it came to raising us. If I did the dishes and didn't quite get them clean she wouldn't complain. She was just mostly concerned about how we behaved. That was the most important thing for her... (24-year-old female patient with sex disorders resulting from conflicts in the behavioral areas of orderliness, cleanliness, politeness, exactness, frugality, and patience)

Love

What we call love is the emotional relationship that can be directed to a series of objects in various forms of expression. It is a capability that every person has. Its earliest form is in the relationship between the mother and child. In the course of his development a person learns to love and to act in such a way that he will be loved in return. The parental model in its relationship to other people and to religion plays an especially important role here.

CHURCH WAS THE ONLY CONTACT WITH THE OUTSIDE WORLD

Sexuality was taboo in our house. There wasn't even a hint of it. But in school my father gave talks on how parents should teach their children about sex. My parents were always embarrassed if we kids happened to see them in their underwear. There were no physical signs of affection in our house. I can't remember a single time that my father or mother kissed me. My parents were like a united front against us kids. I had the feeling that they were enough for each other and that we kids were just in the way. And when we got older we couldn't bring any of our friends home. In our parents' eyes, parties were almost obscene. The older my parents got, the more they shut themselves off from the world. Their only contact with the outside world was church. (28-year-old female teacher, disinterest in sex, contact disorders, marital problems)

Experiences in the primary environment of the family are expanded in the course of one's development through further experiences with the social environment.

The two dimensions of love, the ability to love and the ability to act in such a way as to be loved, can become separated from each other if the development is somehow disturbed:

AT ALL COSTS NOT BE ATTRACTIVE TO MY HUSBAND

Since I found out my husband cheated on me, things are topsy-turvy. At home I'm a real slob. I can't even bring myself to put on makeup or comb my hair. And I couldn't care less how the house looks. I have absolutely no sexual desire, and I don't want my husband to have any either. Just the thought of his touching me almost makes me sick to my stomach. (34-year old mother of three children)

MY WIFE IS DIFFERENT TO MY MOTHER

I have no confidence in my wife anymore. Instead of hanging the clothes in the closet, she carelessly lets them lie around on the chairs. And while my mother stooped over to get every speck of dust, my wife lets it pile up inches thick. (33-year-old civil servant with stomach troubles)

Just the opposite can also happen. Many people consciously act in a certain way so that they will be loved. They spend a good part of their income on makeup, massages, jewelry, and fashionable clothes. They go to a lot of trouble to look attractive, but are still unable to establish contact with a partner or to develop a close relationship with him.

Love has another quality aside from sex and sexuality. One identifies with the person one loves. One trusts and stands by one's beloved, sometimes even going so far as to overlook that person's faults, or to not even see them in the first place. One accepts the partner in his uniqueness and tries to idealize him beyond all comparisons and doubts. Only through mutual love, which recognizes the partner in his uniqueness, is the «product quality» and hence the «replace-ability» of the partner limited. Love is thus a force for evaluating the other person. It exerts a counterbalance to the personal weight given to sex and sexuality. In an intense love relationship only selected features are perceived, namely those that fit in with one's image of the beloved. But love's influence here is not untouched as if in an ivory tower. Rather, it constantly receives reports based on experiences. If there are repeated disorders and disharmonies, if undesired physical characteristics develop, if there are problems of interaction, love will be weighted down by these negative factors. For if the energy expended is greater than the benefits derived, the emotional relationship can begin to totter: *I don't trust men at all, because my boyfriend was unfaithful to me.* Or: *How can I ever trust my girlfriend again, now that she's lied to me?*

The ability to love and to be loved thus requires that constant attention be paid to physical and behavioral characteristics. Getting a driving license does not mean you no longer need to watch out for traffic. In the same way, the marital vow or even the feeling of being loved by your partner does not mean you no longer need to pay attention to yourself, your physical appearance; or your behavior. You must continually monitor these things and be willing to make necessary changes.

Love proves to be dependent on the dimension of time. When we speak of love and view it as dependent on time, there are four situations that become particularly important: We can be happy, we can seem happy, we can become happy, we can remain happy.

Being Happy
It is precisely now that we are content; perhaps we have a partner who pleases us physically and because of his other qualities. Will we like him tomorrow too? If we're still single, it's easy to be happy. Weekend and vacation romances encounter few difficulties. And who knows whether a happy long-term relationship might not develop from an enjoyable weekend?

Seeming Happy
Although a person has enough problems, he gives the world the impression of not being troubled. A kiss in public creates the illusion that everything is fine.

Becoming Happy
A person tries to work through existing problems by discussing them openly. This is done with the hope that the future will be better. But a person could also expect that the problems will solve themselves while he, so to speak, buries his head in the sand.

Staying Happy
Even if a person is happy and hopes for continued good fortune this is no guarantee that one's happiness will continue. Being happy does not mean clinging to the present. Rather, it challenges us to get to know our partner and ourselves again and again, and to continually make new decisions about the partnership. The desire to remain happy in a partnership requires the willingness to see the partner in elegant dress in the evening, and perhaps in hair rollers and with no makeup the next morning. And that's not just once, but for perhaps 40 years. For the woman, it means being willing to accept her husband, whom she admires when he's all dressed up

for the day, also when he's relaxing at home in the evening in patched jeans and with a stubbly beard. And this too, if need be, for 40 years.

When we get to know a partner we know him mostly on the basis of a few typical qualities: physical proportions, facial expression, and some pleasant and unpleasant behaviors. When we are in love we tend to see only the qualities that we treasure; we do not notice other things. This can easily lead to disappointment: What did I see...? Partnerships where at first only sex was the important thing will later on have problems with sexuality. However, partnerships that were founded on strong personality characteristics can be torn apart by the problem of sex.

Disorders and Conflicts
Too much emphasis on the partner's physical characteristics; idealization of individual character qualities; gigantic expectations; naïve optimism; emotional dependency; disappointments; nagging; conflicts in the partnership; separations; divorces; frigidity; disinterest in sex.

Comment

Sex is associated with the body. It orients itself to physical functions and features. It is important here that accurate and objective information about the body be transmitted at an appropriate time. Physical qualities should not be underestimated in the partner relationship. Sexuality is associated with the qualities and capabilities of a person insofar as they concern the sexual relationship in the partnership. Social norms and hence the actual capabilities enter into this area. Love is the global capability, present in every person, to develop emotional ties with himself and his environment. Parental models play a critical role in the development of a person's ability to love and be loved. In its consistency love leads to the recognition of human equality and to a sense of responsibility.

Taken by themselves, sex and sexuality make people interchangeable. In such an instance a person is merely the bearer of qualities that are judged to be valuable or worthless. When sex and sexuality are overemphasized, the uniqueness of the personality is ignored. Love, however, in connection with sex and sexuality, confirms the uniqueness of the individual.

Antidote

Learn to distinguish between sex, sexuality, and love

LOVE IS THREE QUARTERS CURIOSITY. (Casanova)

CARICATURES OF LOVE

Misunderstanding: *I need love for relaxation*
There is hardly a word that is more widely and differently interpreted than the word love. It includes such diverse things as motherly love, love of animals, and fondness. Even sexual love has a number of different meanings that serve as a measure and as a guideline for the individual person. Along with this spectrum of meanings of love there is a spectrum of misunderstandings:

Love as Recreation
Sexuality is experienced in connection with the feeling of inner excitement and tension. This tension finds its release in sexual activity, particularly in intercourse. Here there are not just sexual tensions, but also tensions resulting from our need to achieve, particularly in our careers. This psycho-physiological fact can become a misunderstanding if the sexual release becomes highly stylized as the exclusive goal of the sex act: *After five busy days at work I need sexual release. Who I use to accomplish that is nothing more than a matter of taste.*

Love as a Product of Curiosity
We must admit that curiosity is an important motivation for love, but it is not the only factor.

Love as Conformity
A person thinks that he has to act just like the others: If I don't do it, the others don't give me any recognition.

Love as Accomplishment
A person thinks that our need to achieve in society has to be carried over into sex and sexuality. Intercourse becomes a sport where you have to win: *If the man or woman didn't have an orgasm, the whole thing wasn't worth anything.*
If I had a climax only three or four times I was in bad shape.
If I'm successful in my career, why shouldn't I also be successful when it comes to sex?

Love as Rivalry and Power Struggle

Just as in the situation where accomplishment is important, here, too, the person involved is making a comparison: *If I hadn't gone to bed with him right away, he would definitely have looked for a new girlfriend immediately.*

Love as Proof of Ownership

Sex is frequently used to tie a person down. Often this tendency is associated with pregnancy.

If he has slept with me, he belongs to me.

If I have his child, he's obligated to me.

In these situations the partner often promises to be careful. Or the partner claims she's on the pill, even though this is not true.

Love as a Duty to Other Generations

Here one thinks one should be married by a certain age and have a child. Quite often the parents are the driving force behind this idea. They want their children to marry well, and they want grandchildren they can spoil. When the marriage finally takes place, hundreds of guests are invited. The wedding becomes a life goal.

Love Out of Courtesy

A young man who completed his studies and returned to Iran, was stormed by all his relatives upon his return. Every aunt had her own selected bride for him. His favorite aunt, whose property he would inherit some day, spoke to him in glowing terms about a particular girl she had in mind. The aunt reminded him that she had only his best interest at heart, and she had been providing for him all these years. Now she had found a charming bride for him, a decent, neat, and loyal housewife type. This woman, and none other, was the one he should marry. He couldn't say no, the aunt insisted; after all, she was his aunt, and knew a lot more about life than he did. Out of pure courtesy to her, and without knowing the girl better, he said yes.

Love out of gratitude is associated with love out of courtesy. A patient once told how she had gone to bed with a man because he had helped her get a job when she was young. Another woman had married a man who had helped her family financially.

Love as Confirmation of One's Own Worth
To feel good about himself, a person might develop acquaintances and have sexual encounters. The problem here is that the emphasis is on how the person feels about himself, not on the relationship.

Intercourse as a Logical Consequence
An example of this is the situation where a couple may start necking and petting. Although the need for sex is not in the foreground, the two move more and more toward sex because they think it has to end this way, and what would the one partner think if the other one suddenly avoided what seems like a logical conclusion for them?

This is much like what happens when someone starts flirting and thinks that the other person expects that it has to lead to sex. In this case attraction, tenderness, etc. don't seem to amount to much if they aren't capped off with intercourse. One woman complains:

Whenever my husband gets romantic with me, or when I'm sweet to him, for instance, when I sit on his lap, he expects me to sleep with him. Now I'm actually scared to touch him or to be nice to him.

Love Out of Business Interests
A man marries a woman because he thinks she'll be of help to him in his career, in his business, or in his work. Or she will be a tax brake. Or her appearance and pleasant manner will mean bigger profits in his business. A patient reports:

I'm nothing but a billboard for my husband. He takes me everywhere and I have to represent him. At home he treats me much differently than when other people are around.

Quite often it happens that once a person's business is going well, the man loses interest in his wife and looks for a new partner. Women's liberation can produce similar results for a wife: After many years as a good and devoted wife she gets an education and suddenly feels the need for freedom. She wants to divorce her husband after he has paid for her education.

Love as Liberation
The phenomenon occurs mostly in adolescence. To escape from parental control, a young person will look for a short-term relationship, usually with the first available person who comes along. Sexual relationships

serve to confirm the person's break with the parents. Sexual activity is often carried out as a way of defying the parents.

Love as Protection

A person loves his partner because she is on the same wavelength. She likes the same things, and has similar attitudes and qualities: *We are well suited to each other because we both know how important it is to be tidy.* In this way people protect themselves from unpleasant confrontations. By choosing a partner with the same likes and dislikes, a person is able to avoid those situations that would force him to question his own position.

Love as Equalization

A person chooses a partner who has the qualities that he himself lacks. *I'm a very reserved person. I've always admired my husband because he asserts himself with other people and is so popular.* To balance out his own deficiencies, a person chooses a partner who appears to offer this balance. To give an example: The blind man chooses the lame. The one can't see, but can walk. The other can't walk, but can see. Together they complement each other's talents. This aspect of choice does indeed give a lot of people an opportunity, but it can become a misunderstanding if the person isn't really sure of his own strengths, or if he seeks to even things out through a partner simply because this is a convenient way for him to deal with his problems: *I don't need to worry about the things that my partner brings to the relationship.* A woman would marry a man, who, through his success and his protective manner, helps her in her lack of self-reliance, in her childish dependence. A man marries a woman who can make up for his lack of talent in the kitchen and in the house.

Love as the Blind Leading the Blind

The partnership is chosen because the partner does not have characteristics that, as model, could become a burden over the course of time: *Neither of us can hold something up to the other person. My husband isn't a genius either.* A partnership usually requires a considerable amount of work, namely that of consciously dealing with the thoughts, interests and characteristics of the other person. A person can accomplish this easiest if his partner does not surpass him in any area. The partner can even cause the person to feel: I'm even ahead of him. In other words, it's a case of the blind leading the blind.

As we have already seen at other points in this book, love is not a one-dimensional event that takes place only between two people. The phenomenon of love includes the relationship to one's self, to other people, to social groups, and even to the realm of religion. Against this background we must understand the distortions of love, as they appear in the form of egocentricity, depressive dependency on a partner, social hyperactivity, and exclusive religious ecstasy. Despite the many levels in operation here, special emphasis is given to the partnership relationship at this point. We found that the parental model was a main source of disorders within the partnership. Parents are even a model when they don't understand each other, when there are disharmonies. Here the child learns how to act with a partner, how to treat a wife, how to value a husband.

In psychotherapy it is frequently found that marital problems, often linked to frigidity and depression, can be traced back to the patient's father - the epitome of man - who had treated his wife unfairly. For a man, the reverse holds true: He will take the childhood expectations he had of his mother, and transfer them to other women. Since the other women won't necessarily be like his mother, this can lead to conflicts.

HOW COULD MY MOTHER GO AND MARRY MY FATHER?
My mother had neither the ability to love nor the ability to love my father. In general she turned away from men because of the way they acted sexually. There was nothing about my father that my mother failed to criticize. I've never understood how she could have married my father. I used to often suggest that she divorce him. But material things and her own pride, as far as relatives and acquaintances were concerned, kept her from taking that step. (31-year-old secretary, anxiety and fear of sex)

THE DIRTY OLD MAN
My mother was critical of my stepfather mostly because he was too fat, too dirty, and always smelled of sweat. Any time he approached her, whether it was just a kiss or little hug, she was overcome with a feeling of disgust. And when he did kiss her, she said it was a filthy thing to do, and as she said this, she'd wipe off her mouth with her hand. We lived in pretty cramped quarters,

so sometimes I could hear what went on at night. She didn't at all want him to come near her. She said he was a dirty old man with only one thing on his mind. She claimed he had also ruined her sister, because he just couldn't get enough of it. During the day she'd fuss and fume about all men. She said they just wanted one thing, regardless of whether the wife was sick or not. And if a woman was on her deathbed, the husband would think only of himself and even crawl into bed with her. (29-year-old housewife with aggression, stomach and intestinal problems, disinterest in sex)

The caricatures of love should not just be judged negatively. In the motivations that form the basis for a relationship there are always forces that remind one of this or that caricature of love. Love should not be kept in a platonic purity that is often confused with emotional sterility. If an inhibited woman marries a strong man as her protector, a man who is also successful and open to contact with others, this is not negative. We all compensate like this or in similar way. The real issue here is the willingness to work together to deal with threatening, acute conflicts. The woman in our example can continue to stay in her husband's shadow, living like a wallflower and specializing in things related to the couple's internal world, such as doing the laundry, keeping things tidy, and baking cakes. But through her contact with her husband she can learn the kinds of behavior that gave her so much trouble before she met him. She can learn the behaviors that were her reason for marrying him in the first place. In order to accomplish this, however, her husband must be patient and give her the time and space to develop in her own way.

I MANAGE MY TIME VERY CAREFULLY

My husband says I have no sense of time. Because of me we are often late when we are invited somewhere. I was not raised to be independent. I like to let my husband take the initiative in most things (just like I used to do with my father), and early in our marriage it was customary for him to take responsibility for almost everything. So now, I find I can hurry only if he's urging me on. He used to be a very domineering person, and I was to a certain extent just his pretty companion. (I also have the feeling he buys me pretty dresses just so he'll get the attention too.) When I have the feeling that I am pursuing my own interests independent of him, I manage my time very carefully and I am never late. (38-year-old patient with depression)

I DARED TO CONTRADICT MY HUSBAND

My husband won't allow anything lying around. Everything has to be in its place. But with two kids that's not always possible, so then there's trouble. Sunday morning he counted five things in the kitchen that I hadn't put away. For the first time, I turned around and told him to have a look at all the things he leaves lying around. And I told him he could just pick them up himself. He was speechless. It was the first time I had ever dared to contradict him.

Disorders and Conflicts
Jealousy; too high expectations; fear of being tied with a partner; separation anxiety; fear of freedom; self-recrimination; masochism; disappointment; escape into illness; substitute satisfaction; tendency to cling to others; reluctance to accept responsibilities; disinterest in sex.

Comment
A good partnership is not necessarily one where there seem to be no conflicts. A good partnership is marked by a willingness to work together when problems occur.

Antidote
Learn to distinguish between love and its caricatures.

LOOK AT THE WORLD AS AT A HUMAN BODY WHICH, ALTHOUGH CREATED PERFECT AND COMPLETE, HAS SUCCUMBED, FOR VARIOUS REASONS, TO SEVERE DISORDERS AND ILLNESSES. (Baha'u'llah)

LOSS OF UNITY

Misunderstanding: *Why does God allow this injustice?*
Conflicts and neuroses develop out of disharmonies in the necessary relationships between body, environment, and time. We define a neurosis as a disturbed relationship to reality and hence as a loss of unity. The conflict becomes a constant psychological burden. At first the body is not deprived of anything; something alien to the system is given to it.

MY HUSBAND, THE MOST PRIMITIVE MAN

Politeness is a very important thing to me. When my husband goes beyond what is considered polite, or when he uses rough language at home, he's the

177

Nossrat Peseschkian, M.D.

most primitive man as far as I'm concerned. And then I think to myself, you sure married something there. It takes a while before I get over it.

... THEN I JUST SEE RED

If my daughter doesn't clean up her room, I see red. All my attention is devoted to the mess around me; I can't see anything but it, and can't react rationally.

When the actual capabilities take on a strange form, this can be disturbing for a person, for it forces him to deal with unfamiliar actual capabilities. This calls his self-esteem into question: Can there be other attitudes about orderliness or other actual capabilities than the ones I learned, than the ones for which I am punished and rewarded, than the ones I've been successful with?

On what basis are we to understand this danger, this threat of loss of unity? Man can be viewed as a system in which various elements and components stand together in definite functions. If one component or functional relationship is disturbed, it affects the entire system.

We recognize the drive toward unity in the processes of defense, healing, and regeneration. This kind of tendency is found at all levels of existence, including numerous examples in the animal world. Heschler reports that a rain worm can reproduce its head, even after it has been cut off five times. Bonnet demonstrated that ringworms, when cut in two, become two completely new worms. Some grasshoppers can form a new leg to replace one they've lost. At the same time, this regeneration is combined with a forced growth.

Unity includes an organism's tendency to maintain itself. We clearly see this in normal development and self-preservation. Hunger points to a lack of nourishment, a condition in which the person also experiences in a mental sense. He starts to look for food, and with finding it he not only alleviates the deficiency, but also has a feeling of satisfaction. From this example from the physical domain we can clearly see why experiences as well as things not experienced can lead to mental and psychosomatic disorders.

What is experienced includes a person's confrontation with behavioral norms that seem particularly important to his partner. For example, some people might place of importance on how industrious a child is; a person might give the child a lot of tasks and keep him busy all the time. But this limits his ability to develop his fantasy and sense of play. It thus removes him from a source of experience necessary for his particular age. In this case the potential for conflict lies in what has not been experienced. In other cases it is precisely an experienced event that can cause conflict. Here we can mention traumatic experiences like mistreatment, sexual abuse of a child, accidents, or mutilation. But there can be other important experiences that are not so sudden: imbalances produced by the withdrawal of love; an excess of certain qualities of experience, for example scolding when things go wrong or when the child is messy, impolite, dishonest, or late.

Conflicts therefore are not a necessary part of development but the result of the confrontation between actual capabilities and the demands of the environment. The conflict situation can be regarded as *static*. A person is confronted by the norms of his partner; his actual capabilities do not meet his partner's requirements. But it is more appropriate to look at the situation in a *dynamic* way, viewing the behavioral patterns of both people as changeable. The behavior of the child is not the only thing that can change within the upbringing situation; the behavior of the other people involved can also be changed.

Then how do we interpret the discomfort that occurs when our own behavioral norms are suddenly confronted by unusual behavioral patterns in other people? A mother who places a lot of importance on cleanliness will not know how to deal with her child if the child does not respect her standards of cleanliness.

She can react in a number of different ways. She can try to use every means available to establish her concept of cleanliness, but there are risks involved. Either the child may become totally obedient, thereby losing some of his personal freedom. Or the child may become defiant, thereby destroying the basis for trust. However, this conflict between mother and child can also be looked up on as an opportunity. The mother examines her own behavior and that of her child, and realizes that she values cleanliness very highly, but that she is also impatient. Looking at it more closely: The child upsets the mother, causing her to feel insecure. But this enables her to recognize her loss of unity. This, in turn, offers her the opportunity to re-establish her sense of unity. By expanding and extending her differentiation, she will see the conflict with her child in a new light, and will deal with it appropriately A person brings his partner conflicts, difficulties, problems, and crises. But at the same time he brings the partner the opportunity to expand his or her own personality and to find appropriate solutions to the conflicts. Confrontation has validity in many other areas of interpersonal life: in the relationship between children and their parents, in the relationship between the parents themselves, in their relationships with their in-laws, and in their relationships with other people. It is a mistake to see only suffering in suffering, and only danger in a conflict. This mistaken view has unforeseen consequences for parenting and psychotherapy.

It is not enough to inquire into the «why» of a disorder, sorrow, or test. These problems remain a mystery if there is not also a question as to the «wherefore.» The question about the «wherefore» that is, the question of the purpose, means reintegration, the move toward unity and further development.

Disorders and Conflicts
Escape into loneliness; escape into activity; escape into illness; poor ability to make differentiations; one-sided criteria for a relationship to a partner; absolute standards and ideas about the world; sectarianism.

Comment
Illness and disorders, interpreted as the loss of unity, are not meaningless. They have their meaning in the fact that they help re-establish unity in the personality, or can help to develop the personality even further.

Antidote
Learn to distinguish between a crisis as a danger and a crisis as opportunity.

YOU MUSTN'T HATE A SICK PERSON BECAUSE HE IS SICK.
(Abdu'l-Baha)

HEALTH - SICKNESS

Misunderstanding: *I get furious when our child wakes us up in the middle of the night with his inconsiderate screaming.*

I CAN'T UNDERSTAND SUCH A BORING THING AS THAT
I already get upset in the morning when I go into the nursery to say good morning to my daughter and she doesn't even reply. I've scolded her for this

a number of times and said she was being unfriendly. Instead of taking her bath, she stands up in the tub and plays in the water, dances around, or watches every move I make in the kitchen. I have to tell her again and again to hurry up. If that doesn't work, I threaten to give her a spanking. I just don't understand such slow and boring behavior. When she's finally finished getting dressed at snail's pace, she dawdles the same way through breakfast. She chews and chews and stares out into space, without swallowing her food. Once she's done with all that she throws a tantrum, talking constantly the whole time. I'm really glad when she's finally off to kindergarten. When she's singing and making a lot of noise in her room I go tell her to be quiet or she'll wake up Mark or Dad. She says yes, but the minute I close the door she starts right up again. I feel then that she's blatantly defying me.

I could give lots of other examples. They are all really little things, but from morning to night they create a very tense atmosphere between us. Things have gotten so bad that every time I start to say something to her, my husband butts in right away and asks what's wrong. (32-year-old mother of two children)

For many parents the parenting situation is a battlefield that is littered with confrontations, provocations, disappointments, discouragement, insecurity, and hopelessness. These parents feel helpless in dealing with their children, and wonder how such behavior could ever get started in the first place. They appeal to the child's goodwill: «Be nice, be good, be neat, don't always interrupt,» etc., and are baffled by the fact that these appeals don't do any good. In reality the child's misbehavior, as in the above example, cannot be traced back to good or bad intentions. It represents a disorder that the child cannot intentionally affect unless something else is done.

In our society it is common to consult a doctor even in the case of relatively minor symptoms. If a child has a stomachache, fever, an infection, or a headache, it is assumed that he is sick and needs special attention. But if a child does poorly in school, is cheeky and disorderly, displays a lot of incomprehensible defiance, and doesn't keep himself clean, his parent's react mostly with resistance and dislike. To some extent a physical illness is considered an extraterritorial area where the demands of socialization no longer completely apply. A behavioral disorder, however, creates a very sharp reaction. Almost immediately some form of punishment is administered. But the «educator» himself is not really certain that the other person's unusual behavior has a special character to it.

The automatic connection *behavioral disorder - punishment,* stemming from the belief that everything is a matter of will, overlooks other alternatives. It sees only the deed itself. It judges only the individual behavior, without knowing of the dynamic conditions that gave rise to it.

In the example of the child who was slow in getting dressed, eating breakfast, etc., there is a complex network of conditions behind the child's disorderliness, messiness, impoliteness, and disobedience. Several factors played a role in the dynamic interaction within the family. The girl was a stepdaughter who did not feel completely accepted by her stepmother. Before her marriage the stepmother had found out she couldn't have any children and for this reason had insisted that the child be part of the family. Two years later, as if to spite the medical diagnosis, the woman became pregnant. Now she was busy with her own baby almost all the time and regarded her stepdaughter as a necessary evil. This is the situation that led to the girl's behavioral disorders. It was her way of saying, «Pay some attention to me.» In her action we find a certain resignation. The mother did not understand the behavioral disorders. The critical relationship between mother and daughter came more and more to a head. In each instance the mother reacted automatically, showing her dislike and scolding and punishing the child. The girl, in turn, saw this as a form of attention, and for her this kind of attention was better than being ignored.

It is expected that a child with behavioral disorders will be able to learn to act differently, and, in no time at all: «The child must develop this behavior on his own.» We know ourselves how hard it can be to solve problems between adults. It must be all the harder for a child to express his problems and to awaken some understanding of them. The adult must therefore ask about the reason, not to find an excuse, but in order to understand. In many cases the child's behavioral disorder is not a character disorder, but simply a reaction to his environment: *It is normal to act abnormally in an abnormal situation.*

A physically ill person has an advantage over someone who is neurotic, has behavioral disorders, and reacts in a resigned manner: In the case of the physically ill person, other people have some understanding of it and know to whom they can turn to. But a behavioral disorder is tainted by the belief that it is somehow improper, indecent; in other words, it's something that simply should not be. It seems to be a kind of punishment. It causes the uncomfortable feeling that one is dealing with someone who's kind of crazy, an asocial person or someone with mental illness. For this reason a person is reluctant to go to a therapist, a doctor who treats idiots, a doctor who uses straitjackets and padded cells.

Disorders and conflicts

Too many demands; too few demands; jealousy; envy; rejection; disappointment; experiences of failure; aggressiveness; forcing others to pay attention; self-recrimination; hopelessness; despair; bad moods.

Comment

There are no bad people. Some people can't help, but do what they do, because they haven't learned any other way. They must be led and taught, even if this process is harder than simply uttering the judgement that they are bad, stupid, evil, and rotten.

Even if a person with behavioral disorders is not a sick person in the sense of classical medicine, he is not a criminal over whom the rod should be broken. He needs the same understanding as is shown to a sick person.

Antidote

Learn to distinguish between a normal and an abnormal situation.

NOTHING PREVENTS US FROM IDENTIFYING THE WORLD ORDER OF NATURAL SCIENCE WITH THE GOD OF RELIGIONS. (Max Planck)

FAITH - RELIGION - CHURCH

Misunderstanding: *When I envision God, I always see my father.*

Now, probably more than at any other time in recent history, many scientists from diverse fields - physicists, chemists, physicians, sociologists, psychologists, and anthropologists - have adopted a positive position regarding the significance of religion within society. But there has also never been another time when theologists, almost irrespective of their particular direction, have consciously or unconsciously tried to give religion a bad name and accuse it of being meaningless.

Nossrat Peseschkian, M.D.

It is an interesting phenomenon of our time that many people are unable to find meaning in anything. In earlier times the burning question was «Where from?» Today that question has been replaced by «What for?» a question that is posed in all realms of life. In therapeutic practice this problem is reflected in the question of the meaning and meaninglessness of religion.

It has been shown that there are many misconceptions about the word religion. The concepts «religion» and «faith» lead to emotional resistance and intellectual renunciation. One hardly dares even speak of religion at all, and then only in a castigating sense. This phenomenon also occurs in psychotherapy. It used to be that sex and sexuality were taboos. Today it's religion. In connection with a series of mental disorders we find conflicts that deal with religion in the broad sense of the term.

In psychotherapy there are three attitudes that occur as basic conflict, and in respect of religion these attitudes give rise to the following three types:

The Mummified Type
He identifies with learned religious norms and depictions of faith and dogmas to such an extent that he avoids necessary changes and updates. He reacts in an aggressive way; he defends himself by attacking or

184

withdrawing in order to evade a disquieting temptation. Since faith has often taken the place of awareness and knowledge, since there is thus only semi-knowledge, one can refer to him as a *bigoted* type rather than a mummified type. (He makes assertions, but without knowing.) Bigoted people are tragic figures because they always avoid putting themselves in a position where they would have to face the fact that they are clinging to a prejudice.

I NEED THE POMP AND CIRCUMSTANCE OF THE CANDLES

My religious attitude is expressed by the fact that I go to church with my family at Christmas because I need the festiveness of the candles in order to really get into the Christmas mood. I become very emotional and find that I can once again pray fervently. (29-year-old secretary)

THE TRUE CHILD OF GOD

I can still remember today how my pious aunt drummed it into my head not to smile when my picture was taken for first communion. She said that smiling would be too vain and proud. As a true child of God I could only have an inner joy. I was told a lot of things like this. It was often very hard for me to be a good and devout child. (31-year-old translator, unmarried)

The Revolutionary Type

He has come to the realization that the prevailing religious norms do not meet the demands of the times. Since outdated norms tend to repress the individual, people of the revolutionary type tend to repudiate these norms. They set forth to overthrow them and often end up putting the cart before the horse. Depending on the individual's personality, a person in this category will react with intellectual resistance, in the extreme social forms of active manipulation of others, for instance militant violence, or in the form of passive self-manipulation, for instance the use of drugs.

RELIGION IS SOMETHING FOR OLD PEOPLE

Religion is for old grandmas and people who can find nothing in our contemporary world. Whoever clings to the life raft of religion will drown anyway. Relying on religious faith is like jumping headfirst into a swimming pool and not knowing whether there's really water in it. If a guy wants to bust his skull that way, let him, but not me. We create our own heaven and hell right here on earth, and there's no place for God except in the narrow minds of religious fanatics. Religion throws a veil over the actual conditions in society and keeps people from doing what is necessary. (28-year-old student of sociology)

The Indifferent Type

He is usually characterized by a shift in responsibility. On the one hand he wants to change traditional religious contents, or those that are in need of improvement. He sets himself to this task, but on the other hand is unable to separate himself from certain religious traditions he has acquired.

This group includes people who are basically interested but uncommitted. They may be open to changes in religion, but do not follow them through. If they make a decision in a particular direction they soon reveal themselves to be unstable. They change their minds less because of actual necessity than because of the authority of the rest of the social environment. As soon as someone says, «How could you hurt your parents by giving up your old religion?» they begin to waver. The indifferent type of person is marked by a weakness in making distinctions between what is essential and what is nonessential in a religion. He sees the errors of individual members of the religion and attributes them to the entire body. For him religion is an obligation of his upbringing, but he is unable to really identify with it.

LET THE OTHERS BE HAPPY WITH IT

Without a doubt people have soured religion for me, because I simply can't stand that sort of person. I find that they are too hypocritical. It bothers me when they act so well, but you can plainly see that they do it in word only, they don't practice what they preach. I'm turned off by people who want to embody the church. Let them be happy with it if they want, but not me. I deal with religion by myself, and I have better results. (35-year-old employee)

It seems that the misunderstanding of religion is not really a religious weakness, modern man's inability to believe. The problem seems to be one of being unable to differentiate between faith, religion, and church.

Faith
Religious faith means essentially a spiritual relationship to what is unknown and cannot be recognized. Since the creator (God, Allah, Jehovah, the Original Being & the Totality, the Primal Energy) is by His very nature incomprehensible, there must be faith in order to enter into a relationship with Him. Faith is one of the human capabilities.

Religion
Since man has a particular attitude about the unknown, he has always turned to the founders of the religions and world views. As communal faith, religion is a cultural phenomenon closely linked with the development of history. The form in which the truth of the faith reveals itself depends on the particular developmental level, the needs, and the comprehension of the people in a particular historical situation. The religion the person adopts is largely dependent on his mentors and the prevailing tradition. The child believes the contents that are transmitted to him.

The one part of religion is spiritual, transcendent, and essential *(first level* religion). It can exist independent of the development, since, as the truth of belief, it deals with the essence of being. The second part of religion *(second level* religion) consists of temporal values and social norms. These change according to the socio-cultural development. Included here are the commandments and prohibitions of the individual religions.

Church
The church is the institution of religion, its organizational form and administration. This term covers all forms of religious or philosophical institution. When it comes to religion, the church tends to be something obvious, requiring no explanation. It deals with the first and second level religions much like the skin, pulp, and core of a fruit. If the influence of time and history is not given consideration in the religion, first and

second level religions can easily be confused with each other, thereby distorting the relationship of faith - religion - church: The skin and the core are not differentiated. The religious externals that are influenced by time, the rituals and dogmas - the skin - are put in the foreground while the actual religious contents - the core - are put aside. This produces a shift in form and content: a misunderstanding.

This misunderstanding seems to underlie the three types of reaction described above. It doesn't simply affect the individual and personal attitudes about religion, but can also become the source of conflicts.

I WAS AFRAID OF BEING SINFUL AND GUILTY

For me God was not a loving God, but a God I had to be afraid of. I was always afraid of being sinful and guilty. Because of this, when I went to confession, I was afraid I'd forget some of my sins and end up receiving communion in a sinful state. So I'd make up sins to confess, especially ones having to do with sex. But I felt guilty and decided to do penance and be good. Everywhere I went I was plagued by the thought that I could give myself over to the devil. (32-year-old engineer with anxiety conditions, depression, compulsive ideas, and sexual disorders)

I MAKE A MARK FOR EVERY SELF-DENIAL

Back then I made all sorts of sacrifices to be pleasing to God. Here's an example: To get to school I had to ride a bike into the next village. I made a trip four times a day. But in the dead of winter I would make the trip without wearing gloves. This was my sacrifice: I froze for God. On a card that I kept only for this purpose, I would make a mark for every self-denial. (31-year-old female patient, unmarried, with sexual disorders and anxiety conditions)

WHENEVER I ENVISIONED GOD, I ALWAYS SAW MY FATHER

If I can make a comparison - church, family, home - I should say that the church embodies on a large scale what my father embodies in the family. A power of command built on love, which gave the children some instruction, and now and then a little freedom or fun within its bounds, accompanied by the words: What lucky kids you are! (32-year-old single teacher, with sexual disorders and inhibitions)

The parental model plays a decisive role in the formation of this attitude. They give their stamp to what later becomes a basic conflict and makes the person susceptible to conflicts of a definite type. In the above case the patient didn't just confuse faith, religion, and church. The shift had established itself and had crept into the key experiences via the style of upbringing.

Religion is like a medicine that works in accordance with the nature of the person. It can be meaningful only if it takes into consideration the demands, needs, and requirements of the individual, development (the principle of time), relatively, and unity. If a falsely understood religion leads to disorders, fixations, inhibitions in development, rigidity, or intellectual resistance, it must be nonsense: It is in this sense that Feuerbach called it pathology instead of theology, Marx and Engels spoke of the opiate of the masses, and Freud created the caricature of the insurance agency.

In earlier times science was the opponent of religion, but today this view has changed considerably. In the same way that photography had a liberating effect of painting, so our scientific progress, at least in terms of possibilities, has freed the spirit. Religion and science no longer represent insurmountable opposites. In view of the de-humanizing threat of technology today, it is imperative that they work together.

On the basis of the psychological material at hand, it is not the therapist's task to try to reconcile the patient with his religion or faith, or to divert him from his beliefs. Rather, he should help him make distinctions. Ability to differentiate will allow a person to find his own way.

Disorders and Conflicts
Religious fanaticism; superstition; resistance maneuvers; illusions; fixation; bigotry; anxiety; aggression; resignation; escape into externals; escape into a substitute religion; overestimation of oneself; escape into work; unshakeable convictions which have no basis; sadness; feeling of having been abandoned; feeling of annihilation; mistrust; lack-of involvement in life; distance from reality; dissolution of social ties; withdrawal into one's own inner life; great interest in metaphysical

questions remote from reality; decline in achievement; feeling of inner emptiness and dying away; anxiety feelings; fears of becoming mentally ill; depression; irritability.

Comment

Every person has the ability to believe. Faith is basically the relationship to the unknown and unrecognizable. Faith therefore comprises more than simply religious questions and the question of life after death. It also touches on the questions of private life and science.

Religion addresses man's basic capabilities. His upbringing and the traditions surrounding it usually determine which religion he will adhere to. His relationship to religion is largely dependent on his experiences with his parents and his social environment. Religion is a cultural phenomenon closely linked to the development of history. Church is the institution of religion, an instrument that has often made itself autonomous. Distinctions must be made between faith, religion, and church, and between first and second level religion. The task of religion is to represent values, purpose, and meaning. Science, on the other hand, searches for explanations, establishes logical connections, and finds new meanings. To be beneficial to man, religion and knowledge should compliment each other and form a unity. Religion does not replace psychotherapy, and psychotherapy is not a substitute for religion.

Antidote

Learn to differentiate between faith, religion, and church.

ALTHOUGH EVERYONE IS FATED TO DIE AT SOME TIME, DON'T PUT YOUR HEAD IN THE LION'S MOUTH. (Saadi)

CONDITIONAL AND DETERMINED FATE

Misunderstanding: *What of it, we all have to die sometime.*

Upbringing must not be viewed simply in terms of the normal psychological development and as a way to correct acquired behaviors. People often overlook the obvious fact that upbringing offers the opportunity to influence, positively or negatively, how the so-called inborn defects affect the life of the individual.

HE CAN'T BE ANY DIFFERENT

A 17 year old, the son of an official in the postal department, had suffered brain damage at birth. He wasn't able to walk or talk as early as other children. The parents were particularly aware of this delay when they had a lively and normally developed little daughter with whom they could compare the boy's development. The boy was slightly spastic when he walked, and was slow in both physical and mental development. The parents paid careful attention to his uniqueness. They bathed and dressed him and led him here and there. In the sense of basic primary care they spared him every difficulty. This kind of attention went on until his treatment began. Because of his birth defects this young man, now 17 years old, was treated like a 3 year old. His parents justified it by saying, «He can't be any other way.»

In the therapeutic situation the parents and the adolescent worked through the situation step by step. The crucial matter was to be able to distinguish what the boy could actually do and what he couldn't. The demands placed on the boy had to be neither too great nor too small. It was important that they help the boy develop his potential by giving him appropriate tasks, but first his potential had to be recognized. Already in the first ten weeks the boy was able to put on the simpler pieces of clothing, tie his shoes and eat with a spoon and fork. The change of attitudes associated with this was actually harder for the parents than for the boy. Eventually the boy progressed so far that he was able to begin working in a sheltered workshop. The «prescription» for the parents was: *Don't help your son with activities that you think he can handle on his own. Wait till he does it himself, even if he does it wrong. Only in this way can he learn step by step to be independent.*

Helen Keller is a famous historical example of the potential that can exist despite born defects. Through the patience of her teacher, the deaf, dumb, and blind girl grew from a helpless, animal-like creature into a highly differentiated, admirable personality. In her were seen not just the handicaps which would have created an almost hopeless picture; her hidden potential, which existed despite her handicaps, was also recognized. To replace sight, hearing, and speech, she came forth with strong sense of touch and expressiveness through her hands and with her face.

There are two things one can do to intervene in the case of so-called congenital handicaps: One can try to change the condition itself, for instance through an operation, medication, or physical therapy. Or one can summon other capabilities. Through patience and a consistent attitude a handicapped child, even one with severe disorders can develop many social areas such as orderliness, cleanliness, politeness, creative abilities, and the ability to achieve.

DOES MY DAUGHTER HAVE NERVE DAMAGE?

Irene is driving me up the wall. She doesn't pay attention in school and recently has been bringing home bad grades. She doesn't even listen to me sometimes, either. When I tell her to tidy up her room, it just goes in one ear and out the other. And when we have company she just sits in the corner, stares into space and acts as if the guests weren't even there. Sometimes at night she wakes up screaming, and is bathed in sweat afterwards. After this description the mother posed this anxious and expectant question: *Does my daughter have nerve damage? Can't you examine her for that once?*

Cases like this occur every day. Parents ask: *is our child mentally ill, does he have a split personality, because sometimes he gives away everything and tells such strange stories, is disobedient and untidy. Is that inborn in him?* Behind such questions there is usually hidden a disturbed interaction, distorted awareness of one's self and others. In the consultation, which addresses the problem of difficult and occasionally inborn defects, people involuntarily get to talking about a problem that concerns everyone, particularly the mentor and the child: *...I was convinced that I had to pay for the sins of my parents and the wrongdoings of my ancestors.* Examples like this clearly illustrate the importance of the misunderstanding inheritance - upbringing. Ideas of this sort are closely connected to two questions related to hope and despair in the upbringing. *What cannot be changed, what must one learn to bear?* And *what can one influence, correct, treat?* These questions are aimed at the *determined* and the *conditional fate.* Determined fate is that which is unavoidable: Every person is born and dies; there's no getting around it. One faces the question of the essence of birth and death just like one faces the questions of whether there is life after death, what the origin and purpose of all existence is, what the essence of the creator is, and what the purpose of suffering is. Every individual, without exception, must face these questions.

Conditional fate, however, is fate that has its own history, would have been avoidable, and was or is open to change. The relationship between conditional and determined fate can be shown in this example: For a candle, the determined fate is that its wax burns and is consumed. Its eventual extinguishment is thus a destiny that cannot be changed or modified. But the conditional fate can be compared to the following process: While the candle is still high enough, a gust of wind comes and extinguishes it. This is a conditional fate, for there would have been a lot of ways to prevent the candle from going out.

Except for the problems mentioned in the questions of the determined fate, all events are under the category of conditional fate. This means: Through proper upbringing one can raise the child for a happy life. If because of some influences this is not the case, if disorders or undesired developments occur, one can affect their course if the problems are recognized in time. One can bring about an improvement or a healing. Other disorders, however, which are also conditioned by certain events, cannot be taken care of by science in its current state. In such a situation, it is a question of accepting the disorder and adopting a positive attitude to it. This can make it possible for the person to at least develop his other capabilities.

A child had lost the sight of his left eye in a car accident. From a medical standpoint the child's sight could not be restored. This was a fact that the child would somehow have to come to terms with. The interesting thing in this case is that the child made a good adjustment and developed with relatively few conflicts. The mother, however, who had been driving the car, never did get over it.

The experiences of the past belong to a fate that cannot be changed. What has happened cannot be undone. But a person can influence the attitude he takes to that event. In the same sense the determined fate cannot be averted, but our relationship to it can be changed. These attitudes will determine whether our perspective for the tasks at hand will be differentiated or limited. Which attitudes are chosen, and which are repeatedly preferred, is itself a conditional fate which depends to some extent on the type and form of the upbringing.

Confusion of «conditional» and «determined» fate is significant not only for the person's attitude toward the child. It is also found in the person's attitude toward himself: *I'm just unlucky. That's my fate. It's always been like that, and always will be.* The assertion becomes subjective. The person involved identifies with specific qualities and output potentials and does not see beyond them to become aware of other possibilities.

The statement «I'm just unlucky» is basically a lot different than «I had bad luck.» The latter statement refers to single events, which are not confused and intertwined with the personality itself.

I had an accident, and after that just one accident after another. I'm just an unlucky guy. For a long time people gave me large amounts of suppressive drugs. I thought I was a slow learner.

Before tests and exams in my profession I always said to myself, «You won't make it!» And I always did fail.

Others have things easier than I do, for instance with women. It's hard for me to make contact. No one talks to me. My mother was very phlegmatic and I got it from her. You can't change that. There's nothing you can do about it. What have I accomplished up to now? I look around me: the one guy built a house, the other has a nice wife and I don't have anything.

Disorders and Conflicts

Excessive optimism; bitter passivity; resignation; fear of failure; fear of disappointment; dissatisfaction; existential anxiety; self-recrimination; lack of self confidence; interpersonal conflicts; mental anguish; «a failure.»

Comment

The conditional fate presents a path that a person can choose, but doesn't have to. We've already mentioned a particular form of the conditional fate: the fate that is conditioned by the past. Events of the past are over with and cannot be undone. But a person can have an impact on the current results of the past events: the past can be viewed as a mirror for the future. A mother is doing little to help her child if she simply complains constantly that she didn't have enough time for him. In fact, her guilt feelings are more likely to do more harm than good. It is more important to ask the question: What can I learn from the past? How can I meet the demands of the present? There are alternatives that one can come at any time. This is saying nothing other than that a person's fate lies to a great extent in his own hands; in childhood it lies mostly in the hands of the parents and mentors.

Antidote

Learn to distinguish between being unlucky and having bad luck.

THE COWARD DIES MANY TIMES BEFORE HIS DEATH. THE BRAVE TASTE OF DEATH BUT ONCE. (Shakespeare)

DEATH

Misunderstanding: *The rest is silence*
In our lives we face death not just once, but in many forms and with various degrees of participation. Death as an event belongs to our everyday life. Every minute a lot of people die without it deeply touching us or even arousing our sympathy.

«Everything that science teaches me - and doesn't stop teaching me - confirms my belief in the continuation of our spiritual existence in life after death. Nothing disappears without leaving a trace, and death is only a transformation.» (Quote from a speech by W. von Braun at a meeting of the Nobel prize winners in Lindau, 1971)

The Attitude Toward the Death of Other People
The meaning of death usually first becomes conscious for us when someone dies who we knew and with whom we had some kind of emotional ties. The experience of the death of another person then becomes an outburst of experience.

A big difference exists between a person with whom one has emotional links, and a person who does not mean anything to one, and this difference is most noticeable when there is an accident. One automatically thinks, «I hope it was someone else, hopefully not my family or friends». The degree of emotional involvement depends on how well we know someone, what experiences we had shared, what he meant to us, and what the consequences of his death will be. A person can become precious and dear to us if we miss him, although we hardly missed him while he was alive. Despite the unspoken agreement that we should say only good things about the departed, we value the death of a person according to his accomplishments, in other words, according to the impressions he had made on us. A 55-year-old mother gives this description of her 19-year-old daughter who died. Here is an excerpt:

I never had to keep after her to do her homework. Not at all like her older sister, who did her work only when she felt like it. H. lent me a hand with everything. I didn't even have to ask her. For instance, before she'd go out with her boyfriend in the evening she'd help me wash and dry the dishes. By the way, I find it impossible to imagine that he's already met another girl and even got engaged. I had cooked and taken care of the two of them for months. For me orderliness is a very important thing. My father used to always say, «Learn to be neat, and practice it. Being neat saves you a lot of time and trouble.» In that respect H. was really a model for the others. When I see how my youngest boy keeps his room, I go through the ceiling. She was always sweet and friendly, never said an ugly word. I can't stand how my husband is so blunt sometimes. After all, you have to get along with people and learn to swallow some things. Our family is my one and all. H. felt very comfortable at home; and with her boyfriend it was the same. He liked being here with us. The oldest girl was a lot different. She just had to get out of the house. By the time she was 18, 19 years old she was usually gone in the evening and on the weekend.

We involuntarily weigh the qualities that we experienced in the other person. We measure whether their death was fair or not, whether they deserved it, or whether they should have lived longer. We use the actual capabilities as our standards:

You just couldn't trust him. Every other word was a lie. He was a fraud. We can be happy that he can't cause us any more sorrow.

He was a splendid person. You could always turn to him. He always had time for you and tried to do you justice. With his loss we'll have a lot to bear. For him I hope there is a paradise.

This old bum. He was a sly one, always trying to win your confidence, but he always took sides and was always looking out only for himself. He was concerned only with his own success, and now he can just bum in hell. And that's not to mention how stingy he was. But I won't treat him shabbily. I'm buying a big funeral bouquet out of pure sympathy.

These examples were all collected after the death of one man, and are the spontaneous statements of people who knew him. They clearly show that different attitudes about a person, based on the actual capabilities, influence the attitudes about his death. People often come to say that death was a blessing for someone. They usually say this in reference to situations where a person was suffering from a severe physical illness, or if his inner and outer conflicts produced such a great amount of suffering that even other people in his environment sensed it and understood it.

Age, too, causes death to be seen in a gentle light: *After I saw him for the last time I knew that death was a blessing for him.* Here death appears as the natural and desired result of a series of events. It seems to be the best alternative for the dying person and for the people around him. In such cases the perspective for the future is limited for all people involved. Sooner or later it has to happen.

But when people have long-range expectations of a person, either because of his young age, his responsibilities, or his personality, his death brings a strong sense of disappointment. Even if it wasn't his fault, the departed, after all, did not live up to people's expectations of him:

We wanted to take on so many things, and now he's dead. She died too young.

I'd have wanted to see him get married and have children. Now it's too late. He was at the height of his success when he got sick and died.

As we can see, a person's preparation for the death of another person plays an important role in the way he processes his experiences. If we expect a person to die soon, and he does die, this event is not as shocking to us as when a person is suddenly taken away from us. In our thoughts we play out the event in all its details. In our minds we become used to the possibility and are thus not so susceptible to the effect of a surprise. This is much like the case where a child is prepared for the absence of his mother: people play the game of «Mommy in the hospital» and thus make the event more comprehensible or at least more perceivable for the child. The loss of a person we were close to automatically evokes the feeling of sadness. The separation from a person must somehow be processed. Psychoanalysis speaks pointedly of the mourning work that must be done. If one accepts the fact that the death actualizes the early childhood fears of separation and abandonment, the emotional, affective basis for the mourning becomes comprehensible.

This type of mourning reaction affects nearly everyone in a certain situation. If the term «normal» were not suspect, one could speak here of a normal mourning reaction. If the mourning goes beyond a certain period of time, which, in our culture, is identical to the year of mourning, or if the mourning takes on such significance that it is detrimental to the personality or health of the mourner, we refer to it as an abnormal mourning reaction.

I suffer from depression more and more. I shy away from people and have few friends. For nights on end I don't sleep. I've become very unsure of myself around people and tell myself that I'm really no longer at one with them. I've been suffering from all this since my mother died two years ago. I have the feeling that my depression is simply sadness and emptiness inside. Everything seems so meaningless to me. (34-year-old mother of two, with abnormal mourning reaction)

The abnormal mourning reaction can come immediately after the death of a loved one, but it can also first occur a long time afterward, long after the death has lost its importance for other people. An excessive reaction to the death of a loved one is usually more than the socially expected demonstration of love and concern. Rather, the person himself is faced with the problem of breaking away, a problem which seems to overwhelm him, a problem which is greater than he can bear.

This situation can stem, from various sources:

- Frequently the deceased person had a special importance for the person he left behind. He wasn't just an ordinary person, but a confidant, protector, or one who took responsibility, or, on the other hand, one who needed protection, or needed to depend on others. His importance is measured by his actual capabilities. It is especially hard for us to deal with his loss if we identified with him in various areas or projected our own expectations onto him. In such a case a part of us dies with him.

- The loss of a person close to us often requires us to make considerable adjustments in our own lives. If, for instance, a person was able to share his concerns with his spouse, and to thus relieve himself of some of the burdens, he bears sole responsibility and faces all the problems by himself after his spouse dies.
  How can I take care of the two kids all by myself?
  How can I face life alone?

- Things we used to love to do suddenly become meaningless when we lose our partner. It is precisely these everyday customs that confront us with the emptiness of our new situation. Instead of the certain reactions we could expect from our partner, there is nothing.

Society gives mourners a special role. Dressed in black, they are pitied by others and are subject to a great many limitations. The person in mourning is expected to refrain from certain pleasures and must show his loyalty to the deceased. Related to this is the unspoken command that a widow or widower refrain from sexual activity during the mourning period. Even though this limitation may be in harmony with the mourner's inner needs at the beginning of the mourning period, there often arise guilt feelings, aggression, anxiety, and internal and external conflicts.

- The social and religious norms for mourning behavior can encourage or inhibit the mourning process. In certain religions and societies it is desirable or expected that a person will bear his grief as composedly as possible. Since the forms of public mourning are thus curtailed, the inner processing of one's grief is intensified. This attitude favors the development of a delayed mourning reaction. On the other hand there are mourning rituals that produce excessive outbreaks of grief. The mourner may beat himself with his fists, pull at his hair, accuse God and man, or wail at the deathbed of the deceased, backed up by hired wailing women. The giving of flowers fulfills a similar function. These donations serve as a sacrifice to the dead, a sign of gratitude or indebtedness.

Psychotherapy finds that guilt feelings are at work in the development of abnormal grieving reactions. This guilt covers a wide range - from the feeling that a person caused the other person's death, and didn't help him enough, to the idea that one was not nice enough to the deceased and perhaps even once in a while wished that he were dead. This is a reflection of the conflicts that had gone on between the two people. These burdensome guilt feelings can either be worked out step by step, or they can be suppressed. A part of this suppression process is what psychoanalysis calls idealization: The departed is raised far above the conflicts they had had. The departed, who had made mistakes, becomes the best, the purest, the most perfect man; this image grows, because one thinks one could not deal with the conflicts if they were to be admitted openly. And acknowledging the departed's shortcomings would be a reminder of those conflicts. Idealization creates a chasm in terms of other people with whom we can make comparisons. In the eyes of a grieving mother, the siblings can never be as good as their dead sister. In many cases, the outspoken comparison with the deceased, and the attempt to outdo him in terms of good qualities are viewed negatively. They are considered a disparagement, an abasement of the deceased. We thus see that there is a close link between idealization of the one partner and under-evaluation of another.

In an abnormal mourning reaction the survivor tries not to acknowledge the death of the departed, or tries to overplay or annul it. While the normal mourning reaction ends after a certain amount of time, the abnormal reaction continues of its own energy until the point of exhaustion.

Treatment depends on the particular case. Medication and measures such as sleep therapy and treatment at spas have been shown to be particularly effective where the mourning work was hampered primarily by physical and mental exhaustion. In other instances, however, such physical measures accomplish little. Meditation or a stay at a health spa then have only limited success; afterwards, the patient falls right back into his anxieties and depression. This can be the starting point for psychotherapeutic treatment aimed at strengthening the patient's ability to make differentiations. In this way we make it possible for the patient to work through the conflict situation and to recognize the conditions and opportunities of the unavoidable event he has experienced. The opportunity hidden in death can best be illustrated with an example:

AT LONG LAST HER OWN FREE PERSON

A twenty-six-year-old woman had gotten married at the age of eighteen, right after she finished school. As the only daughter she had been very sheltered at home, very dependent on her parents. When she got married she switched her dependency from her parents to her new husband. Twelve years older than she, the husband took care of everything that concerned the social aspects of the marriage. The young woman had to do nothing but conform to her husband. But when he suddenly died in a traffic accident the wife had to confront herself. She now noticed that she had no interests of her own, that she had spent her time the way her husband had, and that she was now living as a mere shadow of her departed husband. As she said, life no longer had any meaning for her.

After a suicide attempt she started therapy, and there, under the guidance of the therapist, she learned to create her own plan for living. She went back to school and, as she put it, finally became *her own free person.* She came to realize that she could carry on her husband's mission in her very own way. This realization was a comfort in which made it easier for her to deal with her grief and with the guilt feelings she had had for wanting to assert herself.

The Attitude Toward One's Own Death

We soon run into barricades when we think about our own death. To understand the process of death we must rely on the testimony of people who are dying; the situation after death is something that evades our attempts to imagine it. Death is a part of man's determined fate, but each person's attitude to it is different. In addition, a person's attitude changes with age.

Many people avoid being touched by death. They want to ban this fearful event from their consciousness and from their experience.

Why should I concern myself with such things? I'm still young and have my whole life ahead of me. I just want to enjoy it while I can. We've got money, a nice house, good friends, and a car. What more do I want? (28-year-old employee)

Others, particularly those with child-like, naïve attitudes, view their life as a «passageway,» as a «waiting room,» and their death as the «gateway to life.» For them, death offers a profound consolation, although they often seem to be standing somewhat apart from life.

THIS LIFE IS NOT EVERYTHING

Despite all the blows that fate has dealt me, I'm still very humble, just going along in my own way. My life isn't everything, and death is not the end. What life has denied me here, I'll be given in the life after death. (68- year-old widow)

THANK GOODNESS IT'S NOT ALL OVER WHEN WE DIE

My daughter is like a tyrant. If I cook cauliflower, after she asked for it, she later says, «No, I don't like that now, I want to eat noodles.» Then I fix that for her, and in spite of that she doesn't come home when she's supposed to. She comes when she feels like it, and by then the noodles are cold. Then she throws a fit. I always have to force her to take a bath. She doesn't get an allowance anymore, because she always blew it on candy. She'll just have to learn to do without. And then she's always asking for a new dress. I don't think much of that junk that is fashionable today. I have very different attitudes about things. Yesterday I went out and got my hair cut because I was at my wits end with that girl. Patti is so messy and cheeky. Since my husband died I just don't enjoy life any more. Thank goodness it's not over with when we die. Just knowing that there's something more helps me put up with all these problems with my daughter. And maybe I'll earn a bit higher place in heaven if I'm good here in spite of everything. I do try to be nice to everybody. (36-year-old mother of 9-year-old daughter. Mother has depression and anxiety conditions.)

Others see death as the final blow. Fearing it, they live by the motto: Take what you can get, without thinking about losses. Today is the only thing that counts.

EVERYONE IS HIS OWN BEST FRIEND
Precisely because I know that death is the end of it all, I really try to enjoy my life. Everybody is his own best friend. I'm not at all interested in this

gobbledygook about «the meaning of life and death.» I'd rather spend my time on other things. I know I'm self-centered, but other people elbow their way around, too. (38-year-old manager whose son was in therapy because of problems in school and conspicuous behavior)

Still others see death as the ultimate end, but they still live their lives intensely and with ethical motivations.

I CHANGE FROM DAY TO DAY

My life has meaning because I change from day to day and I can directly follow how I am developing. Sure, I backslide once in a while and fall into my old narrow achievement acrobatics again. But I also have friends, am interested in politics and aid to the developing countries, and get a lot of satisfaction from the arts. (43-year-old female teacher)

We can call the death wish a special attitude toward death. The death wish can occur as an aggressive thought directed against other people. «If only you'd never been born.» «If only that old geezer would finally kick the bucket.» We often find this attitude in the background of people who feel guilty about the death of the person they disliked and then develop a severe mourning reaction. The death wish directed against one's self is, as a rule, something of an escape reaction. The motive behind it is frequently the desire to draw attention to a particular situation in one's life, or to punish someone for his lack of attention, his messiness, tardiness, and unreliability.

SINCE YOU DON'T LOVE ME, I'M GOING TO DIE

A 46-year-old woman was found in a wooded area. She had been unconscious for a long period of time. Next to her was a bottle of cognac and several containers of sleeping pills. Her eyes were crawling with ants. The woman was able to be revived and treated medically. In the first discussion she said she had wanted to kill herself because her boyfriend had left her. Life no longer had any meaning for her, and she wanted her boyfriend to feel guilty.

Fear of death is certainly a normal thing, but, as we have seen in various instances, it is not an inevitable reaction, nor does it have to occur in its most severe form.

Fear of death is not simply the fear of the concrete event of death. It can occur independent of death, as, for instance, at night or in the event of an imagined heart attack. In this sense it is correct to say that man dies several deaths.

What does the fear of death actually refer to? As a relatively incomprehensible event, death is often the object of the fear only in a remote sense.

Fear of Death and the Body

The idea that death is associated with pain, or the experience of the death situation itself can be disturbing. The extent of the anxiety or discomfort is closely linked to the person's ideas about his body and its pains, and thus, in a broader sense, to his upbringing. If someone has learned to pay attention to the slightest pain, and to associate it with illness, he will be more likely to be afraid of death.

I'M VERY AFRAID OF DYING

As in the case of severe illness, operations, etc., I am also afraid of death, and I think a lot about how I will act when my last hour is finally here. Even though I've sometimes wished it were all over with – especially when things are going bad for me – I really don't want to die, because, as I said, I am afraid of death. This is probably the reason why I'm very fearful of being sick.

Maybe I run to the doctor too often to get rid of little problems, and maybe I just check myself too much. Ambulances, sirens, and hospitals always remind me of death. It's hard for me to face the fact right from the start our lives are headed toward death. (26-year-old sales manager)

By constantly watching how their bodies are doing, these people are always facing death. They are dying all their lives. Suffering, that is, the sense of a near yet far away death, gives their lives meaning. What is characteristic of these people is that they frequently go to doctors, but rarely follow their advice. The central thing for them is that they know they are suffering, and that no one can help them.

Sickness and suffering are a part of the reality of life. Despite the care that must be given regarding illness, too much attention to illness, particularly in the form of a «search for illness» can be the source of attitudes like those described above.

For some people the event of death is not as frightening as is the idea of the decomposition of the body. One does not like the idea of one's old, familiar flesh turning into something rotten and disgusting. In this case the person is identifying with the body itself and is subjecting the lifeless body to the standards of cleanliness.

THE IDEA OF MY DECAYING BODY GIVES ME NO PEACE OF MIND

I feel a lot of disgust just thinking about how my body, the flesh on my hands, my chest, my stomach could decay into a stinking mess. Although I know I won't experience it myself, it's an idea I just can't get out of my mind. I'm terribly frightened by it. (24-year-old good-looking female model)

Fear of Death and the Environment

Normally death is associated with the body. The organs stop functioning, and the body enters a new condition. But what do death and the fear of death have to do with a person's surroundings? We frequently hear complaints like these:

Your sloppiness is going to be the death, of me.
I won't even have peace in the next world when I think of how irresponsible and sloppy you are.
If I just knew that you could take care of yourself and lead a good life, I could die in peace.
I'd rather be dead than to have to discover that you are cheating on me.

In these cases a person's attitude about the actual capabilities becomes the reason for fearing death or for wishing for death.

IF ONLY I HAD RAMMED INTO THAT CONCRETE PILLAR

For eighteen years I worked as a technician in a big company. As part of the company's reorganization I was going to be transferred to the lab. But how was I supposed to handle that? I had gotten so used to my old assignment. Now I could see that I would be a failure. The change would be the end of me. Recently I went tearing down the highway. Somehow I wanted to run away from all the pressure I had gotten myself into. I kept thinking it would be best

206

if I just ran into a concrete pillar at about 90 miles an hour. Then at least I wouldn't have to face all this pressure. (38-year-old engineer)

In such cases death is the way out of a difficult situation that has grown out of internalized behavioral norms. But it is just as likely that the actual capabilities can be the cause of the fear of death:

If I don't fulfill my purpose in life, my whole life will have been meaningless. I can't die in peace until I have finished my work.

I've worked hard enough all my life. Death holds no fear for me any more.

Depending on the emphasis that was given to the actual capabilities in one's upbringing, the attitude toward death - the death wish, fear of death, or indifference toward death - will take on a different shape.

Fear of Death and Time

A person's attitude to his body and to his surroundings, as well as their relationship to death, develops in the course of his life. This causes the formation of certain conflicts and susceptibilities to anxiety, as reflected in the emphasis or suppression of certain areas. But one's relationship to death is not determined simply by the crucial experiences in one's individual or collective past, nor by momentary experiences. Rather, to a great extent it gets its particular stamp from one's attitudes and expectations regarding the future. Bilz (1967) tells of an experiment carried out by an American physiologist. The researcher tossed rats into a glass cylinder filled with water. Unable to escape from it, the rats swam around in panic for several minutes, then sank to the bottom and drowned. One could not assume that they had exhausted themselves in such a short period of time. With another group of rats the scientist placed a stick in the cylinder so that the rats could save themselves. Rats that had undergone the experience in this cylinder were later able to swim around for 80 hours when they were placed in the cylinder from which there was no escape. Only total exhaustion caused them to stop swimming. The rats in this second group had discovered that there could be a way out. Their «hope,» had enabled them to keep swimming until they were totally exhausted. The «hopeless» rats of the first group, however, had quickly died after just a few minutes of terror and fear.

Although the results of this experiment cannot be completely transferred to the human condition, they do demonstrate how important the future is in shaping our perspective. Our experience in surgery has shown how crucial the patient's mental attitude, his feelings about the operation, and his thoughts on life are to the success of the operation. The way one deals with an illness is also determined by the person's attitude toward the future. If life doesn't have meaning any more, if the person does not find a «stick in the cylinder,» a way for him to get out of his situation, then even the slightest illness can cause tremendous suffering. And through pain, inner unrest, or apathy, new crises can develop in the course of the illness.

For many patients, the physician's diagnosis has the same function as did the glass cylinder for the rats. It can provide hope, or it can take away all hope and let them resign themselves to their fate. It is obvious that the doctor must be very careful in how he handles his diagnoses.

Some diagnoses are made because there doesn't seem to be any other point of departure or practical possibilities. The psychiatric diagnosis of "schizophrenia" falls into this group. Although its conditions are still largely unexplained, and the course of the disease proceeds in step with the decline of the personality in only a few cases, the illness stands at the end of the list of illness prestige and occasionally causes the patient to be entirely hopeless.

If the question of the meaning of death or of suffering cannot be answered at a particular, when the situation seems hopeless, this doesn't mean that it always has to be this way. The woman whose eyes were devoured by ants after her suicide attempt was later unable to understand why she had even taken the sleeping pills. So, in very instant where the situation seems hopeless, it is important to ask whether the same event, from a different point of view and at a different time, wouldn't perhaps have a different meaning. In this sense hopelessness means that the dimension of time has shrunk to a single point on which the person's experience is fixed.

Death and Upbringing
As we have seen, the attitude toward death depends on upbringing, tradition, religion, society, and one's own life experiences. Even if people don't openly talk about death, the child will develop certain attitudes from the behaviors he sees in his environment. If, for example, a mother

has an abnormal mourning reaction to the death of her mother, if she is depressed and break into tears for a long time afterward, the suffering she displays will become a model for the child. The child will then experience a personal loss not simply as an incomprehensible event, but also as a threat to his own personality. This, after all, is what he has seen happen to his mother. From all appearances mourning rituals are not the only things that are transmitted; a family tradition of mourning reactions also seems to exist.

Strong models such as the one described above are not the only ones that are important for the attitude toward death. Isolated experiences that are associated with death can affect a person's total experience of death: whether the person concerns himself with death or avoids it, whether a person thinks about his own death with pleasure and thus overvalues it. What matters here is the attitude of the parents. Through it, the children develop their own attitudes:

AT LAST I'LL HAVE SOME PEACE

A fifteen-year-old boy commented about the death of his grandmother: *Grandma has died. At last I'll have some peace.* The mother reacted automatically: *You should be ashamed of yourself. People don't say bad things about their dead grandmother.* The mother could have reacted in a different way: *I don't know if you really mean it the way you say. I get the impression that you don't want to admit that Grandma's death affects you the way it does us. You don't think it's right for a guy to show his feelings.*

SINCE DAD DIED, I DON'T SEE ANY SENSE TO LIFE ANY MORE

Carl, seventeen years old, sighs: *I don't see any meaning in anything any more, now that Dad is gone.* The mother reports that her response was; *you think I still find any meaning? I gave up on that a long time ago!* In psychotherapy the mother gave a different answer: *It's not easy for us, losing our father at the age of 42. I don't think he would have wanted us to drop everything, all his life he made sure we were happy together. Now it would be crazy if we saw nothing, but the bad side of things. If we stick together now we can still shape our lives into something meaningful.*

Nossrat Peseschkian, M.D.

Disorders and Conflicts

Fear of death; lack of awareness; crisis of personal philosophy; fears of illness; negativism; nihilistic ideas; excessive optimism; pessimism; existential fear; too many demands; too few demands; insecurity; escape into the future; profession as life goal; inhibition of drives; asceticism; sadness; bad moods.

Comment
Like birth, death is a necessary, determined fate. But the attitude toward death is conditioned by upbringing, and by the experiences one has in connection with this theme. The attitude toward death belongs to the conditional fate. The fear of death is a differentiated phenomenon. It is linked to the body, to the actual capabilities, and to one's relationship to the past, present, and future.

Antidote
Learn to distinguish between death and the attitude toward death.

CHAPTER IV:
EDUCATION - SELF-HELP
- PSYCHOTHERAPY

AN EASY CURE

The nephew of the ruler Ghabus-Woschmgir was seriously ill. All the physicians in the land had already given up hope. Their medicines had been to no avail. Since there was nothing more that the doctors could do, the ruler agreed that Avicena, who was a young man of sixteen at the time, should take over the treatment. When Avicena entered the palace, all were amazed at this courage, for he was determined to help the ailing man, even though all the wise Hakims in the land had admitted their helplessness.

Avicena saw the ailing man, a thin, pale young man, stretched out on his bed. The man gave no reply to questions about his medical condition, and his relatives reported that he had not uttered a word for some time. Avicena took the man's pulse and held his hand for a long time. Finally he raised his head thoughtfully and said, «This young man needs a different kind of treatment. To provide that, I need someone who really knows this city, someone who knows all its streets and alleys, all the houses, and all the people living in them.» All the people were amazed and asked, «What does healing a sick man have to do with the alleys of our city?» But in spite of their doubts, they obeyed Avicena's command and sent for a man who, so it was said, knows the city like the palm of his hand. Avicena said to him, «Name all the sections of the town for me.» At the same time he again took the patient's pulse.

When a certain quarter of the city was mentioned, Avicena felt the man's pulse quicken. Then he asked for the names of all the streets in that quarter, until the sick man's pulse again quickened at the sound of a particular street name. Now Avicena asked for the names of the alleys that ran into that street. The man was naming them one by one, when suddenly the name of a small, little-known alley produced a much greater response in the ailing man. Pleased with this response, Avicena commanded, «Bring me a man who can name all the houses in this alley, along with the people living in them.» When they brought such a man to Avicena, he had him say all the houses, and the sick man's pulse rate revealed which one he was after.

When the man came to the names of the people living in that house, he also mentioned the name of a young girl. Immediately the patient's pulse began to race. The observant Avicena commented, «Very good, everything is clear. I now know the young man's illness, and the cure is very simple.» He got up and spoke to the people, all of whom were staring at him in amazement. «This young man is suffering from lovesickness. This is the root of his physical ailment. He is in love with the girl whose name you just heard. Fetch the girl and woo her as a bride.»

The patient, who had listened to Avicena's words with great attention and excitement, blushed with embarrassment and crawled under the covers. The ruler proclaimed the girl as his nephew's bride, and the young man recovered within the hour. *(After Mowlana Persian Poet)*

Introduction to Self-Help

The previous chapter dealt with behaviors, forms of upbringing, types of reaction and conflict, and misunderstandings in interpersonal relationships. Now we will try to draw conclusions from this analysis and to find ways to apply these conclusions to situations in parenting, partnerships, and interpersonal relationships. A practical point of departure like this should not be misunderstood as being a prescription. Rather, it should present guidelines for reducing the danger of the «child falling in the well,» show how to be of help if the child does indeed fall in.

The purpose of self-help is to provide guidelines. Therefore it deals basically with only a few fundamental processes. These have the advantage of being applicable to a relatively large circle of people and to various kinds of problems. Self-help does not offer instructions that can automatically be applied to the individual case. Every partnership, after all, is different; in self-help these differences must be taken into consideration. The principle of cleanliness - to take an example from the actual capabilities - has validity in every partnership. But the importance that is attached to it will differ from one case to the next: One person may need two shirts a day to really feel clean; another might wear the same shirt two days in a row. Some people shower in the morning, others prefer the evening, etc. A partner might find one or the other behavior likeable or dislikeable, or he may be indifferent to it. This is why we avoid giving directions that set forth every step that must be taken. A partnership needs as much flexibility as possible. Self-help should point the way in this direction.

Three Basic Principles of Interpersonal Relationships

A person goes through various stages in his personal development as well as in a partnership. These various stages are characterized by the following three principles.

The Principle of Development

We have already dealt with this principle in connection with the misunderstanding «Development.» In that section of the book we talked mainly about the distortions of time that can lead to too few demands or too many demands. In interpersonal relationships the principles of development corresponds to the *stage* of *«connectedness.»* The child is dependent on his parents. He needs their example, their patience, and their time. The parents for their part feel tied to the child through love, hope, faith, and responsibility. A similar thing happens in social relationships when we assume responsibility for another person and place our hopes and expectations in him. From this point of view connectedness takes on the meaning of a stage of interaction.

The Principle of Differentiation

Differentiation is a basis function that is centered on the actual capabilities. Only through differentiation can a person learn to distinguish between his drives and the needs of his environment. To put it in general terms: we learn by learning to make distinctions. Applied to social interaction, the *stage of warning* comes to the fore. We don't simply learn to make distinctions in our environment through trial and error. Rather, we rely in large part on information from our social environment. When we give advice, when we want to influence someone, or intend to change his ideas and behaviors, we are in the stage of warning. This becomes the epitome of social needs and of adaptability to the prevailing conditions in the environment.

The Principle of Unity

In relation to a person's development (in which a specific unity can be achieved at every stage), unity is ultimately the integration of capabilities into an individual personality. Associated with this is a certain autonomy that increases in importance as the person grows older. In the early years of his development the child is constantly reminded: «Wash your hands; clean up your room; study hard; behave yourself!» But as he grows older his increasing maturity makes him less dependent on so much information from outside. He determines his own path and makes decisions for himself and others. This means that he frees himself from the people he was especially close to, and begins to seek needed information on his own and bears responsibility for himself. We call this the *stage of detachment.* It is a characteristic of the maturing and mature personality.

INTERACTION ANALYSIS

The stages of human interaction - connectedness, warning/differentiation, discernment, and detachment - provide us with a concrete entry into real interpersonal conflicts. On the one hand they are found in the development of a person, or characterize the momentary need of a partner. On the other hand, they exist as attitudes, desires, and expectations in the person involved. Here we are speaking of stages of expectation. If, as happens in interaction, we relate the possible interaction stages of the partner to the stages of expectation of the other person, we arrive at the following depiction:

MODEL OF THE STAGES OF AN INTERACTION

Detachment			
	Warning/discernment		
		Connectedness	
A	B	--	Connectedness
C	--	D	Warning/discernment
--	E	F	Detachment

Stages of expectation of the person involved

To analyze the conflict one must first determine the partner's stage of interaction. One asks oneself the following questions, which characterize the stage of connectedness:

Does my partner need (precisely now) to be with me?
Does he need my attention?
Has he developed an intensive emotional relationship with me?

Interaction does not consist simply of emotional ties. The partner needs some amount of information and warning.

The following questions point to the stage of warning/discernment:

Is my partner lacking information?
Does he need my advice?
Does he need my help in making a decision?

Finally, the stage of detachment is equated with a diminishment, change, or dissolution of the emotional ties. We speak of detachment when someone leaves home to live by himself, when he tries to put his own ideas into practice, when he'd like to make own decisions. Here we ask:

Would my partner like to make a decision on his own, without my help? Does my advice limit his personal freedom?

Is he demanding independence for himself?

Each of these stages points to a stage of expectation in the other person. One asks oneself:

Do I expect my partner to stay with me, to help me, to feel tied to me emotionally, and to show gratitude? (Connectedness)
Do I feel the need to give my partner advice, to influence his decisions, or to warn him? (Warning/Discernment)
Do I expect my partner to be independent? Would I rather not bear the responsibility for him any more? Do I consider it right that he take care of himself? (Detachment)

If the other person's stage of expectation about connectedness matches the partner's need for connectedness, if the need for warning matches the warning and information that is given, and if both partners have the same degree of detachment, the situations are to a great extent low in conflict. But they can become conflictual if the two people are not in harmony as far as their stages are concerned. In our model there are six of these conflict possibilities.

a. One person's need for connectedness is met by the other person's expectation of and need for detachment.

Situation: A four-year-old girl wants to play with her father, sit on his lap, and cuddle. The father withdraws, explaining that he doesn't have time, and the child shouldn't become spoiled.

Misunderstandings involved: Development; dimension of time and image of man; identification and projection.

Typical disorders: Neglect syndrome, associated with fear of being alone and separation anxiety; intensified emotional dependency; impatience or patience out of fear.

b. One partner needs connectedness, and the other thinks he should provide information and warnings.

Situation: A 28-year-old working wife has been looking forward all day to spending a cozy evening with her husband. When he gets home he complains:

I see the kitchen is still a mess and the kids have their things lying all over the place. Sometimes I wonder why I ever got married.

Misunderstandings involved: Goal of upbringing - content of upbringing; relativity of values; dimension of time and image of man; uniqueness.

Typical disorders: Too many demands; breach of trust; mood fluctuations; aggression; balance between love and hate; fear of disappointments; inhibitions with a repressive model.

c. The partner needs information, warnings, and verbal instructions. But the other person expects him to be independent, to make his own decision. The other person gives the partner no support.

Situation: A 17-year-old boy has a new girlfriend who he likes a lot, but she's rather unreliable. He'd like some advice from his mother. She says to him: *You've never asked for advice before and always wanted to act so independent. Go ask your father. I've got enough to deal with as it is.*

Misunderstandings involved: Development; goal of upbringing - content of upbringing; identification - projection; illness - health; identity crisis.

Typical disorders: Crisis of confidence; over-sensitivity; feelings of insecurity; desperation and overcompensation.

d. The partner feels a need for information, warning, and help in making decisions. But the other person would like to maintain a stage of connectedness through attention and tenderness

Situation: A 35-year-old man is having problems with his career. He'd like to know whether he should be retrained. His mother comes to visit and says: *You've got too much to do already, and you really don't look good. Come stay with us a few days and we'll feed you right.*

Misunderstandings involved: Identification – projection; development; relativity of values.

Typical disorders: Inhibition of aggression; difficulty in making decisions; ambivalent attitudes about love; exaggerated expectations of one's self and the model; conflicts in the family situation.

e. The partner would like to assert himself. The other partner does not acknowledge this desired or achieved independence. Instead, the person tries to control the partner by giving opinions and advice.

Situation: A 38-year-old woman, who has just got married, gets a visit from her mother. The mother looks around the apartment sceptically and says: *There's a lot of dust in the corners. It's a good thing I'm here. Your old Mama can show you what tidiness really is. Your husband will claim I didn't teach you how to keep house.*

Misunderstanding involved: Generalization; prejudice; justice - love; identification - projection.

Typical disorders: Aggression - inhibition of aggression; guilt feelings; hatred; silence out of spite; affective renunciation of the model, unwillingness to listen any more; indecisiveness; inability to take action; discontent.

    f.   The partner feels the need for independence and detachment. But the other person counters this with a need for connectedness.

Situation: The 18-year-old daughter wants to go to college. She's accepted at a college that is 150 miles from home. Her father takes the following position: *It's entirely out of the question. We know what could all happen. You would just fade away there. Besides, going to college is nonsense. Why don't you learn a practical skill and stay here with us?*

Misunderstandings involved: Justice - love; loss of unity; conditioned and definite fate.

Typical disorders: Too few demands; dependence; egotism; guilt feelings; hidden or open aggression; balance between love and hate; mistrust; indecisiveness.

These six forms of interaction can serve as an orientation when one tries to analyze conflicts with a partner. By using them, one can understand current problems quite readily and include one's own attitude as a relevant component. In the following pages I aim to show how one can constructively and systematically undertake self-help by giving consideration to this kind of orientation.

SELF-HELP

Within the framework of upbringing and self-help, differentiation analysis is available as a five-step process. This process refers to the described actual capabilities, insofar as they lead to interpersonal conflicts and to mental and psychological disorders. The process is divided into the stages of distancing/ observation, inventory, situational encouragement, verbalization, and broadening of the goal.

STAGE 1: DISTANCING/OBSERVATION

If someone feels responsible for another person, he automatically sees that person differently than others do. As a rule, he unconsciously and unintentionally transfers his own wishes to that person. He expects that person to act the way he would like to himself. At the same time, he puts himself in the other person's shoes and identifies with him. As a result of this strong emotional involvement, he regards the other person's affairs as his own and intervenes in them.

Under circumstances such as these, the other person is no longer viewed objectively or «impartially,» but subjectively, and with strong emotional attachment. The closer he is, the stronger the involvement: one's own children, grandchildren, spouse, friends, colleagues, and parents. Their closeness to us makes it possible for us to know them intensely. But, paradoxically, this intense knowledge does not help us perceive them more objectively, rather, the opposite occurs. On an unconscious level we give them our own emphasis. Certain personality traits come to the center of our attention. A one-sided view of the personality emerges. A 15-year-old girl laments:

I have a serious problem with constipation, and quite often I don't have an appetite, so lately I've become quite thin. Somehow I'm suffering from a lot of tension between my mother and me. I'm constantly fighting and quarreling with her. After a scene like that I go to my room and cry half the night. At those times I've actually even thought about suicide. Whenever my mother starts preaching to me, I start seeing black spots in front of my eyes and fall on the floor in a faint. And lately I've also been having a lot of trouble concentrating. Some days I just want to run off into the woods.

The symptoms in this case are typical bodily ailments that point to an infection of the large intestine, depression, problems in school, and parental conflicts. The patient was referred to a specialist in internal medicine, who was to provide psychotherapeutic treatment. No organic cause was found. It turned out that there was a definite mother–daughter conflict that was encouraged by both sides. The mother makes this criticism: *She's not industrious and tidy enough. Her bad grades in school prove that as far as industriousness is concerned, she's going downhill:* At every opportunity the mother criticizes the girl for the lack of ambition and her messiness. She gets upset over this, can't sleep, and also nags her husband about it. He reports: *...again and again my wife has gone on about it till three in the morning.* In her conversations the mother often comes back to the fact that she wishes her daughter would do what she herself did not achieve, namely to finish her college degree. The high hopes she had for her daughter are continually dashed. In addition, she would have liked to have the freedom that her daughter now enjoys. The mother complains: *We're at the end of our rope with this Latin and the other school subjects. And my marriage has also suffered because of this conflict with my daughter.*

For a more objective and appropriate view of the partner, it is necessary that one be free of customary clichés. In order to see the partner more as he really is, and to change the behavioral habits that lead to conflict, three steps are necessary at the distancing stage: Observation, absence of criticism, and the foregoing of bringing an uninvolved third person into the situation.

Observation

When people are supposed to give information about the things that disturb them in their partners, they usually retreat into generalizations such as, «He simply bothers me»; «we aren't compatible»; «I get upset over him»; «she's unbearable.» There comes to the surface a considerable sense of discomfort, which, however, seems to emerge out of thin air. There is no reference to concrete behaviors, to the situations in which those feelings of discomfort occur. Instead there are strong emotional overtones, mostly negative in nature. Careful observation of the conflict-laden situation already offers some help. The person observes under what circumstances the quarrels and confrontations develop. These observations are put down in writing.

The mother of a 15-year-old girl writes: *Her room looks like it has been hit by a bomb. Particularly after she's been doing her homework. She doesn't put things back where she got them. Her books pile up on her desk so that there's hardly any room to write. That's the way she leaves the room, even when she's done with her homework. When she cooks in the kitchen she leaves the dirty bowls and pots sitting right where she last used them. When I see that, I just want to explode. I just need to look at it... She has a real need for keeping herself absolutely clean. She won't wear her clothes unless they're spotless. But now it's getting to the point that she doesn't wand to clean her clothes herself. When her things get dirty, she doesn't want to wear them, of course, but she doesn't do a thing to take care of them. But I'm not the laundry lady for her royal highness, my daughter. If I don't do anything, she doesn't do anything. She thinks it should just all fall right into her lap. When things don't work out the way she wanted, she gets depressed and goes around pouting. If my husband and I didn't sit right next to her and keep telling her what to do, she wouldn't do anything about her homework. That's when I lose my patience and we end up screaming at each other. Last week she came home with a D in French. I didn't sleep a wink the whole night...*

These simple remarks, a written record of the woman's observations, can serve to some extent as a mirror. By giving shape to a vague feeling of discomfort, it is possible to acquire new perspectives and thereby to introduce a relearning process into the partnership.

The Suppression of Criticism

Criticism is the epitome of the educational means associated with the secondary capabilities. It comprises verbal actions as well as concrete ones such as reward and punishment, praise and criticism. Through criticism in the wider sense of the word a person learns what is desirable and what is undesirable behavior. One learns to make distinctions. Criticism can be carried out in various ways: Constructive criticism helps a person develop a better sense of self and others, and enables him to expand and refine his ability to make differentiations. One

223

the other hand, constant criticism that is one-sided casts doubt on the person's self-image and sense of personal worth. Nagging creates a barrier between people. People don't just want to hear how bad they are; they also need positive confirmation.

Working Out the Problem with One's Partner
Many things don't become a big problem until they are dealt with in front of a lot of other people instead of just with those directly involved. The others take sides, give advice, which is partially contradictory, or get the people involved riled up against each other. The conflict fails to come to an end, not because the parties involved wouldn't have found a solution, but because the others can't let them forget about it:

I'm ashamed to go to my relatives or to my mother's acquaintances. They all know about my problems, know what my weaknesses are, and are just waiting for me to do something wrong again. They hang around me like vultures, eager to bombard me with advice.

A conflict is first of all a private thing. Discretion is the prerequisite that must be there before someone involved in the issue can win the confidence of the other person.

Distancing means that one tries to create some room to see the other person more clearly. It is much like the case of a mountaineer who must get far away from the mountain to see its whole outline. From nearby he can only see a few slopes. In terms of upbringing, distancing in a concrete sense means: For a certain time we refrain from criticizing the people with whom we are in conflict. In place of criticism, of judgment, there is observation regarding:

The spouse, who doesn't have enough time for us, or who is messy or unclean;
The boy whose sloppiness and defiance are driving his parents to desperation;
The girl whose rudeness will cause the neighbors to «mount the barricades»;
The adolescent who comes home too late;

The mother-in-law who pokes her nose into every little thing;
The friend who is always late; the colleague who seems arrogant, etc.

It's not always easy to suddenly accept someone you've previously reacted to emotionally. It's not easy to simply observe. Mere observation and the attempt not to criticize and to limit the extent of the conflict can produce a definite effect. The confrontation is now perceived from a new point of view. Another effect, the meaning of which must be properly understood, is that one can hardly believe one recognizes the person any more. The expectations that had built up as a result of the constant criticism are suddenly no longer fulfilled. Now there is suspicion and mistrust: «What's gotten into my wife all of the sudden?» «What are my folks driving at?» The child who is used to nagging and criticism is suspicious of his parents' new behavior. He doesn't trust the peace that he now finds around him. The mother of a 15- year-old girl reports:

This week I tried several times to be nice to her instead of criticizing her. In several cases I succeeded, but she has the feeling that my behavior is not genuine. And I still get upset about everything, but I try not to let her see it. In this way we avoided a lot of friction. If I don't scream at her, she's also a lot more subdued in her tone, too. But I've never made it all the way through an evening, because my anger just builds up and I have to let it out. Then I'm really disappointed with myself, because I tried so hard.

Stages of Observation
Observe your partner's behavior.
Write down what makes you angry.
Describe exactly the situations in which you get upset.
During the observations, do not criticize your partner.
During this time, do not give any advice; even though it might be well intended.
Problems are private matters. Do not discuss them with people who are not involved in the situation.

Nossrat Peseschkian, M.D.

Focal capabilities
Justice - Love.

Pay attention to misunderstandings
Generalizations, projection, prejudice.

STAGE 2: INVENTORY

Observation alone is incomplete. Along with its function as a mirror it has a perhaps even greater function as a valve: one gives vent to what is in his heart, but without having intervened in the conflict directly. What counts now is to describe very carefully the conflict situation and the behaviors that were perceived as being disturbing. In so doing, one must find an appropriate form for representing them. How good the observation is depends on how systematically it takes place and how encompassing it is. In other words, it must be appropriate.

The *Differentiation Analysis Inventory* (DAI) can serve as a guide for the observation. This inventory makes possible a systematic of characteristics, behaviors, and capabilities that play a central role in a person's life and every stage of life. This description helps create an adequate and encompassing picture of what we face, and enables us to proceed confidently and with a clear goal in mind. Along with its applicability and ability to make things more comprehensible, the methodology of the DAI has a further advantage.

The DAI is an encompassing system of description and gives content-based criteria for a therapeutic process and for self-help. In the inventory the person gives concrete statements as to which of the actual capabilities are positive and which are negative. Differences in degree are shown with several positive (+) or negative (–) marks. In addition, situations should be noted in detail: with whom, when, and how often which behaviors were in evidence. In this way the DAI serves as the primary aid to observation.

The Differentiation Analysis Inventory Filled Out by the Mother of S

Actual Capabilities	Positive (+)	Negative (-)	Area (Who-where-when-frequency)
Punctuality	+++		Nothing conspicuous
Cleanliness	+	-	Great demand for cleanliness, no individual efforts for cleanliness
Orderliness		- - -	Her room is as messy as a pigpen
Obedience	+	- -	Stubborn, especially toward her mother
Politeness	+	-	Often rude toward her mother, polite toward her father and others
Honesty/loyalty	+++		No problems
Justice	+	-	Expects justice for herself
Industry/achievement		- - -	Only when her parents keep after her
Thrift	+	-	Handles her own money well, but is wasteful out of carelessness
Love		- - -	Is loving to her dolls and her dog
Patience	+	-	She gets angry when people remind her of the rules
Time	+	-	Most of the time she is busy with the dog
Contact		- -	She is reserved and has few contacts
Sex-Sexuality	+	-	She's interested in sexual questions. She prefers to be caressed by her father
Trust	+	-	Trusts her father more than her mother
Confidence		- -	Throws in the towel at the slightest lack of success
Hope		-	She's often pessimistic; makes comments about suicide
Faith-Religion		- -	Has actually not been evidenced in her
Doubt		- -	Doubts her own capabilities and the trustworthiness of her parents
Certainty		- -	Like a passing fancy
Unity		- -	That's the main problem in our family

The DAI makes it possible to see the partner limited not only to a few negative areas, but also to take into consideration a multitude of his capabilities. The DAI thus gives rise to a discovery, which is a primary discovery for some people: «My partner is really not as bad as I thought. He's even got a whole range of positive qualities that I hadn't really seen until now.» This distinction makes it possible to approach the person in a more just way, and creates the basis for mutual trust: «At last my partner doesn't just see my shortcomings!» Since a partnership does not depend solely on the one partner, but also on the person involved, the DAI is appropriate for both members of the partnership: «Which actual capabilities are developed positively or negatively in me personally? What are my attitudes and expectations?» This method can also be used to get a grasp of the conflicts in an individual. A person can set up a DAI for himself and thereby differentiate his own capabilities insofar as this is possible through «self analysis.» *«I'm not at all the failure I always thought I was.»* (24-year-old student suffering from strong inhibitions). In the case of external conflict situations, as mentioned previously, the partner's DAI can be drawn upon.

By comparing a person's DAI with that of his partner, it is possible to look at the conflict in a differentiated way. Differences in relation to individual actual capabilities can serve as a typical clue to conflicts.

Stages of the Inventory Process
Transfer your observations to the DAI
Mark the positively oriented capabilities with a (+), the negative ones with a (-).
The inventory won't really become comprehensible to you until you make brief remarks for each individual actual capability, as to where, when, how often, and towards whom the behavior takes place. Fill out a DAI for yourself as well as for your partner. Evaluate your own actual capabilities. Determine which actual capabilities are markedly conflictual, once for your partner and again for yourself, and finally for a comparison of the two profiles of the actual capabilities.

Focal capabilities
Justice; time; orderliness.

Watch out for misunderstandings
Justice - love; development.

STAGE 3: SITUATIONAL ENCOURAGEMENT

Now, instead of criticizing the other person, we can encourage him when he does something that in our opinion is right and good. It's not enough to make a general statement like «You're a nice person» or «I love you» or «You have pretty eyes.» All too often assertions like this do not have a concrete basis. The assertion should be directly related to the particular situation and should be expressed immediately after the positive behavior has taken place.

At first the encouragement is given as «reinforcement» after each occurrence of the selected positive behavior. Later it is given only after the second, third, or fourth time, and finally, only on an irregular basis. The following function as reinforcements: a friendly glance, a smile, words of praise, a hug, and occasionally (1) material rewards (favorite foods, money, etc.).

Frequently the process of «encouragement» faces the danger of becoming diffuse, indistinct, and thus inefficient in the long run. A *plan of encouragement* can help to avoid this development. In the process, the observations noted in the DAI can serve as documentary aids. We can illustrate the process by using the case of S. as an example.

Positioning the Extreme Evaluations

For the selective encouragement, the person writes out the three capabilities which received the most extreme evaluation in each column, and places them opposite each other:

Positive	Negative
1. Punctuality	1. Orderliness
2. Integrity	2. Industriousness
3. Frugality with money	3. Frugality at home

The Most Crucial Pair of Capabilities

It has proven to be ineffective to simultaneously go into all the behaviors that received extreme positive and negative evaluations. Such a method would make the person feel unsure, and the pedagogic effect on the partner would be diminished. This is why it is recommended that of the six extreme evaluations, one selects the pair of positive and negative capabilities that seem the most important ones on the basis of their significance for the person involved. For the mother of the 15-year-old girl, at that time the most positive quality, punctuality (+ + +), and the most negative, orderliness (- - -), were the pair that, in her opinion, were causing the most difficulty.

Punctuality (+ + +)/Orderliness (- - -)

The Corresponding Capabilities
Since difficulties in upbringing are a matter of conflicts in social interaction, and since the DAI takes this interaction into consideration - by looking at the partner's capabilities through the eyes of the other person - that person positions his own attitudes about the conflict opposite those of his partner. The mother herself was tidy and industrious. But with regard to her daughter's orderliness, she was - according to her own judgment - impatient. She usually got very riled or tidied up the place herself. In this case we have the following depiction:

Daughter: Punctuality (+ + +)/Orderliness (- - -)
Mother: Patience (- - -)/Orderliness (+ + +)

The Practice of Selective Encouragement
During a period of at least three days to a week at the most the other person encourages the positive trait in the pair of capabilities. The person praises the partner in this area and thus reinforces a concrete behavior. In connection with the pair of capabilities, the person has already worked out which behavioral patterns can be rewarded. This process made the person aware of and sensitive to them. The corresponding negative capability is not criticized. Indeed, when it appears in the partner, it is simply ignored.

For the other person, the corresponding capability must be the center of attention. He must heed the positive behaviors of his partner and his own capability which corresponds to the negatively marked quality of his partner. In our case example, the following motto holds for the mother:

Punctuality Week - as confirmation for the daughter;

Patience Week - as a way for the mother to check her ability to make distinctions.

The mother's report: *This week I often tried to encourage my daughter. At first she was downright critical and didn't want to accept anything I said, perhaps because she knows that when I'm angry I would just do the opposite again. That same day, when she came home on time, I told her I was happy about that. She took in my words of praise without comment. At other times when I gave her some encouragement, she would say she already knew she had done it well, and that she was surprised that I hadn't noticed sooner. It hasn't always been easy for me to be patient. And there were still times when I could barely hang on. But, to the surprise of my daughter and myself, I've usually managed to stay calm and patient.*

In a similar way other capabilities can be thematicized and worked through one after another. The person observed the behavior of his partner, created some distance to it, and then achieved some insight into the partner's positive capabilities. Through selective encouragement the person was able to confirm the self-worth of the partner. At the same time, that person could work through the corresponding capabilities for himself.

Stages of Situational Encouragement

The three extreme evaluations in the DAI are written out.

To determine the pair of capabilities to be dealt with, the positive and negative, extreme evaluations are chosen which seem most important at the time.

The corresponding capability in the other person is positioned opposite the partner's pair of capabilities that are most pressing at this time. The corresponding capability is the behavioral area in the other person that corresponds to the negatively marked capability in the partner.

For a week, the positively marked capability in the partner is praised in concrete instances. There is no criticism. During this period the corresponding capability occupies the foreground for the other person. That person, for instance, practices patience throughout the week.

Nossrat Peseschkian, M.D.

Focal capabilities
Confidence - trust.

Watch out for misunderstandings
Generalization; justice - love.

STAGE 4: VERBALIZATION

Through systematic observation on the basis of the DAI, the person involved can obtain clues as to the relationship between his own behavior and that of his conflict partner. The verbalization stage is marked by the attempt to establish verbal communication between the two partners. Verbal communication may seem an obvious thing, but in interpersonal conflicts it is usually disordered. The structure of the communication in the case of undifferentiated criticism generally has a typical form. A person limits himself to short utterances and commands which are repeated frequently. He speaks in telegram style. The communication is predominantly one-sided: «Have you done your homework?» «Why aren't you finished yet?» «Your slowness is getting on my nerves!» «Can't you see that?» «You're unbearable.»

The partner, in turn, produces statements that are equally undifferentiated. These are often replies in telegram style also, such as «No,» «Yes,» «Maybe,» «Leave me alone.» Because of their defensive character these are usually interpreted as indications of defiance. As such, they themselves become the cause for criticism. It's a vicious circle. We call this form nonverbal or limited communication, because an actual verbal exchange is usually missing. Criticism, combined with insufficient verbalization, indicates an emotional, aggressive attitude. The opposite of it is a communication disorder that we refer to as «monologizing.» In this situation one of the partners speaks almost constantly, giving the other person no opportunity to really answer.

When a partner is challenged or summoned to a discussion, it depends largely on *when, where,* and *how* this happens. For example, it doesn't make much sense to call a child in from playing, just to tell him how messy he is. Similarly, it is not appropriate to open this discussion in the presence of relatives, acquaintances, and friends. With good reasons the partner would immediately recognize this behavior as a defamation and as a challenge. It merely provokes his resistance.

The monologue is equally problematic as an attempt at verbalization. If the person simply wants to give a lecture and preach, the conversation, which really isn't one at all, is of no interest to the other person. A 39-year-old female white-collar worker reports:

I was always forced into an inferior role. I had no right to have an opinion of my own. I always had to listen and take in all these lectures. If I wanted to defend my position there was an immediate quarrel and temper tantrum. There was nothing else I could do but protect myself from this domination. I did this by always adopting a role that I really didn't want to play.

How Does One Begin a Conversation

First there must be preparation (distancing, inventory, and selective encouragement). Only then can the discussion, as verbalization, hold promise of an open confrontation, that is, a confrontation that is not hampered by misunderstandings. As soon as this basis for trust is established or re-established, the conflictual behaviors can be addressed. At this point a lot can be blurted out. The following procedure is more favorable: The discussion is begun with some encouragement, there is mention of a positive behavior, and the partner's success is addressed. After this, the critical topics can be tackled. This procedure has two advantages: first, the other person is reminded of his partner's positive qualities. Second, it creates a basis of trust for the partner. Once he sees that he is accepted, he is in a better position to accept criticism. Here's how it could look in practice: «You know, I'm really happy that you helped me with the shopping. But you also know that we both have some problems with how messy the house is. What do you think we can do about it?»

Factual Criticism

The other person speaks in concrete terms about the problems that have come up. He states concretely what he is angry about and gives examples. He doesn't merely make general statements like «You lied to me.» He cites the specific instance that caused him to feel the way he does. Several examples can be mentioned to make it easier for the other person to understand. Frequently we hear parents complain, «We've tried lots of times to start a serious discussion with our kids because we were angry about something. But when we got the discussion started we had long forgotten just what it was that had upset us. So, we'd just throw out a lot of general complaints, such as «You were being a smart aleck» or «You don't know how to behave.» There is a simple remedy for situations like this. If you write the events down, you will be able to remember them better. If the situation is then discussed in detail, everyone will know what the issue is. In this way you can minimize those misunderstandings that stem from statements that are too general and too imprecise.

Even if the other person makes an effort to give only factual criticism and acknowledges the partner's positive qualities, he can now and then expect that his partner will not reciprocate factually and with detachment. Though aware of the dynamic processes of the confrontation, it is sometimes hard for that other person to remain calm and fair. And to an even greater extent one cannot expect this objectivity from the partner, who, after all, has suddenly received the opportunity to speak candidly about his problem. The 15-year-old girl in our example had taken notes about her mother's behavior. When the mother, through her preparations, had created a «safe» place for her daughter, that is, one where she could feel she would not be punished, the girl read her notes to her:

The drapes in my room were hanging crooked. Mom said I should go straighten them out right away. I told her she shouldn't sniff around in my room all the time and always complain. Then she went around the house screaming that I should shape up and do what she said, since I didn't live there alone. She said I had no right to talk back to her and tell her what to do.

When I got home tonight at 7:00 after walking the dog, I forgot to brush the dog before letting him back into the house. Immediately my mother started screaming that I didn't take care of the dog. Then she said I should find a place where I could buy inexpensive meat for him, because otherwise she would take the money out of my allowance. This, she thought would finally teach me!

Today she went shopping with Dad. When she got home she screamed at me again, saying I should please not stand there and do nothing, but help her out because company was coming at 3:00, and I certainly had time to lend a hand. I replied very emphatically that my time off from work was for rest and recreation, not for tearing around the house like a cleaning lady. Eventually, I said, I'd end up working the whole morning, cleaning, cooking, doing dishes, just because she didn't want to damage her fingernails. But she would never acknowledge something like that. When she heard me say that, she really exploded and said that it was all very obvious.

Today is her birthday. I went to her to wish her a happy birthday. Her only comment: hope you shape up. I can't keep going the way it has been.»

Advice Unwanted

In the first phase of the discussion the other person had taken on the more active role. Now it is necessary for him to simply listen. This means, don't interrupt the partner, don't make any comments, don't start with well-intentioned advice, and don't try to justify yourself in front of your partner. We should keep in mind that we are dealing with a confrontation, and that we cannot expect the same opinion from both partners. On the contrary: the expression of differences in opinion can be a sign of openness, candid discussions, and trust.

Game Rules for a Discussion

Both parties present possible solutions, which are then written down. If the mother scolds her daughter for her messiness and demands that she put everything back as soon as she's finished playing, the daughter can make a counter proposal. She will straighten everything up when her playing is really over, namely late in the afternoon, or right before she goes to bed. To the extent that the child's suggestion is compatible with external circumstances (size of the home, siblings, etc.), it is agreed upon by both parties. Otherwise, they can continue to look for a solution. It's also possible that they will agree to postpone the discussion to another day. Every evening they should talk about the situation and discuss the success or failure they've had in carrying out their agreement. It has been our experience that 15 to 20 minutes are sufficient for a discussion of this type. In any event, the two decide themselves when the discussion will take place. Right before bedtime seems a particularly good time.

Until now we've proceeded under the assumption that the partner, having gone through the phase of distancing, inventory, and encouragement, is open to a discussion. But if there is a lot of rigidity, one must consider the possibility of a defiant reaction. In our case example the mother reports:

My daughter showed absolutely no interest when it was first suggested that we have a talk. She preferred to pull back into her shell and just read. Yesterday she joined in after a lot of resistance, and then only to let loose with all her complaints, which, by the way, are completely unjustified. For instance, she just can't see why we stupid adults can stay up later at night and she has to go to bed. When my husband gave some polite and reasonable explanations, she replied that no one can boss her around, and no one can make her go to sleep. When we asked her how she thought we could keep the house neater, whether I could perhaps help her, etc. she didn't give it much thought. She just said she felt comfortable without all the house cleaning, and that I could go ahead and do it. She is not interested in improving the situation. She just wants to solve her own problems to her satisfaction, without being considerate of others. Maybe I was dissatisfied with the way the conversation went, because she's not used to this type of thing. My husband and I want to really work at it and have frequent discussions with her now. Maybe then things will get better.

The girl wants to test her mother to see if the new behavior is just a fad or if she's really serious about it. After a certain period of time the mother can repeat her offer to have a discussion. During this period she should continue with the situational encouragement. If, after long and intensive attempts, they don't have the discussion, they can seek help from a psychologist or therapist.

Stages of Verbalization

At this stage there are thorough discussions of the current conflicts.
In order to establish a basis of trust, the discussion is begun with encouragements that are justified by the circumstances.
One partner relates his complaints; the other person listens.
The partner listens to the complaints of the other person.
The two look for common solutions to the problems that arise. The people involved promise to keep quiet about their discussion.

Focal capabilities
Politeness - honesty.

Watch out for misunderstandings
Generalization; projection; relativity of values.

STAGE 5: GOAL EXPANSION

The communication disorders in the partners' situation usually severely limit the contact between them. The partner is punished in that the other person forbids him something or withdraws something from him. This punishment, which was originally used as a means of education, becomes taken for granted and represents a fixed component within the relationship («Because of your messiness and your lies we won't go on a picnic Sunday.») Out of this can develop a general lessening of the activities the two undertake together. But this is no longer interpreted as simply a form of punishment. It is also seen as a cooling off, a diminishment of their relationship. We call this process goal limitation. It doesn't just happen with the child, but also has an impact on the life of the other person in a relationship. For instance, a mother may have had an upsetting day because of her children's messiness and problems in school. But the mother might take it out on her husband, in which case their sexual relationship can be affected. The wife is silent with her body. But the reasons for this are not known to her. A reaction like this does not have to be provoked by the children. There can be other causes, such as in-laws, neighbors, parents, problems at work, and, lastly, the husband himself.

The limitation is due to a lack of differentiation: People confuse justice and love. The criteria for reward or punishment are the valid behavioral norms of the actual capabilities. In those cases where the educational means become autonomous, there is a limitation of the goal. This limitation affects both partners.

S's mother says to her daughter: *Because of you I cried all afternoon, because you're so lazy in school. Now just don't expect me to go into town with you. I'm too wiped out for that...*

In this case the mother gives up something she would have liked to do, simply to punish her daughter. She limits her own possibilities and goals, to some extent consciously but also unconsciously. This form of punishment is a nonverbal means of upbringing where the actual problems are not discussed openly. One exerts punishment by forcing the partner to give up something. Or, he gives up something himself and speculates on the other person's guilt feelings. It is characteristic of goal narrowing that people see only the current problem and nothing else. The narrowing of the goal is thus also a narrowing of the field of vision. The basic principle for expanding the goal is the realization that the relationship with the partner isn't simply under the unlucky star of the immediate conflict. Rather, this problem is just one of many aspects of the relationship. There are always a number of other ties to the partner besides the one that is causing so much trouble at the moment.

Methodology for Goal Expansion
After a basis of trust is established through the measures we have already discussed, and when the partners are ready and able to verbalize their feelings, the limitation of the goals can be removed. There is little sense in giving the partner a prescription for what he would like to do. It is more effective to give consideration to his initiatives, which one can then help him develop further. The expansion of the goal deals with the three realms of the human personality: body, environment, and time. One doesn't just sit behind a desk, but rather takes walks or participates in a sport. One doesn't just sacrifice oneself for the household, but reads a book or goes to a concert. One doesn't limit ones social relationships; rather one invites friends, and sometimes also their children, to the house. One doesn't just see that the children do their homework; one also plays with them, and preferably not just the same game all the time. The prerequisite for all of this is that one or other of the partner has learned to know what he wants and to express these wishes.

Report on the Case of S, One Year After the Start of Treatment
In S's case there was therapeutic consultation and family therapy as described above. The focus of the treatment was the conflict-laden mother-daughter relationship. Since the father was the key figure-both mother and daughter needed his attention- he was included in the therapeutic process. After just three months of treatment the pains in the large intestine disappeared.

Similarly, the idea of suicide disappeared. And at the time of the follow-up examination, the considerable underweight had balanced itself out. The girl reports that she feels fully accepted by her parents, and that she no longer has such difficult quarrels with her mother. When problems occur, both she and her mother are able to control them. Her schoolwork, she says, has also improved. And what both mother and the daughter are happy to report is that the father now has more time for them. The mother is concerned that the daughter demands to be allowed to stay out later, but this problem was dealt with in the family group. The daughter reports: *«My mother used to scold me at every opportunity. It started when I got up in the morning and didn't even end when I went to bed. Today my mother is a different person. It's not that she wouldn't have anything to say any more. If she doesn't like something, she says it, but only in the family group. I think it's terrific how she keeps herself under control.»*

The goal expansion is not decided by one person alone. To the extent it affects a group of people, everyone has a right to put in his two cents' worth. The most appropriate forum for this, and the forum that actually ought to be the most obvious, is *the partner* or *family group*.

Stages of Goal Expansion
Interpersonal conflicts are characterized by a narrowing of the goal (one withdraws, reacts one-sidedly).
In goal narrowing, individual actual capabilities are used as a weapon (one sees nothing, but messiness, etc.).
Goal expansion takes place in the four areas of human relationship to I, to you, to we, and to the primal we.
In goal expansion one tries to overcome the imbalance by seeking new activities and goals for oneself and one's partner.
The establishment of family, parental, or partner groups makes it possible for individual family members to confront their own wants and goals systematically.

Focal capabilities
Hope and unity

Watch out for misunderstandings
Loss of unity; time

FAMILY GROUP - PARENTAL GROUP - PARTNER GROUP

OTHER PEOPLE'S PROBLEM

A woman was dissatisfied with her fate. She was poorer than everyone else. She never had enough bread for her seven children. Her husband had died at an early age. One night, after desperate prayer, there appeared before her an angel who gave her a sack and told her to toss all her sorrows and needs into it. The sack was hardly big enough to hold so many worries, problems, and fears. But the angel took her by the hand and led her, moaning, mumbling to herself, into heaven. When she arrived there, the woman was amazed, for she had imagined heaven to be much different. The clouds were all made of sorrow sacks like the one she had carried with her. And on the biggest sack there sat an old man, a very honorable gentleman whom she recognized from the pictures she had seen as a child. The Omnipotent One knew about all her troubles - after all, he had heard all her prayers and curses day after day. He commanded her to put her sack down, and then said that she could open all the other sacks and have a look inside them. But she would have to choose one and take it back with her to earth. She opened one sack after another and found aggravations, problems, urgent conflicts, boredom, and all sorts of other things like that. Some of them were new to her, others were familiar, and in the case of others, she didn't really know whether she had ever seen them before or not. With great effort she worked her way through all the clouds till she came to the last sack. She opened it, spread out its contents, and began to organize them. Then she recognized that it was her sack. But when she picked up the sack it seemed much lighter than before. And more than that, her problems didn't really bother her any more, and she no longer felt her pains. Instead of all of that, she now saw genuine misunderstandings, objective threats, and rewarding goals. *(Middle Eastern story)*

As a social being, man is dependent on other people. Living with other people takes place within a constant interplay of give and take.

The social group offers us many advantages, in which to some extent can be of major significance for us. But in some cases we might see them as a threat. In each case, both aspects of the social contact must be taken into consideration. There are countless people who find it hard to take part in a social group and to feel comfortable in it. They are awkward or shy, or feel rejected by the group. Frequently they react by withdrawing from the group (shyness, resignation), or else they demonstrate an exaggerated liveliness and try to dominate the group (troublemaker). But then there are also others who neither cause a disturbance nor cooperate; instead, they are passively tolerant and indifferent. A person's attitude toward his social environment isn't a mere coincidence. Over the course of time it develops as a result of his experiences. The process is much like that of water that gradually warms up instead of suddenly coming to a boil.

THE FAMILY GROUP

The so-called primary group, usually the family, is the basic form as well as the model for all other social groups. A primary group comprises father, mother, siblings, the child, and other people who are closely connected with this unit.

The family is the site of the first and, in some situations, the fundamental social experiences. Here there are common interests, relationships, and interactions between the individual members of the family. Each member has a special role in the group. The members of the family all have the ability to weigh their own interests in comparison with those of the family as a whole. In other words, they are able to make distinctions and to forego some of their own wishes. The functional capabilities of the family depend on the range of communication among the members. If there are communication disorders, the group cannot function as a dynamic and open system. Instead of dynamics and flexibility, there will be rigid behavioral patterns («As long as you live in this house you'll do as I say»), rigid role divisions («I'm the boss in this house»), and narrowing of goals («Each of us has his own area of interests»). But where the opposite holds true, a functioning family offers the opportunity for development on many levels. In this sense it can actually be shown that most disorders are marked by conflictual relationships with the parents or siblings. Since a child's interests, wishes, and even problems, as expressed in connection with goal expansion, touch on a wider social area than merely the two-person relationship, it is a good idea to solve these problems by drawing on the entire family. In a practical sense this can best be done through the family group.

How does a family group take place?

All the members of the family meet regularly at a certain time to have a discussion. This can be on a weekly basis. But a meeting can also be called for a particular situation. The group should meet late in the afternoon, while the children are still alert. All the members have input as to when the discussion should be held. The time they agree on (for example, Saturday afternoon at 5:15) is binding on everyone in the family. If unforeseen events make it impossible for someone to attend the discussion, the other members of the group should be informed in advance, and a new time should be set. The meeting should last from 45 to 60 minutes.

Equality Among the Members of the Group

Each member is accepted as an equal partner. To conduct the family group the parents do not need any academic or special training. Children from the age of two upward can take part, even if they don't understand every word of what is being dealt with in the group. They will see what is happening, they will observe how people talk with each other, and they will get an idea of the opportunities that are available for solving a problem. The child will see the family working together, not just eating, watching TV, and being outdoors.

The Group Assistant

In the family group, as in other groups, it is a good idea to select a group assistant to see to it that everyone has a chance to speak and that no one, not even the father, dominates the conversation. The group assistant also tries to hold the group to the topic and to prevent serious digressions. Lively discussions of the problems in the family should be viewed positively. This vigor can be attributed to the various structures of the actual capabilities in the individual members, and to the division of roles within the family. Any member can become the group assistant. The group can set a minimum age of 5 for the assistant. Since a child of this age cannot write, the task of keeping records can be delegated to someone else. Each week the group assistant is determined by sequence. The sequence should be put down in writing.

The Group Notebook

Each member keeps his own notebook. In it he records topics he'd like to bring up, as well as the agreements and decisions made by the group. The members of the group should write down their problems. If the child is too young to write, he should try to draw his problem and explain it to the group. If he is even too young to do this, his mother should write it down for him, but without adding her own comments, and without deleting anything. The child should also use the notebook to keep track of how he spends his money, and how he uses his time. In this way he will learn more about handling his money and his time and can develop a more systematic approach to his tasks and his interests. The notebook also helps him be more prompt, orderly, clean, and exact and to develop a more differentiated attitude toward things and events in his daily life.

The Daily Plan

By using a daily calendar the child can learn to divide his time into segments. A systematic approach to time can then become a model for a systematic approach to his own being. By completing his tasks on time he finds a certain confirmation of himself. On the other hand, a vague relationship to time stems to be reflected in a vague relationship to himself, just as too much structure and too much planning is the expression of a strict and defensive nature. The segmentation of time by means of a daily agenda has proved to be a good way to shape one's attitude to time in general. How does such a daily agenda look? In general it covers the span of time from getting up to going to bed.

Our daily agenda did not develop overnight, as it were. Six weeks earlier, the boy had begun to write down some ideas. Each evening he worked through these ideas in his discussions with his parents. Additions were made to the plan while other items were deleted. The boy set up an agenda for each day. After a while, certain recurring events began to crystallize, such as getting up, eating lunch, and going to bed. Attention was given to the individuality of the child. There was no question about his doing his homework, but the boy himself determined when he would do it. One example of this 11-year-old boy's daily plan is given below:

Daily agenda for 11-year-old school boy

6:30	Get up
6:30-6:35	Toilet
6:35-6:40	Shower
6:40-6:50	Exercise
6:50-7:00	Get his school books together
7:00-7:15	Breakfast
7:15-7:30	Free
7:30	Leave home
7:35	Catch the school bus

8:00	School
10:00	Recess. Don't forget to bring a snack
3:00	School is out
3:30	Arrive at home 3-30-4-00. Snack and Rest
4:00-5:00	Play baseball
5:00-6:00	Homework
6:00-6:45	Dinner
6:45-7:30	Free
7:30-8:00	Homework
8:00-8:30	Meet with parents etc.
8:30-9:30	Television
9:30	Bed

Weekly Plan – Checklist

If a person doesn't want to deal with minute planning, he can instead use a checklist where daily tasks can be marked off. With this, he himself or the child has an overview of the important achievements and can thus avoid having important tasks pile up on him. The checklist is a kind of self-check which replaces the unpleasantness of having someone else do the monitoring. As a weekly plan the checklist can be used for an entire week.

The family group plays an important role in this process. The family discusses the agenda and rewards the individual for adhering to it. The daily, checklist, and weekly agenda can become very meaningful instruments in the life of the family.

<u>*The process in a family group*</u>

The family group meets promptly at the determined time and, if possible, forms a circle around a table. The group should see to it that the individual members do not have to sit too close to each other. The television, radio, and other sources of disturbance should be turned off. The group should wait until everyone is there. The group assistant then asks, «Who would like to say something today? Who's got a particular problem?» The problems that are mentioned are then gathered and worked through. The group assistant asks each member for his opinion on the problems. In doing this, he should raise these questions:

What is the problem?
What are the causes, sources, goals, and interests hidden behind this problem?
What possible solutions exist?

The theme that seems to be the most important one for the group becomes the theme for the week. There can be a week of courtesy, week of tidiness, week of honesty, week of punctuality, etc.

The Memo Card
In the stages of distancing, inventory, encouragement, and verbalization the interaction involved only the relationship between two people, for instance, the child's sense of order, the mother's patience. In the family group, however, the theme of the week is valid for all members of the family. To keep that theme in mind and to make the learning more intensive, all the members of the group receive a little card containing the theme of the week, e.g., Courtesy Week (memo card).

In connection with this the parents have the task of becoming informed on the history, theory, and practice of the particular theme. They should read the appropriate chapters in this book. This orientation will help them to better recognize the conscious and unconscious conditions and connections behind individual problems. In this way they will be in a better position to lead the discussion in the group. By confronting the conditions and causes of the problems they not only deal with the conditions in a punctual manner, but also introduce and present connections such as the corresponding capabilities. These can be treated as a supplementary problem in the following week. If, for example, they chose politeness as the theme of the week, and worked through it intensively, they can then deal with the corresponding capability, namely honesty, which to a certain extent grows out of excessive politeness as a form of dishonesty. The theme for the following week would then be, as decided by the group: Honesty Week (memo card). The week after that, the themes of the two previous weeks could be combined.

The theme would then be: Politeness and Honesty Week (expanded memo card). One shouldn't try to pick a fight with the theme and try to teach the child a lesson without good cause. Only through timely development in the group is it possible to focus on an actual capability or a problematic behavioral area. For instance, the child will probably not actively participate in a discussion on honesty until he has actually ridden public transportation without dropping in this token. Another example: Unless the child complains that his parents are too impatient, or do not take enough time with him, there really can't be a meaningful discussion about patience, time, and their corresponding capabilities.

The Division of Functions and Role Exchange
The sharing of functions can be considered a basic principle within the family group. Only when the child can share in the problems of the adults in the group, will he be able to have a fuller understanding of those persons. The reverse is also true: Rigid divisions of roles can distort the parents' views of their children's problems. In the family group the children have as much right to be critical, as do the parents, if someone in the family does not abide by the decisions of the group.

But criticism must take place only in the family group. Until then, the members should simply record their observations in the group notebook. The exchange of roles is the most direct way to dynamically shape the structure of the family. Each member of the family can actively push for those wishes that he has presented to the group. In this way he can take over the planning and execution of their decision. If the group agrees on the planning, the child can direct the execution of the plan on his own or in conjunction with an adult (mentor system). In practice it looks like this: The child wants to go somewhere in the country on the weekend. He mentions a particular destination. The group discusses this suggestion and if there is agreement, the child can be given the responsibility of carrying it out. In this way the group supports the process of further planning through suggestions. The child prepares a hiking map, checks into public transportation, and makes suggestions as to where they can eat and spend the night. At their destination the child places the orders and takes on other tasks that are traditionally handled by the father. At their next group meeting they talk about this adventure. After they have evaluated how successful it was, they can discuss individual aspects of it. By delaying any criticism until this point, they avoid inhibiting and intimidating the child then and there. But we must keep in mind that this kind of behavior is not easy: A child, after all, thinks, speaks, and acts differently than an adult. It's not always easy for an adult to refrain from jumping in and showing that he knows how to do something better.

Examples of Goal Expansion within the Family Group (from Reports of Activities Carried Out by a Family Group)

Thomas would like to spend the evenings building models with his father. Barbara suggests that she go into town with her father once a week.

Larry mentions that he'd like to stay up a half hour later one night a week. The mother suggests that she shouldn't be the only one who wakes the kids in the morning. She thinks that she and her husband should take turns doing it.

The parents want their kids to prepare breakfast on Sundays and holidays. The mother says she wishes her son and daughter would help do the dishes. The mother wishes her children would make a better job of sticking to a schedule and not come running to her so often with their last minute demands.

Susan wants to watch a particular wildlife series on TV. Her father gives her an animal book that contains information on how the animals live.

Barbara says she'd like to help cook on Sundays. She wants to learn how, and even has a few new suggestions on how to prepare some foods.

Matthew complains that his father is too fussy. He asks whether it's really necessary that they straighten out the fringes on the carpet after they've had company.

Suzy complains that they can hardly play, and that her mother always says they shouldn't mess up the room.

Tony would like the whole family to go swimming so he can show them what he's learned in swimming class.

Billy doesn't just want his father to play with him all the time. He also wants his mother to play with him.

Amy complains that her father only has time for TV in the evening.

Dan wishes his father wouldn't start working on the papers in his briefcase the minute he gets home from work.

Mary doesn't like to go to bed by herself. She wishes one of her parents would come along, at least to tuck her into bed.

Record of a family group meeting
A mother of two reports on her first experience with a family group:
We got together on Friday evening at 6:30. This time it worked well, probably because the kid's had helped decide on the time. The kids wanted a nice dessert and candlelight so it would be nice and cozy. They also liked the idea of the notebooks. I was chosen to be group assistant.

Our daughter Erika (9 years old) was the first to speak:

Erika: I'm getting too fat. You all say that, but you don't help me do anything about it. Mom and Peter always sit right in front of me and eat chocolate, and I'm supposed to only watch. I wish you'd be more helpful. You know, we could all cooperate and just eat fruit and vegetables on Sundays, for instance.

We decided to get a calorie guide and to ask the pediatrician about a possible diet. Peter came up with the idea that from now on he would eat chocolate only by himself (he doesn't have a weight problem at all). Then our 6-year-old son Peter wanted to talk.

Peter: Erika never lets me sit on the chair.

Erika: Peter always wants to have the chair where I'm sitting; this triggered a debate that went on for a half hour. The day before, we had been in a shop. My daughter sat down. But when she offered to let her brother sit on the other half of the chair, he wasn't satisfied. He wanted to sit on the other side. He really let her have it, and she fought back with all she had. In our discussion of this problem nothing was decided. There was no agreement as to how the problem began and how it could be solved. Each child made a suggestion, but the other one didn't want to go along with it. They both thought they were right. And I made the mistake of trying to give advice.

Peter then talked about a similar quarrel he'd had with Erika. The incident had taken place weeks earlier, but he hadn't been able to put it out of his mind. He had let her play with his ball and later he wanted to use her hula-hoop. But she wouldn't give it to him, and they got into a flight. At our discussion about this Erika explained that she had only wanted to show him how it worked, that's why she hadn't immediately given it to him. At that point Peter left our meeting for a while. It was boring for him, and he wanted to do some painting.

I spoke up on the topic the children's allowance. My daughter had also made a note about this.

Erika: Why do I only get $.80? All the kids at school get more than that.
I: How much more do you need, and what would you like to get with it?
Erika: I'd like to get a dollar. Once in a while I'd like to buy something just for myself. I'd like to buy it on my own and show it to all of you, afterwards.
I offered her $ 1.50, but she said that was too much. If she can't make do with $ 1, she intends to talk to us about a possible increase.

Erika then said she wished we would play together in the evening more often. We agreed on this immediately and suggested that the children come inside in time to eat and have their baths. Sometimes they don't come in from playing until 7:00. Then they want to watch TV, eat, take their baths, and at 8:30 they want to play with us.

Erika then offered another suggestion: She'd like to make a daily plan with me. I agreed to that right away, but we postponed it till the end of the week because the usual rhythm of the days would start again then with school.

We all found the discussion to be very good, and we plan to continue it in the future. But for my part it hasn't worked quite right. I still give advice now and then and tend to interfere too much. And the questioning – when, why, what do you suggest – hasn't really become a part of me yet.

In school our 9-year-old daughter wrote an essay about her own experiences in the, family group:

We had a family council. Why?
Sometimes we had problems and didn't really want to talk about them. For instance, when we did something wrong. We just didn't say what was on our minds. Partly because we were scared, partly because we were embarrassed. We were all like that, we kids and also our parents. It went on like that until one day Mom said, «My neurologist told me that if people don't speak their minds, they should set up a family council where everyone can give his opinion.» So we each bought a notebook and wrote down what the others had done wrong (my brother just drew pictures). We agreed on a time and then at the end of every meeting we picked a new leader to keep the whole thing going. Since we started this, things have been a lot better at our house.

Significance of the family group
Current problems aren't the only things that are dealt with in the family group. The group meeting is also an opportune time to plan all sorts of activities - weekend trips, purchases, travels, company, holidays, gifts, etc. In this way the child learns to take an active part in the family and becomes aware that the family group is more than a formal arrangement or instrument for dealing with problems. The child comes to learn that within the family group he can have an impact on the family's decisions. The child is therefore not merely the object of decisions made by the parents. Rather, the members of the group, as subjects that play an active role in making decisions. There is another dynamic consequence of this group process. In the family, which to a certain degree functions automatically, that is, without conscious control, there are usually unconscious divisions of roles, rigid dislikes, and special preferences. We find, for example mother-son relationships, or the father-son conflict. The family group functions simultaneously; in

other words, all the members are there at the same time, actively taking part in the group. As a result, there are a lot of different transferences going on at multiple levels. Along with these transferences, there are emotional connections through which the family ties and conflicts can be managed more effectively.

The ideas, views, and decisions resulting from the group are not the property of individual members, but are the product of the group work. The situation here is much like what happens with a pot of soup. Many different vegetables (carrots, onions, celery, etc.) are cooked with water, seasonings, beans, peas, salt, and pepper to yield a dish, which, according to the connoisseur, has a flavor that is more than the sum of its individual components. The same holds true for the creation of ideas in the consultation process. The cooperation and interaction in the group coalesces into a newer, higher unity having characteristics (qualities) that hadn't existed before. The flavor of the vegetable soup can't be traced back to one particular vegetable. Nor can the attitudes, behaviors, and decisions of a group be attributed exclusively to the contributions of one or a few members of the group. The credit must go to the group as a whole.

Summary
The family group is concerned with man as a social being; it involves more than two members, particularly within the biological family.

The members meet on a regular basis at a predetermined time. The members take turns leading the group as group assistant.

Their meeting should not last more than 45 to 60 minutes.

Each member keeps a group notebook of conflicts and suggestions that should be discussed in the group.

The group discusses problems affecting the entire family and also makes plans for family activities.

Problems are worked through in accordance with the secondary and primary capabilities. This takes place by assigning the problem as the theme for the coming week. If, for instance, the child has been telling lies, the next week will be honesty week. During the week, each member of the family should watch himself in terms of his own behavior in this area.

Helpful aids are: the daily plan, the weekly plan, the checklist, and the memo card.

By sharing functions and exchanging roles, the members of the group have an opportunity to become familiar with the role tasks of the other people in the family.

Focal capabilities
Patience; model; time; contact; trust; confidence; punctuality; orderliness; conscientiousness.

Watch out for misunderstandings
Justice - love; uniqueness; generalization; anxiety; aggression; imitation.

THE PARENT GROUP

We have been concerned with how one works through a problem with a child, how a family group is constructed, how it functions, and how the relationships between parents and children are regulated within the family group. Until now we have not dealt with the question of how the parents face problems between themselves.

In the professional literature this problem is all too often neglected. Generally, parents are referred to as a homogeneous and unified institution. But the relationship between the parents - be it positive or negative - plays a critical role in the child's development. The parents' problems can affect the children or a narrower or broader environment; they can be personal problems of the individual parents, or they can refer specifically to the parents' relationship to each other. Such problems should not be dealt with in front of the children unless they are discussed within the framework of the family group. In the case of problems which concern the children, the parents should come to an agreement - at least in principle - before the family group. Otherwise it is recommended that the parents confront the problem at a definite time, for instance, in the evening. In this way they can solve the problem at an early stage and simultaneously keep the children from being drawn into the conflict unnecessarily. A parent group meeting should not last longer than 15 or 30 minutes. It is much better to talk about a problem every evening for 15 minutes than to thrash it out once a month from 9 p.m. to midnight. The differentiation analysis inventory can be used as an aid for the parent group. In its structure and techniques the parent group is much like the partner group. As we have seen, the parent group is, in principle, coordinated with the family group. The parent group deals with problems that extend beyond the family group and concern only the parents. The establishment of the parent group alongside the family group is therefore necessary because the parents live not only with the family, but also as a couple.

Maxims for the parent group

A good marriage is not one where there are no problems and conflicts, but where there is a willingness to talk about problems openly, honestly, and factually, and to work through them in a like manner.

Marriage is not an insurance agency. Rather, it is a balancing act between love and justice.

Spouses should learn to discuss problems in various areas of life (such as raising children, problems at work, sexual problems, and conflicts with in-laws and acquaintances). There is no one who doesn't have time, for such discussions, provided he is really ready and willing to enter into them.

If a person feels unable to cope with marital problems on his own, he should seek professional help.

Divorce is a question of responsibility: toward the spouse, oneself, and the children.

Summary
A distinction must be made between conflicts which concern the entire family, and ones that only affect the parents.
The parents should not voice their arguments in front of the children.
The parents should talk on a regular basis, preferably in the evening, to work through their problems and make necessary plans.
Length of the parent discussion: 15 to 30 minutes

Focal capabilities
Patience; time.

Watch out for misunderstandings
Man - woman; relativity of values; justice and love; the unconscious; health - illness.

THE PARTNER GROUP

The partner group is the place for dealing with problems and conflicts that develop within a partnership. Like cancerous tumors, conflicts tend to grow beyond their bounds and to spread into areas which are not really affected by them. The partner group is designed to counter this tendency. When problems arise, they can be limited in their time and location and then be dealt with by the people involved. In its basic features the procedure for the partner group corresponds to the methods that we have already become familiar with in the family group.

In the partner group the members are faced with a difficult task that will make it seem to some people as if they must constantly try to jump over their own shadow. After all, it is not easy to suddenly talk to a partner whom you've been punishing with your silence. Quite often a reversal like that is accompanied by a loss of status: You thought you dominated that person; now you are supposed to accept him as a partner. This idea alone can cause the division of roles in the relationship to become unsteady. To counter these difficulties, the partners can use the process of differentiation analysis, with its stages of distancing/ observation, inventory, situational encouragement, verbalization, and goal expansion. As a further aid, the exchange of roles within the partnership frequently works miracles.

Exchange of Roles
This lends support to mutual understanding and empathy. The technique is a simple one. For a week at a time one partner takes on some of the role activities of the other person. The male partner does the shopping; the wife takes care of the car. In the sexual realm as well, the partners take turns being the initiator. The woman learns not be a passive recipient. The man learns to distance himself from sexual performance and the compulsion to conquer. The partner group itself decides just how the exchange of roles will be carried out. This does not mean there is a loss of spontaneity and romance. Indeed, the process is an adventurous attempt to discover new areas of behavior and forms of interaction with one's partner

Memory Aids
Human memory is weak. We remember only a small part of what we experience. And then this small part is modified by our expectations, desires, and other discoveries and experiences. This is particularly the case when we recall critical behavior on the part of our spouse and want to utter a judgment on it. But we have at our disposal excellent memory aids that can screen out any subjective colorations. What we are talking about here is the written records of critical events: «When was I upset with you? In what situation did that take place? What were the causes, and how did I react?» With these conflicts written down, it is much easier to discuss them with your partner objectively and to create a more factually based relationship. Our memory of events may be weak, but our memory of good intentions is even weaker. Here we can use the memo card, which we discussed earlier in our section on the family group. By looking at the memo card «Politeness» we can avoid insulting or hurting our partner. The memo card «Orderliness» reminds us that we can be more careful and thus avoid an angry situation caused by carelessness.

The partner group (and other forms of self-help group) deal with more than anxiety and aggression. The important task for these groups is to look beyond the anxiety, aggression, and guilt feelings, and discover the insufficient discernment of actual capabilities that brought them about. The member of the group is put into a position where he can understand his other partners in the group, evaluate the conflicts according to their situational significance, and appropriately integrate the actual capabilities that are involved in the conflict.

Questions that each partner should ask when there is a conflict in their partnership:
- Can the problem be changed?
- Can my partner fulfill my expectations?
- Does he want to solve the problem?
- Have I already attempted to move toward a solution?
- Am I viewing our situation honestly and openly?
- Am I expressing my opinions honestly?
- Am I ready to listen to my partner? Am I even ready to give my partner some time and to take time for myself? Or do I expect change to take place immediately?
- If we can't solve this by ourselves, are we willing to seek professional help? Do I expect my partner to do all the changing, or am I ready to make some changes as well?
- Am I giving us another chance? Do I stand by my partner even during a serious conflict?

Maxims for the partner group
Every person, by his very nature, is capable of having a partnership. But not every person can enter a partnership without preparation. How a person learned to enter into a partnership plays a decisive role. There must be fundamental distinctions sex - sexuality and love. These represent a unity in the life of every person.

Training and preparation for partnership begin in early childhood.

We should guard against transferring our own ideas of partnership or divorce to other people and situations just as each person is unique, so every partnership is also unique.

Well-intended advice from friends and relatives has destroyed more than a few partnerships.

Separation offers an opportunity. During a separation we learn a lot of things. We can use these new insights if we end the separation. If the separation continues, we can use these insights with a new partner.

<u>*Summary*</u>

The partner group is the place for dealing with problems that arise between adult partners.

The partner group rests upon the assumption that the partner is ready to abandon the role position that had been a natural one for him. The exchange of roles is a central method used in the partner group. The one partner takes on the tasks and functions of the other.

It has proved helpful to use memory aids such as the memo card and written records in the group notebook.

Focal capabilities
Time; patience; trust; loyalty.
Watch out for misunderstandings
Man - woman; justice - love loss of unity.

DIFFERENTIATION ANALYSIS PSYCHOTHERAPY

In many cases astounding success has been achieved through the process which we have described in the section on self-help. But sometimes problems occur that seem to block the way to self-help. Among these problems are a partner's unwillingness or inability to discuss the problems, his resistance to any attempts to influence him; relativity of values; generalization, apparent inability to express his feelings, and deeply rooted fixations.

It is particularly hard for a layman to re-educate himself through self-help if the problems are less acute and if their origins were experiences in early childhood. Character changes, neurotic developments, and psychosomatic disorders are particularly resistant to self-help. This is an area which is treated by psychotherapy, particularly by differentiation analysis psychotherapy.

Psychotherapy, the control field of differentiation analysis, offers a five stage therapeutic process. It is particularly appropriate for brief therapy. In a shortened form, differentiation analysis can be used as the basis for therapeutic discussions oriented toward an inventory of the actual capabilities. Marriage counseling, help with raising children, and social interaction counseling in schools and work places all play an important role here. The intensive form of differentiation analysis therapy can take place in an institutional setting or on an outpatient basis. In an individual plan of treatment, sometimes also incorporating group work and group therapy, the differentiation analysis therapy can be completed within four to six weeks. As a form of sensitivity training it can also take place as a weekend group. One example of its application is the following case, where differentiation analysis was used with a woman suffering from frigidity. (Peseschkian, 1974)

Case study

A 28-year-old married patient, the mother of one child, was referred for psychotherapy by her gynecologist. The woman was frigid and depressed. Organic, gynecological, and endocrinological tests yielded negative results. In her initial interview the woman reported:

When I go to bed I always hope my husband won't wan t to have sex. If he does want it, I feel very guilty and give in as if sex were something I just have to endure. Right from the start I resist it to my very core. During intercourse I resist all his caresses. I just want to get it over with as fast as possible. After a short time, he tries to penetrate me, and this is very painful for me because I am all tensed up. I feel such disgust when his penis touches me down there. That makes me resist him even more, and it just gets worse...

The woman's problems had become much worse about two years before beginning therapy, shortly after the birth of her child. The following factors played a role in the development of the actual conflict:

- The patient had worked as a secretary. Successful in her work, she had managed a lot of responsibilities and helped financially in building their house. But after her child was born, her husband didn't want her to work any more. She reports that this made her feel dependent and doomed to being a housewife.
- The husband had a new job on the road, making it impossible for him to always get home at a regular time. The wife complains:

If he says he'll be home at 7:00, I can be happy if he shows up at 9:00. He always has an excuse for being late. I don't know any more what I should think of his coming home late. Every time he's late, it just destroys my trust in him.

The two frequently fight over money. The husband accuses her of spending too much.«*You can't keep throwing money away the way you used to. You know I'm the only breadwinner now.*» When the wife hears comments like these she bursts into tears. She had invested all her savings in their new house.

The husband's need for tidiness and cleanliness is a particularly important factor. Previously, when the patient was still employed, the two of them had shared in taking care of the house. Now that the wife is home all day, the husband relies on her to do it all. «*You're home all the time. You take care of it.*» The patient reports, «*Instead of hanging up his clothes or putting them in the laundry basket, he leaves his socks and shirts and other things laying around on the bedroom floor. Unless he's getting ready for work, my husband doesn't keep himself very clean either. I think personal cleanliness is important, but he neglects it. When he crawls into bed all smelly and with bad breath, I just want to get out of bed and go away.*

From the differentiation analysis inventory of a 28-year-old patient with sex disorders:

Actual capabilities	Patient	Husband
Ambition	+ + +	+ + +
Punctuality	+ + +	-
Orderliness	+ +	-
Cleanliness	+ + +	- -
Obedience	-	-
Politeness	+ +	+
Honesty	-	+ +
Thrift	+	+ +
Trust	- -	+

+ Positively marked   - Negatively marked

Differentiation analysis depicts the actual conflict as follows: In her relationship with her husband, the potential for conflict lies in her restriction to the role of housewife, coupled with dissonances with her husband related to punctuality, time, thrift, orderliness, and cleanliness. These factors represent a considerable problem, but they alone do not account for her severe symptoms. Aside from looking at the actual burdens she feels, we must inquire into her ability to bear them, and hence into her basic conflict.

The patient grew up in a family where ambition and achievement were the criteria for emotional attention. In addition, the patient had to assert herself with her brother, who was two years younger. Here again, the main criterion was her accomplishments. In her childhood she had to stand out, particularly as far as ambition and orderliness were concerned:

«Whenever I was untidy, my brother was held up as an example for me, and that really got to me. My mother could get terribly upset if things weren't where they should be. She'd either nag a lot or give us the cold shoulder for hours on end, and then she'd withhold our allowance. I got a lot of compliments for keeping clean and taking good care of my clothes. Dirt was the worst thing that could happen to me... I was also terribly shocked when I started menstruating.

Nossrat Peseschkian, M.D.

I had no idea what was happening, because no one had ever explained it to me. My mother said it was necessary so that my body could get rid of waste products. It was generally a rule around our house not to talk about dirty things or problems that could offend someone. So, we kept a dignified silence about a lot of things.»

The actual conflict addressed itself to the following areas of the basic conflict:
- Ambition and achievement as criteria for self-esteem.
- Punctuality as the criterion for trust.
- Orderliness as the criterion for attention and recognition.
- Thrift as a sign of maturity and independence.
- Cleanliness as the criterion for self-respect and integrity.
- Politeness as the family's traditional way of inhibiting aggression.

Through politeness, problems were directed inward. No physical causes for the woman's disorder could be found. The conflicts were centered on the areas of the actual capabilities as described above. The dispositions for conflict appear partly as basic conflict (the past) and are actualized by the conditions of the actual conflict (the present). The existing conflicts are of an interpersonal nature and are based on attitudes with a strong affective component.

After twelve sessions over a 6-month period, the woman's therapy was successfully concluded. A year later, a follow-up examination was made. The patient and her husband agreed that there was no longer a sexual problem. They were able to handle and control any difficulties as they arose. Their lifestyle also changed as they both developed new interests in common and established stronger contacts with other people. Sexuality was, as the husband put it, «no longer the be all and end all.»

This strategy for treatment should not be understood as a rigid scheme for all cases. Individual modifications of the plan for treatment must always be considered case by case. Factors to be considered are the age of the patient, the nature of the particular conflict, and the internal and external motivations of the people involved. Depending on individual conditions, the treatment can focus on analysis, hypnosis, or group psychotherapy.

At the present time there are data on 80 patients (52 women, 28 men). With the women, the diagnosis deals mainly with fear of sex and general and selective frigidity. The men suffered mostly from premature ejaculation, impotence, and fear of sex. In every case there was considerable improvement. In 74% of the cases there was a lasting cure (following-up interval approximately one year). The average therapy ranged from 12 to 21 sessions, depending on the individual diagnosis.

As a short form of therapy concentrated on conflicts, differentiation analysis has been used for the following illnesses:

- Sexual disorders (in women, fear of sex, frigidity, hyper-sexuality; in men, impotence, premature ejaculation, fear of sex, masturbation, and homosexuality perceived as illness).
- Vegetative functional disorders with psychic etiology and organic neurosis (sleep disorders, cephalalgia, asthma, colitis, ulcers, rheumatic problems, heart neurosis, prostate problems, anorexia nervosa, obesity, neuro-dermatitis, vegetative dysfunction, stuttering, and bed-wetting).
- Psycho-reactive mental disorders (phobias, depression, behavioral disorders, compulsiveness, learning disorders, alcoholism, drug dependency, and abnormal mourning reactions).

In the case of psychotics and psychopaths the differentiation analysis was carried out in varying degrees. To some extent there was promise of success. In differentiation analysis education and psychotherapy are separate only in terms of their methods; as far as content is concerned, they are related in the sense that psychotherapy is a continuation of and aid to education (re-education). When education and psychotherapy work together, anxiety and aggression are channeled, inhibitions are broken down, generation conflicts are weakened, and the possibilities for communication are increased. We view all of this as the prerequisite for world peace and a world unity built on a unity in multiplicity of education and psychotherapy.

In education and interpersonal relationships the goal of differentiation analysis is to expand the partner's abilities to make distinctions based on the secondary and primary capabilities. The task of the educator and the therapist can be summed up in this way:

We can lead the person to the fountain, but he must drink of it himself. The way to a more mature attitude toward life is:

Learn to differentiate!

Inventory sheet for the reader: to check himself and his partner *The Differentiation Analysis Inventory (DAI, short form)*			
Actual capabilities	**Patient**	**Partner**	**Spontaneous comments**
Punctuality			
Cleanliness			
Orderliness			
Obedience			
Politeness			
Honesty/openness			
Fidelity			
Justice			
Ambition/achievement			
Thrift			
Dependability/exactness			
Love			
Patience			
Time			
Trust/hope			
Contact			
Sex-sexuality			
Faith/religion			

Heavy Burdens

Persian mysticism tells of a wanderer who trudged along on a seemingly endlessly long road. He was loaded down with all sorts of burdens. A heavy sack of sand hung on his back; a thick water hose was draped around his body. In his right hand, he carried an oddly shaped stone, in the left hand a boulder. Around his neck an old millstone dangled on a frayed rope. Rusty chains, with which he dragged heavy weights through the dusty sand, wound around his ankles. On his head, the man was balancing a half-rotten pumpkin. With every step he took, the chains rattled. Moaning and groaning, he moved forward step by step, complaining of his hard fate and the weariness that tormented him. On his way, a farmer met him in the glowing heat of midday. The farmer asked, «Oh, tired wanderer, why do you load yourself down with this boulder?»

«Awfully dumb» replied the wanderer, «but I hadn't noticed it before.» With that, he threw the rock away and felt much lighter.

Again, after going a long way down the road, a farmer met him and asked, «Tell me, tired wanderer, why do you trouble yourself with the half rotten pumpkin on your head, and why do you drag those heavy iron weights behind you on chains?"

The wanderer answered, «very glad you pointed it out to me. I didn't realize what I was doing to myself.» He took off the chains and smashed the pumpkin into the ditch alongside the road. Again, he felt lighter. But the farther he went, the more he began to suffer again.

A farmer coming from the field watched him in amazement and said, «Oh, good man, you are carrying sand in the sack, but what you see far off in the distance is more sand than you could ever carry. And your big water hose as if you planned to cross the Kawir Desert. All the while there's a clear stream flowing alongside you, which will accompany you on your way for a long time.» Upon hearing this, the wanderer tore open the water hose and emptied its brackish water onto the path. Then he filled a hole with the sand from his knapsack. He stood there pensively and looked into the sinking sun. The last rays sent their light to him.

Nossrat Peseschkian, M.D.

He glanced down at himself, saw the heavy millstone around his neck and suddenly realized it was the stone that was still causing him to walk so bent over. He unloosened it and threw it as far as he could into the river. Freed from his burdens, he wandered off through the cool of the evening to find lodging.

BIBLIOGRAPHY

- Abdu'l-Baha (1977) Tablets of the divine plan: revealed by 'Abdul-Baha to the North American Baha'is, rev. edn. Baha'i Publishing Trust, Wilmette, pp 39-40
- Alexander F (1950) Psychosomatic medicine. de Gruyter, Berlin
- Baha'u'llah (1976) Gleanings from the writing of Baha'u'llah (trans. Shoghi Effendi).
- Baha'i Publishing Trust, Wilmette
- Baha'u'llah (1939) The hidden words of Baha'u'llah (trans. Shoghi Effendi). Baha'i Publishing Trust, Wilmette
- Battegay R, Rauchfleisch U, Graf von Schliefen H (1972) Sozioökonomische Determinanten der Inanspruchnahme der Psychiatrischen Universitätsklinik Basel. Schweiz Arch Neurol, Neurochir Psychiatr 111:67
- Bowlby J (1973) Separation. Anxiety and Anger. Hogarth and the Institute of Psycho-Analysis, London
- Brobeck JR (1979) Best and Taylor's physiological basis of medical practice, 10th edn. Williams and Wilkins, Baltimore
- Erikson EH (1950) Childhood and society. Norton, New York
- Freud S (1912) The dynamics of transference. In: Standard edition of the complete psychological works of Sigmund Freud, vol 12. Hogarth, London, pp 98-108
- Fromm E (1973) The anatomy of human destructiveness. Holz, Rinehart and Winston, New York
- Gellhom E, Loofbourrow GN (1963) Emotions and emotional disorders. Hoeber Medical Division, Harper and Row, New York
- Klein M (1940) Mourning and its relation to manic-depressive states. Int J Psychoanal 21:125-153. Die Trauer und ihre Beziehungen zu manisch-depressiven Zuständen. In: Klein M (ed) (1962) Das Seelenleben des Kleinkindes. Klett, Stuttgart
- Luban-Plozza B, Pöldinger W (1971) Der psychosomatisch Kranke in der Praxis. Lehmanns, Munich

- Peseschkian N (1973) Kosmetische Chirurgie - und dann? Medical Tribune 42:37
- Peseschkian N (1974) Actual capabilities as aspects of connotation in interpersonal and social origination of conflicts and conflict handling. 5th International Congress of Social Psychiatry, Athens, 1-7 September 1974
- Peseschkian N (1974) Zürn Beispiel Höflichkeit. Sexualmedizin 3:506-510
- Peseschkian N (1975) Herzrhythmusstörungen unter psychosomatischem Aspekt. In: Verhandlungen der Deutschen Gesellschaft für Innere Medizin, vol 81. Bergmann, Munich
- Peseschkian N (1975) Kopfschmerz in Abhängigkeit von sozialen Normen und Konflikten: Was hat Pünktlichkeit mit Kopfschmerz zu tun? In: Barolin V, Saurugg GS, Hemmer D (eds)Kopfschmerz-Headache
- Peseschkian N (1976) Differenzierungsanalytische Aspekte zum Weichteilrheumatismus. In: Verhandlungen der Deutschen Gesellschaft für Innere Medizin, vol 82. Bergmann, Munich
- Peseschkian N (1976) Neue Behandlungsmöglichkeiten autonomer Fehlsteuerungen dargestellt an einem Fall ulcus duodeni. In: Gross VD, Largen D (eds) Fehlsteuerungen des autonomen Nervensystems. Hippokrates, Stuttgart
- Peseschkian N (1977) Positive Psychotherapie. Theorie und Praxis einer neuen Methode. Fischer, Frankfurt
- Peseschkian N (1978) Vom Mut, eine Probe zu wagen. Erfahrungsheilkunde 27(10):622-630
- Peseschkian N (1979) Der Kaufmann und der Papagei. Orientalische Geschichten als Medien in der Psychotherapie. Fischer, Frankfurt
- Peseschkian N (1979) Krankheitsmodelle: Jeder sieht etwas Richtiges aber nicht alles. Erfahrungsheilkunde 28(91:718-722
- Peseschkian N (1980) Positive Familientherapie. Eine Behandlungsmethode der Zukunft. Fischer, Frankfurt
- Peseschkian N (1982) Positive psychotherapy in medical practice. Hexagon Roche 10(3)

- Peseschkian N (1983) Psychosocial norms in medical practice - minor emotional trauma. Hexagon Roche 11(2)
- Peseschkian N (1984) Auf der Suche nach Sinn. Psychotherapie der kleinen Schritte. Fischer, Frankfurt
- Portmann A (1944) Vom Ursprung des Menschen. Reinhardt, Basel
- Spitz RA (1965) The first year of life. International Universities Press, New York Stern D, Beebe B (1977) Engagement-disengagement and early object experiences. In: Freedmann N, Grand S (eds) Communicative structures and psychic structures. Plenum, New York
- Winnicott DW (1971) Playing and reality. Tavistock, London

OVERVIEW OF BOOKS WRITTEN BY NOSSRAT PESESCHKIAN

S. Fischer Verlag:

- Positive Psychotherapie - Theorie und Praxis einer neuen Methode *(Positive Psychotherapy – Theory and Practice of a New Method)*

- Psychotherapie des Alltagslebens - Training zur Partnerschaftsbeziehung und Selbsthilfe
  (Psychotherapy of Everyday of Life)

- Der Kaufmann und der Papagei - Orientalische Geschichten in der Positiven Psychotherapie
  (Oriental Stories as Tools in Psychotherapy - The Merchant and the Parrot)

- Positive Familientherapie
  (Positive Familytherapy)

- Auf der Suche nach Sinn - Psychotherapie der kleinen Schritte
  (In Search of Meaning – Psychotherapy of Small Steps)

- 33 und eine Form der Partnerschaft
  (33 and One Form of Partnership)

- Psychosomatik und Positive Psychotherapie
  (Psychosomatics and Positive Psychotherapy)

- Angst und Depression
  (Anxiety and Depression in Everyday Life)

- Das Geheimnis des Samenkorns
  (The Secret of the Seed – Positive Stress Coping)

- Der Nackte Kaiser
  (The Undressed Emperor – How to Understand and Heal the Children's Soul)

- Morgenland – Abendland
  (Biography of Nossrat Peseschkian - Positive Psychotherapy in Dialogue Between the Cultures)

- Mikrotraumen: Das Drama der kleinen Verletzungen
  (Constantly Drip Excavates the Stone: Microtraumas - The Drama of the Small Injuries)

- Die Treppe zum Glück - 50 Antworten auf die großen Fragen des Lebens
  (Steps to Happiness – 50 Answers to Important Questions of Life)

- Lexikon der Positiven Psychotherapie
  (Encyclopaedia of Positive Psychotherapy)

- Das Alter ist das einzige Mittel für ein langes Leben
  (Seniority is the Only Means for a Long Life)

Springer Verlag:
- Wiesbadener Inventar zur Positiven Psychotherapie und Familientherapie – WIPPF
  (Wiesbaden Inventory for Positive Psychotherapy and Familytherapy – WIPPF)

- Psychosomatik und Positive Psychotherapie
  (Psychosomatics and Positive Psychotherapy)

Hippokrates Verlag:
- Positive Ordnungstherapie
  (An Instruction for Holistic Medical Practice)

Trias Verlag:
- Mit Diabetes komme ich klar
  (To Cope with Diabetes)

- Lebensfreude statt Stress - Persönliche Stressfaktoren erkennen und hinter sich lassen. Anstöße, Übungen, orientalische Weisheiten
  (Vitality Instead of Stress)

- Was haben Sie auf dem Herzen?
  (What do You Have on the Heart?)

Pattloch - Weltbildverlag:
- Vom Glück des Suchens und des Findens
  (Of the Luck of Searching and Finding)

Verlag Hans Huber:
- Salutogenese und Positive Psychotherapie
  (Salutogenesis and Positive Psychotherapy)

Herder Verlag:
- Wenn du willst, was du noch nie gehabt hast, dann tu, was du noch nie getan hast
  (If You Want Something You Never Had, then do Something You Never Did)

- Klug ist jeder. Der eine vorher, der andere nachher
  (Everyone is Clever. The One Before, the Other One Afterwards)

- Es ist leicht, das Leben schwer zu nehmen. Aber schwer, es leicht zu nehmen
  (It is Easy to Take Life with Difficulty. But Heavily to Take it Easily)

- Das Leben ist ein Paradies, zu dem wir den Schlüssel finden können
  (Life is a Paradise to Which We Can Find the Key)

- Glaube an Gott und binde dein Kamel fest.
  (Believe in God and Lash Your Camel)

- Goldene Regeln der Lebenskunst
  (The Golden Rules of Art of Living)

Kreuz Verlag:
- Die Familientherapie: Eine praktische Orientierungshilfe!
  (The Familytherapy – A Practical Aid for Orientation)

- Wenn du eine hilfreiche Hand brauchst, so suche sie am Ende deines eigenen Armes
  (If You Need a Helpful Hand, then Look for it at the End of Your Own Arm)

- Glaube an Gott und binde dein Kamel fest
  (Believe in God and Lash Your Camel)

Self-published:
- Fasten in verschiedenen Kulturen und Religionen
  (Fasting in Different Cultures and Religions)

POSITIVE PSYCHOTHERAPY (SUMMARY)

Positive Psychotherapy (PPT after Peseschkian, since 1977)™ is a psychotherapeutic method developed by Nossrat Peseschkian and co-workers in Germany since the late 1960s. It can be described as a humanistic Psychodynamic Psychotherapy, which is based on a positive conception of human nature. PPT is an integrative method which includes humanistic, systemic, psychodynamic and CBT-elements. Today there are centers and trainings in some twenty countries world-wide.

The founder of Positive Psychotherapy, Nossrat Peseschkian (1933-2010), was an Iranian-born German certified psychiatrist, neurologist, psychotherapist and psychosomatic specialist. He was inspired in the late 1960s and early 1970s by different sources, persons and developments:

- The spirit of that time, which brought into existence humanistic psychology and its further developments.
- Personal encounters with prominent psychotherapists and psychiatrists, such as Viktor Frankl, Jacob L. Moreno, Heinrich Meng and others.
- By the humanistic teachings and virtues of the Bahá'í Faith.
- By looking for an integrative method, specially because of problems between psychoanalysts and behavior therapists at that time.
- Based on transcultural observations in over 20 cultures, and searching for an integrative method which is cultural-sensitive.

The method was first called Differentiational Analysis (in German: Differenzierungsanalyse). In 1977, Nossrat Peseschkian published his work "Positive Psychotherapie", which was published in English as "Positive Psychotherapy" in 1987. **The term "positive"** is derived from the original Latin expression "positum or positivus" which means the actual, the real, the concrete. The aim of Positive Psychotherapy and

Positive Psychotherapists is to help the patient and client to see also their abilities, strengths, resources and potentials.

The main characteristics of Positive Psychotherapy are:
- Integrative psychotherapy method
- Humanistic Psychodynamic Method
- Cohesive, integrated therapeutic system
- Conflict-centered short-term method
- Cultural-sensitive method
- Use of stories, anecdotes and wisdoms
- Innovative interventions and techniques
- Application in psychotherapy, other medical disciplines, counselling, education, prevention, management and trainings

The three main principles or pillars of Positive Psychotherapy are:
- The Principle of Hope
- The Principle of Balance
- The Principle of Consultation

1 - The Principle of Hope implies that the therapist wants to assist their patients to understand and see the meaning and purpose of their disorder or conflict. Accordingly, the disorder will be reinterpreted in a "positive" way (positive interpretations):
Some examples:
- Sleep disturbance is the ability to be watchful and get by with little sleep
- Depression is the ability to react with deepest emotionality to conflicts
- Schizophrenia is the ability to live in two worlds at the same time or living in a fantasy world
- Anorexia nervosa is the ability to get along with few meals and identify with the hunger of the world

Through this positive view a change of standpoint becomes possible, not only for the patient, but also for his environment. Hence, illnesses have a symbolic function which has to be recognized by both therapist and patient. The patient learns that the symptoms and complaints of the illness are signals to bring his or her four qualities of life into new balance.

2 - Principle of Balance: Despite social and cultural differences and the uniqueness of every human being, it can be observed that during the management of their problems that all humans refer to typical forms of coping. According to the balance model, the four areas of life are: 1. Body / health; 2. Achievement / work -; 3. Contact / relationships; 4. Future / meaning / goals.

Though these four ranges are inherent in all humans, in the western hemisphere the emphasis is more often on the areas of body/senses and profession/achievement in contrast to the eastern hemisphere where the areas are contact, fantasy and future (cross-cultural aspect of positive psychotherapy). Lack of contact and imagination are some of the causes of many psychosomatic diseases. Everybody develops his or her own preferences on how to cope with conflicts that occur. Through a one-sided mode to the conflict solution, the other modes are getting eclipsed. The conflict contents (e.g. punctuality, orderliness, politeness, trust, time, patience) are described in terms of primary and secondary capacities, based on the basic capacities of loving and knowing. This can be seen as a content-wise differentiation of Freud's classical model of the instances.

3 - Principle of Consultation: Five-stages of therapy and self-help. The five stages of positive psychotherapy represent a concept in which therapy and self-help are closely interrelated. The patient and the family are getting informed together about the illness and the individual solution to it.

- 1st Step: Observation; distancing (perception: the capacity to express desire and problems)
- 2nd Step: Taking inventory (cognitive capacities: events in the last 5 to 10 years)

- 3rd Step: Situational encouragement (self-help and resource-activation of the patient: the ability to use past successes in conflict solution)
- 4th Step: Verbalization (communicative capacities: the ability to express outstanding conflicts and problems in the four qualities of life)
- 5th Step: Expansion of goals (in order to evoke forward-looking orientation in life after the problems are solved, the patient is asked: "What would you like to do, when no more problems are left to be solved? Which goals do you have for the next five years?")

The main emphasis of Positive Psychotherapy during the past 40 years has been treatment, training and publication.

- In 1979, the Wiesbaden Postgraduate Training Institute for Psychotherapy and Family Therapy was established as a postgraduate training for physicians in Wiesbaden, Germany. In 1999, the Wiesbaden Academy for Psychotherapy (WIAP), a state-licensed postgraduate psychotherapy academy with a large outpatient clinic was established for the training of psychologists and educational scientists.
- Most Positive Psychotherapists are working in private office or in clinics. In Germany, Positive Psychotherapy is counted as a psychodynamic method and the health insurance covers the costs.
- Since the early 1980s, seminars and trainings in some 60 countries have taken place. Today, Positive Psychotherapy is practiced in more than 25 countries with approximately 30 independent centers and institutions. The training programs for mental health professionals consist of basic and master trainings over several years.
- The international head office is based in Wiesbaden, Germany. Positive Psychotherapy is represented internationally by the World Association of Positive Psychotherapy (WAPP). This international governing board of directors is elected every three

years. There are national and regional associations in some ten countries.

- PPT and its therapists have been engaged in the international development of psychotherapy, and are active members of numerous international associations

Publications and Research

- In 1997, a quality assurance and effectiveness study was undertaken in Germany. The results show this short-term method to be effective. The study was awarded with the Richard-Merten-Prize.
- Today there are more than 30 major books on Positive Psychotherapy, of which some have been published in more than 23 languages.

INSTITUTIONS OF POSITIVE PSYCHOTHERAPY

International Academy for Positive and Transcultural Psychotherapy (IAPP) – Professor Peseschkian Foundation –

Foundation

The Foundation was established in 2005. It is a non-profit organization which is engaged in the development of Positive Psychotherapy world-wide. Positive Psychotherapy is based on a positive image of man: every person, every family, every society, every culture, and the entire human race have the potential to evolve in the direction of health, justice and peaceful co-existence. The transcultural approach is a practical application of Positive Psychotherapy and the positive image of man.

◆ **Board of Directors** ◆ **Board of Trustees** ◆ **Scientific Advisory Board**

Projects

- **Education**: teacher training and Positive Pedagogic in Germany and abroad; Positive Management for school administrators. Mental Health for schools, teachers, students, parents and society.
- **Self-help:** public lectures and workshops; Books of Positive Psychotherapy in different languages
- **Postgraduate Program**: certified trainings for counsellors of Positive Basic- and Master-Courses of Positive Psychotherapy
- **Transcultural Projects**: Basic- and Master-Courses of Positive Psychotherapy in Ethiopia (Mental Health Project) & social project in Addis Abeba; lectures and workshops at universities and conferences worldwide.

Publications and rights

- Rights administration and promotion of the 32 books by Professor Nossrat Peseschkian, M.D., translated into 26 languages
- Administration of all publication contracts with German and foreign publishing companies (the proceeds from the book sales are exclusively re-invested into the Foundation's projects)
- International library of Positive Psychotherapy

- International multilingual glossary of Positive Psychotherapy Terms

Targets and Goals

- Contribute to creating and establishing a culture of cooperation and understanding
- Encourage and motivate political and religious leaders, scientists, economists and individuals for the purpose of unity in diversity. Exchange and interchange of ideas with other social and therapeutic organisations.
- Science and research, in cases of conflict resolution and stress management as contribution to the development of peace.
- Integral professional and scientifical exchange in the educational and therapeutical work with children, adolescents and adults.
- Practical application for further education and postgraduate education in the form of seminars, workshops, and courses in the field of Positive Psychotherapy.
- Health and well-being as imbedded in a holistic system.
- Self-help as a resource-oriented approach.
- Counsel and guide individuals, families and organisations in terms of education, upbringing, economy- and society-related issues.
- Application of Positive Psychotherapy and psychosomatics as a resource-oriented and conflict-centered short-term therapy.
- Diminish prejudice, advancement of sexual equality, the combat of poverty, structural aid in the fields of demographic, educational and health policy, as well as old-age support.
- Establish and preserve an International Archive on Positive and Transcultural Psychotherapy.
- Maintain and expand an extensive Library.
- Award «Positive Psychotherapy Prize» in different categories.

The Foundation is member in:

World Council of Psychotherapy
European Association of Psychotherapy
European Accredited Psychotherapy Training Institute

Federal Association of German Foundations
Network of Foundations in Wiesbaden

World Association for Positive Psychotherapy (WAPP), Inc.

The World Association for Positive Psychotherapy (WAPP) is the democratically elected **international umbrella organization of Positive Psychotherapy**. It consists of national associations, national and regional training institutes, centers, representative offices and individual members. It was established in 1996 as International Center of Positive Psychotherapy (ICPP) and re-named to World Association for Positive Psychotherapy in 2008.

As an officially registered non-profit organization, it represents the interests of Positive Psychotherapy on the international level. Its Head Office is currently situated in Wiesbaden, Germany.

WAPP **promotes the theory, method and practice of Positive Psychotherapy**. It is engaged in the training of postgraduate professionals in psychotherapy, family therapy and counseling all over the world.

The main training program consists of **Basic and Master Courses of Positive Psychotherapy** offered by officially certified trainers. Graduates of the Basic Course training are certified by WAPP as "Basic Consultant of Positive Psychotherapy". Graduates of the Master Course training are granted the title of "Certified Positive Psychotherapist".

In addition, WAPP organizes
- workshops
- lectures
- conferences
- seminars

pertaining to the different aspects of Positive Psychotherapy as well as transcultural exchange of theories, techniques and research.

The Objective of WAPP and of all institutions of Positive Psychotherapy is to promote the physical, mental, social and spiritual health of individuals, families and groups and the mutual understanding and tolerance between different cultures.

WAPP is **represented by a Board of Directors and a President,** elected every two years by the WAPP members.

Membership in WAPP is offered as:
- **Institutional membership** for training institutions, Positive Psychotherapy Centers and national associations of Positive Psychotherapy
- **Full membership** for all individuals, who have completed a training seminar in Positive Psychotherapy.
- **Supportive membership** for everyone interested in Positive Psychotherapy.

WAPP and its affiliated institutions are members of:
- European Association for Psychotherapy (EAP)
- World Council for Psychotherapy (WCP)
- International Federation for Psychotherapy (IFP)

Contact:

WAPP Head Office
Luisenstrasse 28
65185 Wiesbaden
Germany
Phone: +49 611 34109903
Fax: +49 611 39990
E-mail: wapp@positum.org

www.positum.org

Visit us on Facebook at: Positive Psychotherapy.

CPSIA information can be obtained
at www.ICGtesting.com
Printed in the USA
BVOW02s0217040117

472546BV00001B/58/P